Praise for *The Merging of Two Oceans*

"Pir Netanel's book opens further the doors of Jewish-Sufi cross-fertilization, offering beautiful stories and practices from both traditions, and furnishing interesting background material pertaining to the creation of the Inayati-Maimuni Order and its founding *pir,* Reb Zalman Schachter-Shalomi. If you are someone whose soul is stirred by both the Sufi and Hasidic traditions, this is a book you will want to read."

— Gregory Blann (Shaykh Muhammad Jamal al-Jerrahi), *When Oceans Merge: The Contemporary Sufi and Hasidic Teachings of Pir Vilayat Inayat Khan and Rabbi Zalman Schachter-Shalomi*

"With *The Merging of Two Oceans,* Pir Netanel Miles-Yépez has brought us an important and long-overdue piece of scholarship, as soulful as it is erudite. Peppered with practices, teaching tales, and the history of the Sufi and Jewish mystical traditions' intertwining, *The Merging of Two Oceans* is an accessible and deeply nourishing read that many spiritual seekers will celebrate. "

— Rabbi Tirzah Firestone, author of *Wounds into Wisdom: Healing Intergenerational Jewish Trauma*

"Embracing the ancient maxim that "the height of human knowledge is to know that we do not know," Pir Netanel encourages us to embrace the interspiritual learning that has enriched Jews and Muslims, Hasidim and Sufis, for centuries. He describes how these two "oceans" commingled in the Middle East and Eastern Europe, and in the life of Rabbi Zalman Schachter-Shalomi. *The Merging of Two Oceans* also recounts a story of friendship between *rebbe* and student and beautifully describes the author's ordination. Pir Netanel makes esoteric teachings accessible through references to contemporary literature and film, as well as history and stories, and philosophical, spiritual, and psychological wisdom gleaned from a contemplative reading of scripture. This rich context informs concrete advice on how to meditate and pray. If you find yourself at the uncomfortable 'crossroads of religions,' Pir Netanel meets you there and lets you know you're not alone."

— Father David Denny, co-founder of The Desert Foundation, and co-author of *Desert Voices: The Edge Effect*

"In this book, our dear brother Netanel Mu'in ad-Din has prepared a banquet of wisdom for the soul and mind that overflows with deep and detailed knowledge of tradition and practice. The clarity and mastery with which he explains the meeting and merging of these two traditions, Sufism and Hasidism, allows the reader to become familiar with the central teachings of both traditions in an accessible way, while also becoming acquainted with the nuances of their respective spiritual terminologies. In addition, by sharing details of his personal journey with his spiritual guide and the birth of a new lineage, he provides us with insights into the inner workings of the tradition, something that is often hidden and can only be speculated about. As a work that is at once spiritual manual, history and storytelling, this collection of talks can be seen as inspired by the *malfuzat* ('discourses') genre of Sufi literature."

—Shaykh Issa Farajajé, Chishti-Nizami Sufi Shaykh

The Merging of Two Oceans

Nine Talks on Sufism & Hasidism

Pir Netanel Miles-Yépez

The Inayati-Maimuni Order
Boulder, Colorado
2025

*"The old shall be renewed,
and the new shall be made holy."*
— Rabbi Avraham Yitzhak Kook

This book has been produced for the Inayati-Maimuni Order in cooperation with Albion-Andalus Books.

Albion-Andalus, Inc.
P. O. Box 19852
Boulder, CO 80308
www.albionandalus.com

Design and composition by Albion-Andalus Books
Cover design by D.A.M. Cool Graphics
Cover detail from "Humayun received by the Safavid ruler Shah Tahmasp of Iran" from Abu'l-Fazl's Akbarnāmah, dating from Agra, circa 1602-'03. British Library.
Illustrations by Netanel Miles-Yépez.

ISBN-13: 978-1-953220-09-7 (Hardcover)
ISBN-13: 978-1-953220-10-3 (Paperback)

Distributed by Ayin Press via Publishers Group West

Manufactured in the United States of America

For

'Ibrahim Baba'

Pir Ibrahim Abdurrahman Farajajé

of blessed memory

Contents

Preface	*ix*
The Holy Name of God *(Derekh Ha-Shem)*	*3*
Seeking Internal Seclusion *(Hitbodedut P'nimit)*	*27*
A Hidden Dialogue *(Ma'asiot)*	*49*
Reb Zalman's Journey "Toward the One" *(Likrat Ha-Eḥad)*	*73*
Hyphenating Sufism and Hasidism *(Ani Ma'amin)*	*87*
The S'firot in Sufi Zikr *(S'firot)*	*109*
One God, Many Worlds *(Olamot)*	*127*
Between the Animal and Divine Souls *(Beynoni)*	*149*
Threads of Connection *(Ḥutim)*	*173*
Apprendix A: "Seclusion"	*187*
Apprendix B: Simple Instructions	*189*
Notes	*191*
Glossary	*215*
Index	*229*
Author Biography	

Preface

The nine chapters of this book have their origin in eight talks (and accompanying Q&A sessions) given from 2010 to 2020. The versions contained herein have been edited for publication (adding a little material here and there, as well as some sources), but generally retain the structure, and hopefully, some of the colloquial flavor of the original talks. The quotes I use in the text are largely presented in the adapted forms in which I gave them in my oral talks, often being made gender neutral for purposes of inclusion and accessibility.

The title *The Merging of Two Oceans* is an *homage* to the 17th-century Persian work *Majma al-Bahrain*, in which Prince Dara Shikuh explores the affinities between Sufism and Vedanta. It is also the title of a series of talks I gave in New Lebanon, New York, on April 27-30th, 2017, at the Abode of the Message, for Wisdom of the Prophets: Sufism & Judaism, an Inayati Order event with Pir Zia Inayat-Khan and Rabbi Tirzah Firestone. In using it now, I do not wish to draw attention away from a similarly titled and themed work by my colleague, Gregory Blann (Shaykh Muhammad Jamal al-Jerrahi), *When Oceans Merge* (2019), exploring the Sufi and Hasidic teachings of Pir Vilayat Inayat-Khan (1917-2004) and my own *rebbe* and *murshid,* Rabbi Zalman Schachter-Shalomi (1924-2014). I encourage those who enjoy this work to see the latter volume for further reading.

While I first conceived the idea of writing a book on the parallels between Sufism and Hasidism more than a decade ago, the actual work never amounted to more than a few outlines and

fragments of chapters. The idea was later resurrected in 2015 in conversations with my friend, Pir Ibrahim Abdurrahman Farajajé, of blessed memory, affectionately known as 'Ibrahim Baba.' A Chishti Sufi *shaykh* of vast intelligence and heartfulness, Ibrahim Baba had been a friend of my *rebbe*, and had a deep and abiding love for Judaism which was evidenced by the Jewish-Sufi community that had grown up around him in the Bay Area. At that time, we discussed collaborating on such a work, which no doubt would have been all the more rich and illuminating for his contributions. But sadly, Ibrahim Baba died suddenly in February of 2016 and I abandoned the project.

And yet, I had been giving public talks on the connections between Sufism and Hasidism (or Sufism and Judaism) since at least 2010. These talks increased when I was teacher-in-residence at the Abode of the Message, a Sufi retreat center in New Lebanon, New York, in the Fall of 2015 and 2016, and culminated in the Wisdom of the Prophets: Sufism & Judaism event with Pir Zia Inayat-Khan and Rabbi Tirzah Firestone in the spring of 2017, when I was the spiritual director of the Abode.

In 2020, during the Coronavirus pandemic, I began to gather material from these talks into the book you have before you. It is not the project Ibrahim Baba and I imagined—a deep comparison of stories and teachings from Sufism and Hasidism—but it may still be useful and interesting for some who share our interests and commitments to both traditions. Thus, this book is dedicated to him.

I wish to express my deep gratitude to my lineage brother, Pir Zia Inayat-Khan, with whom I worked so closely from 2015 to 2017, and with whom I also discussed many aspects of the relationship between these traditions. His own work on these connections can be found in the chapter "The Staff of Moses" in his book *Mingled Waters: Sufism and The Mystical Unity of Religions* (also an *homage* to the *Majma al-Bahrain*). Some of

the question and answer responses in chapter nine of my own book are responses to Pir Zia himself and material from *Mingled Waters.*

I also wish to thank my friend (and fellow-student of Rabbi Zalman Schachter-Shalomi, *z"l),* Rabbi Tirzah Firestone, who joined me for the Sufism & Judaism event at the Abode. It was a rare treat to hear the teachings we both had learned coming out with such a unique flavor and new emphasis. I am likewise grateful to Pir Shabda Kahn and Murshid Wali Ali Meyer, with whom I also spoke on these topics at a public event at Mentorgarten in San Francisco in 2017. Pir Shabda likewise gave me permission to use certain material and suggested a few corrections. Murshid Atum O'Kane and Pir Puran Bair also generously granted me permission to use my descriptions of them.

I must also thank my friend and former companion, Jennifer Alia Wittman, who invited me to be teacher-in-residence at the Abode of the Message in the fall of 2015, where I gave part of "Reb Zalman's Journey Toward the One," and who later, along with Pir Zia, also invited me to teach at Wisdom of the Prophets: Sufism & Judaism in the spring of 2017, where I gave versions of most of the rest of the talks in this book. Likewise, Al Bellenchia, who again invited me to be teacher-in-residence at the Abode of the Message in the fall of 2016 (and later its spiritual director), where I gave my "Between the Animal and Divine Souls" talk, and a version of "A Hidden Dialogue."

Other friends, colleagues, and students who deserve thanks for their support and contributions to these talks include: Elyn Tajnura Aviva, Tessa Bielecki, Rev. Adam Bucko, Debra-Sue Cope, Chuck Jameel Davis, Father David Denny, Leigh Ann Dillinger, Darakshan Farber, Murshid Suhrawardi Gebel, Rebbetzin Eve Ilsen, Shaykha Camille Helminski, Shaykh Kabir Helminski, Rabbi Zvi Ish-Shalom, Zachary Amitai Malone, Sarah Leila Manolson, Charlotte Rizvana Maryam Mason, Rory McEntee, Khaldun Mendel, Hallaj Michalenko,

Amina Peterson, Raj Seymour, Taya Shere, Wendy Waduda Welch, Rev. Matthew Wright, Murshida Eileen Alia Yager, and in particular, my friend Shaykh Issa Farajajé, who has so ably taken up his father's mantle and is carrying the lineage into the future.

I would also like to thank my colleagues at Naropa University: President Charles Lief, Dr. Amelia Hall, Nataraja Kallio, Dr. Ben Williams, and Dr. Stephanie Yuhas.

I am especially indebted to my beautiful and heartful murids, who are the true inheritors of these teachings. Among them, special thanks is due to Daniel Jami' (who thoughtfully and diligently proofread the book), Sasha Salika Gaynor (who helped with the glossary and index), as well as Phil Ansell and Peter Halim Schein who served as readers for the book.

And finally, to my loving and supportive partner, Jamelah Nabil Zidan; you are a blessing in my life, and to all of this work.

Netanel Mu'in ad-Din Miles-Yépez
Boulder, Colorado, June 17th, 2021

"The fire of devotion
Purifies the heart of the devotee
And leads to spiritual freedom."

— *The Bowl of Saqi*

derekh ha-shem

The Holy Name of God

Contacts between Sufis and Jews in the Middle East *

In 18th-century Damascus, there lived a holy *tzaddik*, a 'righteous' mystic named Rabbi Moshe Galante, who was a *baki* or 'expert' in what were once called the 'seven wisdoms'—grammar, rhetoric, logic, arithmetic, geometry, astronomy, and music—and who was also the chief rabbi of the Jewish community.

Now, Rabbi Moshe was a caring leader, so he was concerned one day to learn that many of the Jews of his community actually went to a certain Muslim Sufi for prayer when they were sick. "The Holy Dervish," they claimed, would pray on the matter and then tell them whether they would recover, or God forbid, whether they needed to put their affairs in order. Although it says in the Talmud that Rabbi Hanina ben Dosa could also tell if a patient would live or die after he prayed for them, Rabbi Moshe could not imagine that anyone else, let alone a Muslim, could know such things.

Alarmed by the notion of Jews seeking such counsel from a Muslim Sufi, Rabbi Moshe was inclined to denounce this "Holy Dervish" from the *bimah* of the synagogue. Nevertheless, he hesitated, for it is a Jewish legal principle to investigate a

* Edited from "The Merging of Two Oceans: Sufism and Hasidism I," a talk given in New Lebanon, New York, on April 28th, 2017, at the Abode of the Message, and "Sufism and Hasidism," given November 1st, 2016 at the Abode of the Message.

matter carefully before coming to a judgment. Thus, Rabbi Moshe decided to seek out the Holy Dervish to inquire into the matter himself.

Sitting down at his desk, he penned a simple invitation inviting the Sufi 'healer' to come to his home for tea. On the appointed day, the dervish came and the two men sat down to talk. Almost immediately, it was clear to Rabbi Moshe that the Sufi was no charismatic charlatan, but actually a man of great dignity and learning. Thus, he began to probe him on each of the seven wisdoms, discussing grammar, rhetoric, logic, arithmetic, geometry, and astronomy, one after another. In each subject, Rabbi Moshe was amazed to find the Holy Dervish a master. Indeed, in only one of the seven wisdoms was the dervish deficient; he seemed to know little or nothing of music as it is understood in the classical wisdom.

Noting Rabbi Moshe's own mastery of the subject, the Holy Dervish asked the rabbi in humility, "Could you possibly teach me this wisdom?"

Rabbi Moshe was gratified and answered, "I would be delighted to instruct you in this subject. Truly, I like your company, and you seem to me a wise man . . . But I have one condition . . ."

"And what is that?" asked the Holy Dervish.

"After I teach you the seventh wisdom, I would like to make a request, which I hope you will not refuse."

"It is my sincere desire that I may be able to oblige you," the dignified Sufi responded, placing his hand over his heart.

Thus, over the next weeks and months, Rabbi Moshe and the Holy Dervish met to discuss the wisdom of music. When it seemed clear to both men that the dervish had mastered the principles of the seventh wisdom, the Holy Dervish thanked Rabbi Moshe, saying, "I am sincerely grateful to you, my friend; now please tell me what is your request?"

Rabbi Moshe, with some trepidation, now broached the subject that had originally caused him to seek out the distinguished dervish. "I am told, my friend, that you pray for people, and that you are able to predict whether or not they will get well. I would sincerely like to know how you do this."

The Holy Dervish paused at this unexpected question.

"That is truly a difficult request, my friend. It is not easy for me to answer. This is an awesome matter which cannot be shared in an ordinary way. However, as I have already committed myself, I will endeavor to show you how this is done . . . *but* . . . you must be worthy of it."

Taken aback, the rabbi asked, "What must I do to become *'worthy'?*"

"Purify yourself, repent, and return to God."

Though he tried not to show it, Rabbi Moshe was a little indignant that *he*, a deep *mekubal* and *tzaddik*—a righteous kabbalist—should be told to purify and repent by a Muslim! Nevertheless, he was courteous to the dervish and agreed.

Now Rabbi Moshe was actually a profoundly righteous man and used to the deepest devotions, so he thought little of this task. Such practices were part of his daily routine; so he fasted, did *t'shuvah*, repenting of his small transgressions, and came back to the dervish a week later, saying, "I am now ready."

The Holy Dervish looked at him discerningly and said, not unkindly, "No, my friend, I'm sorry, you are not."

Rabbi Moshe was shocked, and asked genuinely, "But why?!"

The Holy Dervish sighed and replied, "Because you still don't believe that I have anything to teach you. It is not a trick I do, not a formula—this is a profound mystery. You have to take it seriously."

Rabbi Moshe returned home deeply troubled; his proud tower collapsed, he was completely humbled. In tears, he

began a real process of *t'shuvah*, of 'repentance,' crying out to God—*"Ribbono shel Olam*, 'master of the universe,' this Muslim dervish sees through me! In the beginning I was afraid that he had nothing to teach me; now I am afraid that he does! What does this all mean?! What if he derives his power from unholy places? I don't want to fall from your service for the sake of my own intellectual curiosity, or God forbid, vanity! Please, God, help me!"

Thus, rocked by this experience, the rabbi recited psalms—praying, questioning, searching—until he returned to the Holy Dervish the next week a genuinely repentant man.

The Holy Dervish looked at Rabbi Moshe this time and said, "All right, come with me."

The two spiritual masters passed through the dervish's house to a magnificent enclosed garden behind it, the kind that is called a 'paradise.' In the garden, filled with all manner of fruit trees, was also a very large pond, in the center of which was an island. On the island there was a brilliant white building.

The dervish pointed to the building, as if to say, *We are going there;* but there seemed to be no way of getting across to it. Near the edge of the pond, however, was a small structure, which they entered.

Once inside, the Holy Dervish said, "Here we are going to disrobe and descend these steps, swimming under the water to the secret entrance to the shrine on the island. The shrine itself has two chambers; in the outer chamber you will find a robe. We will then pass through the door to the inner chamber; but you must keep your eyes closed! I will hold your hand as we enter and we will bow down and prostrate seven times. After the seventh prostration, when I squeeze your hand, I want you to begin to pray for the person who needs your prayers. When I squeeze your hand again, open your eyes, look straight ahead, and then you will see whether the person will live or not."

Bewildered at these instructions, and more than a little afraid, Rabbi Moshe began to disrobe.

Completely naked now, they walk down the stairs into the waters and swim together under the water to the island, coming up on a secret stair beneath the island into a chamber within the shrine where two white robes are hung.

They put on the robes and Rabbi Moshe feels himself trembling inside as he closes his eyes. This is the worst of all possible situations for a Jew, and he thinks to himself desperately . . . *A Jew should have his eyes open! How will I know whether I am bowing before an idol, God forbid?! Now, holding the hand of a Muslim Sufi, I am going to bow down and do seven prostrations in some secret esoteric rite before I know not what! Please,* Ribbono shel Olam, *'master of the universe,' please understand that I am doing this for a holy purpose . . . I am trying to find the answer to a mystery—I hope not in my own vanity, but for the good of this community, to know what is really happening here! I only want to serve you! If there is an idol, please know it is to* you *that I am bowing, and not an idol!*

The two holy masters prostrate once, then a second time, a third time, and then after the seventh prostration, they rise, and the Holy Dervish squeezes Rabbi Moshe's hand. He begins to pray very deeply and seriously for the sick member of his congregation. Then, after a few minutes, the dervish squeezes his hand again. Now, Rabbi Moshe opens his eyes and looks, trembling at the wall in front of him, and sees written in bright letters on the wall . . . *The name of God!* . . . from which an otherworldly light is shining.

He then feels the dervish squeeze his hand again and both men bow, step backward through the door, and humbly bow again. They then take off their robes in the outer chamber and swim back underwater and come out in the little structure near the edge of the pond.

Once there, Rabbi Moshe dries off and puts on his clothes in silence. When he is fully dressed, the dervish turns to him to

speak, but Rabbi Moshe says hurriedly, "I can't talk right now," and quickly rushes out of the structure, through the paradise, and out of the house.

The next *Shabbat,* Rabbi Moshe Galante, the chief rabbi of Damascus, had the *shamash* (attendant) call the community together from all the various synagogues in Damascus and gave them the following sermon . . .

"I have known for some time that you have been going to the 'Holy Dervish' for prayer and counsel. I was at first troubled, as you might expect; but now that I have looked into the matter myself, I want you to know that this dervish is indeed a holy man who has built a shrine to house God's holy name, into which he enters only with great awe and trembling. All of us say the holy name so often, saying the *Sh'ma* and making our many holy blessings, and yet none of us feel as much awe as this holy dervish. We think ourselves such a holy and special people; but I tell you that we do not pay enough attention to the proper way of honoring God's name! We have much to learn from this Holy Dervish."[1]

I first learned this story from my teacher, Rabbi Zalman Schachter-Shalomi, of blessed memory, who first came across it in Eliyahu de Vidas' *Reshit Ḥokhmah.* He loved the deep spiritual exchange between the noble Sufi and the learned Jewish scholar, and told it in much the same way as I have given it here. Once, he even had me tell it at dinner with a visiting Sufi *shaykh* in the last year of his life, stopping me at one point to add an important detail I had missed.

It is perhaps the most positive story of Sufi-Jewish connections I know, and even involves a historical figure, Rabbi

Moshe Galante (d. 1806), the learned chief rabbi of Damascus, a descendant of Rabbi Moshe Galante of S'fat (d. 1608), his more famous namesake.

But such stories are not usually preserved intact. For a Jew of Moshe Galante's position to willingly accept instruction in spiritual matters from a Muslim would, in the eyes of many of his contemporaries, make him an *apikoros*, one who had 'abandoned' his faith; and for Rabbi Moshe to know that he actually *required* such instruction would likewise shake the very foundations of his life and being.

So why would such a spiritually dangerous story be preserved among Jews? Often because it is assumed to prove another point entirely, or because some 'triumphalist' element has been added to make it more acceptable. I suspect that many may have thought, or even told the story as if the divine name written on the inner wall of the dervish's shrine was none other than *Y-H-V-H,* the holy unpronounceable name of God in Hebrew, suggesting that the dervish secretly honored the earlier Jewish revelation. Thus, Rabbi Moshe could say with a clear conscience, 'The dervish honors the name better than we.'

But what was *actually* written on the wall? The Holy Dervish says himself that this is no "trick" or "formula." Likely then it was simply 'God,' *Allah*—the four letters, *'alif-lam-lam-ha'*—painted in Arabic calligraphy on the wall.

Rabbi Moshe would have recognized it immediately. After all, he lived in Damascus, and would have spoken and read some Arabic as the common language of the land.

The story, you see, is not about a special esoteric name; it is about a special reverence that reveals the inner light and essence of God. We do not know what the light that shone through it meant—whether the person for whom Rabbi Moshe prayed would live or die—but Rabbi Moshe understood that protecting the sanctity of the divine name to such a degree might allow it to reveal its truth to us.

In the end, I think we must be grateful for however such stories are preserved, even buried under and obscured by centuries of misunderstanding and abuse; for they have arrived by God's mysterious grace at the moment when they may be seen for what they really are, treasures to enrich our future.

Converts and Apostates

There are actually many suggestive examples of contacts between Jews and Muslims in the historical record, and even of the influence of one upon the other. There are clear examples of Jewish influence on the Islamic tradition, and clear examples of influences from Islam upon Jews in the Islamic world. Unfortunately, some of those influences are born of unhappy circumstances.

There are periods in Islamic history (as in all history) where aggressive military regimes, like the Almohad Caliphate, contrary to the normative teachings of Islam, forced conversions in the Iberian peninsula upon Jews and Christians, failing to respect their sovereignty as *mu'minun* ('believers') and the Qur'anic *dictum*—"There must be no compulsion in religion" (2:256).

In my late twenties, I studied with a Moroccan kabbalist who told me how his grandfather had once taken him to the *suq,* the open market in Morocco, and bought food for them from a Muslim vendor. The boy was aghast, as a Jew can only eat kosher slaughtered meat—Muslim *ḥalal* does not qualify. So the boy pulled his grandfather's sleeve and whispered urgently, "*Saba!* We can't eat this!" But his grandfather only winked at him, exchanging another wink with the Muslim vendor and urged the boy to eat. Later, his grandfather took him to a particular house in the city and knocked on a strange door. The same Muslim answered, and they were led inside the house and

then through a hidden door into a secret chamber beneath the house where a group of Jews were gathered for prayer.

The food had been kosher; these were *anusim,* the descendants of 'forced' converts who kept their Jewish identity hidden. Culturally, and to all outward appearances, they were Muslims, though inwardly Jewish. Some of these *anusim,* my teacher said, came into contact with Sufism, which was liberating for them in many ways.[2]

A more infamous example of conversion involves the Dönmeh, 'apostates.' These were followers of the "failed Messiah," Shabbetai Zvi (1626-1676), a Sefardi Jewish mystic who claimed the Messianic mantle in the 17th-century, leading masses of oppressed and hopeful Jews in Europe and the Middle East to flock to his banner, as it were, sometimes selling their homes and all their possessions in anticipation of the promised messianic redemption. Such profound stirrings, however, could not fail to arouse the notice of the Turkish sultan. Shabbetai Zvi was arrested in early 1666 as a potential political threat, and on September 15th, brought before the sultan and offered the choice of conversion to Islam or death. He chose life and a royal pension, devastating thousands of hopeful Jews throughout Europe and the Middle East, throwing whole communities into a depression.[3]

Nevertheless, many of Shabbetai Zvi's followers refused to see his conversion as apostasy, believing there was a secret mystical purpose in it, and joined him in converting to Islam. Externally Muslim, they remained loyal to a radically antinomian Sabbatean Judaism in private, marrying only within the fold through the centuries.[4] Called the Dönmeh, many of these Jews eventually became Bekashi Sufis, who were already known to be somewhat heterodox Muslims.

Not all Jewish conversions to Islam, however, were coerced; nor did all connections to Sufism follow conversion. There are accounts of Jews who discovered Sufism and converted willingly

to Islam, eventually becoming well-known Sufi saints. There is Shaykh Badi ad-Din (b. 1315), called Shah Madar, whose family were Jews from Aleppo. He received the education of a young Jew, but after his parents died, traveled to Mecca, where he met the Sufi master Ashraf Jahangir Semnani (1285-1386). Eventually, he made his way to India and visited the *dargah* or shrine of Khwaja Mu'in ad-Din Chishti in Ajmer. There, Shah Madar kept company with Yogis and became known as an ecstatic ascetic. His disciples claimed that he shared in the nature of God and kept his face veiled because anyone who saw it fell to the ground in a faint.[5]

Then there is Sarmad (ca. 1590-1661), an Armenian Jew whose Jewish learning before coming to Sufism was considered profound. In Iran, he studied with the great mystic-philosopher Mulla Sadra (d. 1640-41) and attained significant knowledge of the *ishraqi* or 'illuminationist' teachings of Yahya Suhrawardi and the *waḥdat al-wujud* or 'unity of all being' teachings of Muḥyiddin ibn 'Arabi. Some say this led him to embrace Islam.

For years, it seems, Sarmad earned his living as a merchant, traveling widely and amassing a considerable fortune. In India, however, he fell passionately in love with a young Hindu, Abhai Chand, who was forbidden to him. It is said that Sarmad then went mad, stripping off his clothes and wandering the landscape spouting mystical poetry—"In this old round monastery, I know not that my God is not Abhai Chand!" he proclaimed. Later, he would teach Abhai Chand to read and translate the Hebrew of the Torah and Psalms and to compose Persian verse.

Sarmad wandered throughout India, traveling from Lahore to Hyderabad as a naked ecstatic, reciting mystical verse and attracting as many enemies as admirers. He claimed that the

prophet Isaiah had also gone about naked at the end of his life. (Isa. 20:2-3) In Delhi, he came to the attention of the Sufi prince Dara Shikuh (1615-1659), the eldest son of Shah Jahan and a profound student of Sufism. Before the prince, Sarmad wore a loincloth, and the prince listened admiringly to the wisdom of this intoxicated mystic *(majzub)* who saw only God everywhere.

After Prince Dara Shikuh was murdered by his younger brother, the Sufi Sarmad was arrested in a purge of the prince's supporters on a charge of public nudity. Asked by the inquisitorial religious judges why he only recited *La 'ilaha,* 'There is no god,' and not the entire statement, *La 'ilaha 'illa llah,* 'There is no god but God,' he replied that he had become so absorbed in contemplation of the former that he had not yet gotten to the latter!

At his execution, the executioner stepped forward to cover the saint's eyes, but Sarmad prevented him, saying, "Come in whatever disguise you wish, God, I recognize you." The legends say, after his beheading, the severed head of Sarmad finally spoke the words *". . . 'illa llah,"* 'nevertheless, God.'[6]

Baḥya ibn Paquda and the "Duties of the Heart"

Ethnically Jewish mystics who converted to Islam like Shah Madar and Sarmad, of course, have no more place in traditional Judaism than Jewish-Christian mystics like Teresa of Ávila and John of the Cross. However, there are other Jewish mystics of the Muslim world who were profoundly influenced by Islam and Sufism and yet remained committed Jews. Among the most significant is the Spanish Jewish mystic, Rabbi Baḥya ibn Paquda (11th-century C.E.).

Little is known of Baḥya's life, other than he lived in Muslim Spain (probably in Saragossa), that he was a religious judge, or *dayyan,* who composed Hebrew liturgical poems *(piyyutim),* and

despite being a committed Jew, had a significant knowledge of Sufi practice and teaching. The latter fact is attested in his book, *Al-Hidayah ila-Fara'id al-Qulub*, or 'The Guidebook to the Duties of the Heart,' written no later than 1080 C.E.

The book, like many Jewish books of that time and region (including Maimonides' famous *Guide to the Perplexed)* is written in Judeo-Arabic—basically common Arabic written in Hebrew characters (with some Hebrew vocabulary)—making it relatively easy to read by Arabic speaking Jews and no one else. Thus, it was not until the Spanish-born Yehudah ibn Tibbon (1120-ca.1190) translated the work into Hebrew as *Ḥovot ha-Levavot*, or 'Duties of the Hearts,' in 1161, that the book became accessible to Jews everywhere.

It is precisely for this reason that Baḥya's connections to Sufism, despite the popularity of his work, were little known or appreciated until relatively recently; for without a knowledge of Islamic and Sufi sources, Hebrew readers could only be expected to understand it as a highly original contribution to Jewish ethical literature *(mussar)*. Indeed, among the Ba'al Shem Tov's early Ḥasidim, the Hebrew text of the *Ḥovot ha-Levavot* was seen as a profoundly *Jewish* guidebook to the Hasidic way of life as they understood it.

However, as early Orientalist scholars of Judeo-Arabic began to re-read the original with a knowledge of parallel Arabic literature, it became clear that the Judeo-Arabic work was largely based on Sufi spiritual manuals, and contained traces from the works of Sufi authors like Abu 'Abdallah Harith al-Muḥasibi (781-857) and Abu Talib al-Makki (d. 996).[7] It even referenced (in a somewhat disguised fashion) *aḥadith* or 'reports' of the prophet Muḥammad, peace be upon him.[8]

Baḥya's *Hidayah* is organized into ten chapters called 'gates,' each describing a quality and a contemplation leading in succession to the pinnacle of the spiritual path, the true love of God: (1) contemplation of the unity of God *(tawḥid)*, (2) creation

(i'tibar), (3) obedience to God *(iltazam ta'at Allah),* (4) reliance on God *(tawakkul),* (5) sincerity in one's intention *(ikhlas al-'amal),* (6) humility before God *(tawadu),* (7) repentance *(tawba),* (8) self-examination *(muḥasaba),* (9) asceticism or detachment *(zuhd),* and (10) love of God *(maḥabba).*

In his 'Gate of Unity' *(bab al-tawḥid),* Baḥya uses the precise language of Sufi masters, such as Dhu'n-nun, Junayd, and Qushayri, to articulate the classic Sufi teaching that the height of human knowledge is to know that we do not know.[9] This "learned ignorance" is distinguished from common ignorance by a deep desire and endeavor to know, and is particularly applied to our knowledge of God. Unlike the ignorance of one who has never asked the question or sought an answer, those who seek God and come to know God, know more and more that they do not know God at all.[10]

But it is in the tenth and final gate, the 'Gate of Love' *(bab al-maḥabba),* that Baḥya suggests various "signs" and "practices" of those who love God, giving a thorough description in Jewish terms of a well-known Sufi practice of the time, *al-qiyam was-siyam,* 'rising and fasting' during the night.[11] Based on the ideal of *qiyam al-layl,* a prayer practice of the prophet Muḥammad, meaning to 'stand during the night,' Sufis would rise in the night to stand vigil in prayer or recite *zikr* through the long night. Baḥya quotes a number of biblical verses in support of this practice, including—"My soul desires you in the night" (Isa. 26:9) and "I remembered your name, God, at night" (Ps. 119:55).[12] He also tells us that he has composed special exhortations to "rouse and encourage" the soul to rise and pray at night.[13] "Oh my soul! Awaken from your slumber! Recite poems to the one who formed you, chant God's name, proclaim God's wonders, and fear God wherever you dwell."[14] These are recitations for those who wish to rise and do prostrations in prayer both day and night.[15]

Baḥya recommends reciting the exhortation he calls *tokaḥah* or 'reproof' while sitting. But first, he would have us sing some of our favorite hymns and pray using his *bakashah* or petitionary prayer—"alternately standing and prostrating yourself until the end. Then bow and recite whatever entreaties you care to," followed by Psalm 119, and Psalms 120 through 134.[16]

However, more important than the practices themselves, he tells us, is to "purify your soul, focus your heart," and to recite these things slowly, with deep and authentic feeling. "Do not say something without first feeling it in your heart, for a little prayer said devoutly is better than a lot said quickly and empty-heartedly."[17]

Was Baḥya alone among Jews in doing such practices? Was he alone in his awareness of Sufism and Sufi sources? *He certainly was not.*[18] Was there a Jewish communal Sufi practice in the Iberian Peninsula or the Maghreb? *Perhaps.*[19] What we do know is that a Sufi-styled Jewish communal practice, or 'Jewish-Sufism,' did evolve in the centuries to follow.

Avraham Maimuni and the Egyptian Ḥasidim

Without a doubt, the most significant consequence of the exchange between Sufis and Jews in the Muslim world is seen in the Jewish-Sufi sect of 13th and 14th-century Egypt. Though it is among the more unusual stories in the history of Judaism, it is far from an obscure aberration on the margins of Jewish life; for this sect was led by one of the most learned and well-pedigreed leaders of Judaism at that time, Rabbi Avraham ben Moshe Maimuni (1187-1237).

These were not ethnically Jewish converts to Islam, nor a single individual like Baḥya ibn Paquda influenced by the teachings and practices of Sufism; this was a well-organized sect with an integrated Jewish-Sufi communal structure and spiritual

trajectory. Far from abandoning Judaism, they practiced it with a devotion and diligence hardly to be rivaled.

Where did they come from? It is difficult to say. The cultural ferment of Spain in the "Golden Age" yielded a complex and diverse number of movements and creative syntheses among Muslims and Jews. The respected Arabist S. D. Goitein referred to this as the great "Jewish-Arab symbiosis," affecting language, politics, literature, theology, philosophy, and spirituality.[20] New translations of Greek sources into Arabic led to fresh explorations of Aristotelian and Neo-Platonic thought, yielding a variety of competing (and sometimes complementary) rationalist and mystical movements among Jews and Muslims.

Baḥya ibn Paquda's *Hidayah* benefitted from both Neo-Platonic and Aristotelian influences, binding theosophical mysticism and philosophical rationalism with a devotionally-oriented practice borrowed from Sufism. Later, the great Jewish philosopher and legal scholar, Rabbi Moshe ben Maimun (1135-1204), better known as Maimonides, would draw extensively on Baḥya's presentation of negative theology (i.e., establishing what God is not) and his discussion of the love of God,[21] demonstrating the influence and reach of Baḥya's Sufi-styled teachings among Arabic speaking Jews into the next century.

Did Baḥya's *Hidayah* give birth to a Jewish-Sufi movement in Spain? Or was it itself the product of a quiet dialogue between Jews and Muslims in that particularly rich period of cultural exchange? We cannot say for certain. What we can say is that the dialogue that ultimately produced a Jewish-Sufi sect in Egypt probably had its origins in Baḥya's Spain, where such exchanges seem to have been easier and more acceptable.

In the century after Baḥya, the Spanish-born Jew, Yosef ibn 'Aqnin (ca.1150-ca.1220), would write a commentary on the *Song of Songs* that reads like a Sufi treatise on the love of God, his definitions of love drawn from the classic manual of the Sufi

master, Qushayri.[22] Another Spanish Jew, the famous student of Maimonides, Yosef ben Yehudah of Ceuta (ca.1160-1226) may also have studied with Averroes (Abu al-Walid Muḥammad ibn Rushd, 1126-1198), the great Spanish Arab philosopher, making him an heir to the two greatest Jewish and Muslim philosophers of the time.[23]

In the 12th-century, many such Spanish Jews began to arrive in Egypt as refugees, fleeing the Almohad persecutions in their homeland, including the great Maimonides.[24] It is clear that the Jewish-Sufi sect of Fustat (Old Cairo) in Egypt was active during Maimonides' tenure as *rayyis al-yaḥud*, leader of Egyptian Jewry, and that later, the leadership of the Jewish-Sufi sect was comprised of a significant number of politically prominent persons with close family and national ties, many of them of Spanish origin like Maimonides.[25]

It is doubtful that Maimonides himself belonged to the Jewish-Sufi sect, though there are indications that he both knew about Sufi-styled Jewish practitioners and included some aspects of Sufi ideas in his Judeo-Arabic work *Dalalat al-Ḥa'irin* (translated into English as *The Guide to the Perplexed)*. Somewhat critically, he writes about those who repeat the name of God—and here he uses the word *zikr* or *dhikr*—simply because an authority-figure told them to do so, without first pursuing a thorough examination of, and achieving a hard won humility before, God's unknowable nature. He follows this by saying that such practices should only be attempted after this attainment, which might be read as an endorsement of *zikr*, if practiced properly.[26] Maimonides, as we see throughout his *Dalalat* (and particularly in his relationship to his student, Yosef ben Yehudah of Ceuta, to whom the book is dedicated), is almost rigid in his commitment to a systematic course of intellectual and spiritual development (in which no steps are ever skipped). Thus, his criticism may be less directed at Sufi-styled spiritual practice than the practice of it by the unqualified.[27]

There is little other evidence to suggest that Maimonides was involved in the Jewish-Sufi sect. I suspect it was a phenomenon known to him, practiced by colleagues and companions, about which he had personal reservations. However, there is no such ambiguity about his son's involvement.

When Maimonides died in 1204, his eighteen year-old son, Avraham ben Moshe Maimuni, succeeded him as *rayyis al-yaḥud,* the leader of Egyptian Jewry (later *nagid).* In time, Rabbeynu Avraham ('our master' Abraham) would also become the leader and most outstanding spokesman of the Jewish-Sufi sect, who referred to themselves as *"ḥasidim."*[28]

Though he would effectively found a Maimonidean dynasty of Jewish-Sufism, it is clear that Rabbeynu Avraham was not the founder of the Jewish-Sufi sect. In his *Kifayat al-'Abidin* ('Guide to the Servants of God'), he refers to an elder contemporary, "our companion on the path of God" *(saḥibuna fi derekh Ha-Shem),*[29] Rabbi Avraham he-Ḥasid (d. ca. 1223), with whom he worked closely, and who may have been a friend and mentor.[30] Rabbi Avraham he-Ḥasid, along with his brother, Yosef, are alternately referred to as leaders of the Ḥasidim, or "head of the Ḥasidim," *rosh he-ḥasidim.*[31] Likewise, Rabbeynu Avraham's father-in-law, Rabbi Hanan'el ben Shmuel, was also an important Jewish-Sufi leader,[32] and there is even some suggestion that Avraham's maternal ancestors may have belonged to or had long-held sympathies with the Jewish-Sufi sect.[33]

Nevertheless, it appears that something coalesced for the sect under Rabbeynu Avraham's leadership, defining the character of the community, and setting up a dynastic relationship with the Maimuni family that would last at least five generations.[34] No doubt, part of it was the legitimacy offered the sect by the fact that the *mawla* or *shaykh* of the community was also the *nagid* (lit. 'prince' or 'ruler') of all Egyptian Jewry.

Under Rabbeynu Avraham, the Jewish-Sufi practices of the community would become formalized, and in the *majlis* of the *nagid*—the 'private salon' of Rabbeynu Avraham—*de rigueur*, or obligatory. One of the pre-eminent scholars of Jewish-Sufism, Paul Fenton, has nicely summarized the distinctive Sufi-influenced practices of the community (often integrated with traditional Jewish prayer practices), given here in my own words . . .

> *Ablutions:* Going beyond traditional Jewish practice, the Egyptian Ḥasidim valued the Muslim emphasis on washing the feet as well as the hands before prayer (which may have seemed merely obvious in a Middle Eastern cultural context).[35]
>
> *Prostrations:* The once traditional practice of prostration in the Jewish prayer service was restored, but now following the form of Muslim prostrations, touching the 'seven points' to the floor (i.e., the roots of the toes, the knees, palms, and forehead).[36]
>
> *Kneeling:* Likewise, kneeling would become a part of certain portions of the Jewish prayer service, following the custom (if not the exact form) of Muslim prayers.[37]
>
> *Spreading the Hands:* During particular supplications in the prayer service, the Egyptian Ḥasidim would lift their hands in a supplicating manner, palms upward.[38]
>
> *Weeping:* The accessing of deep emotions in prayer, especially those emotions connected with remorse, leading to tears and genuine *t'shuvah* or 'repentance,' was encouraged.[39]
>
> *Orientation:* The etiquette of the prayer service among the Egyptian Ḥasidim was to pray in orderly rows, as Muslims do, in the direction of the *'aron kodesh*, or 'holy

ark,' which benefitted both the general decorum of the service, and also allowed room for prostrations.[40]

Rising and Fasting: Among the major practices of the Egyptian Ḥasidim was the night vigil of *qiyam was-siyam*, 'rising and fasting,' recommended by Baḥya ibn Paquda, in which one rose in the night to pray and make prostrations of obeisance through the night.[41]

Seclusion: Perhaps the peak of spiritual commitments was that of *khalwah*, 'seclusion' or solitary retreat (often in dark places), for periods of up to forty days (which Sufis called the *'arba'in)*, for the purpose of achieving the state of 'internal seclusion' *(khalwah batinah)*, leading to an encounter with the 'divine presence' *(ḥaddral-ilahiyya)* and 'prophetic union' *(wusul nabawi)*.[42]

Incubation: A secret practice related to communing with the divine presence in sleep, referenced by Rabbeynu Avraham, but which is left unexplained.[43]

Remembrance: Though no description of the classic Sufi practice of *zikr* (or mantric 'remembrance' of the divine names or formulae) has yet been found in the writings of the Egyptian Ḥasidim, there are tantalizing references like that already mentioned by Maimonides, and one in Rabbi Avraham he-Ḥasid's commentary on the *Song of Songs*, where he says that one can attain "to the spiritual realm through the practice of inward and outward holiness as well as the extreme love of God and the delight in His recollection *(zikr)* and holy names."[44]

The obvious mirroring of many aspects of Muslim prayer or *salah*, as well as the outright adoption of various features of Sufi culture and practice would be significant enough to raise the eyebrows of any observant Jew in his day or after; but still

more astounding is Rabbeynu Avraham's open and positive references to Muslim Sufis with regard to these practices in his *Kifayat*, suggesting that the Sufis of Islam actually "walk in the footsteps of the prophets of Israel," keeping their practices and offering an example to the Jews of his time.[45] It is an amazing statement, perhaps unprecedented in the history of Judaism up to that point.

The Restoration of the Jewish-Sufi Legacy

Despite the obvious daring of his work, Rabbeynu Avraham finds justification for all the Sufi practices he mentions—such as rising in the night, the master-disciple relationship, and the wearing of the patched wool garments—in the *TaNaKh*, the biblical canon.[46] They are identified, as we have already noted, as traditions of the "prophets of Israel," and thus his *Kifayat al-'Abidin* is filled with references to them and examples from the Hebrew Bible. The portions of the *Kifayat* that are still extant read like a Jewish-Sufi manual, outlining the *maqamat* or various 'stations' along the Jewish-Sufi path, describing qualities to be developed—such as compassion, generosity, contentment, humility, reliance on God, vigilance, zeal—just as one might find in Qushayri's *Risalah*, but here illustrated with specifically Jewish examples. Whether read as a Jewish-Sufi text, or simply as a work of Jewish *mussar*, ethical literature, the *Kifayat* is a masterpiece.

Although hidden in his father's shadow for almost 800 years, Rabbeynu Avraham Maimuni is now appreciated for his own genius and contributions to Jewish thought and practice. The once accepted opinion of the 19th-century Jewish historian, Heinrich Graetz, that "Abraham Maimuni was a man of learning, not of original, intellectual power" who "followed with slavish fidelity in the footsteps of his great father" has now been dispelled.[47] While he maintains his father's philosophical

positions, and his father's mode and style of halakhic or Jewish legal observance, his personal spiritual emphasis is bold, original, and devotionally-oriented in the way of the Sufis.

Today, some believe that had the *Kifayat al-'Abidin* been translated into Hebrew in Rabbeynu Avraham's time, it would have revolutionized Judaism, spreading its influence throughout the Jewish world.[48] Sadly, this did not happen, and the greater part of his legacy remained largely unknown and unappreciated for centuries. It is only in the last fifty to a hundred years, with the uncovering of the Cairo Genizah, that we have really begun to learn something of how revolutionary Rabbeynu Avraham was in his day, and how the Jewish-Sufi community of Egypt operated under the Maimuni family's influence for up to five generations before disappearing from the historical record.

For many Jews today who have found inspiration in Sufism, or who have even become Sufis, the legacy of the Egyptian Ḥasidim stands as a testimony to the possibilities of a marriage between these traditions and a validation for their personal experiences as believing Jews with modern Sufism. It is perhaps also a confirmation of something which Rabbi Moshe Galante learned in his encounter with the Holy Dervish, and something which my own master, Reb Zalman, once said to a group of young Jews on Yom Kippur in the 1970s. Inviting an elderly Palestinian Qadiri-Rifai *shaykh*—Sidi Hasan of Balata—to address and lead the congregation in the Sufi practice of *zikr*, Reb Zalman said to the young Jews present, "Now *kindelakh* (children), I know you are not used to hearing the *Ribbono shel Olam*, the 'master of the universe,' addressed by the name *'Allah,'* but I can assure you, it is truly the same God."[49]

hitbodedut p'nimit

Seeking Internal Seclusion

The Zikr of the Egyptian Ḥasidim *

In the summer of 2008, I drove down to Questa, New Mexico, to do a private retreat at Lama Foundation near the burial place of the Jewish-American Sufi master Murshid Samuel (S.A.M.) Lewis. My temporary 'home' for that retreat was the "Maqbara Hut," not far from the grave, built on the very spot where my own *murshid* Zalman Schachter-Shalomi, of blessed memory, had done a forty-day retreat in 1984. My sole companion was to be the *Kifayat al-'Abidin* of Rabbi Avraham ben Moshe Maimuni (1187-1237) who had founded a Sufi-inspired Hasidic dynasty in 13th-century Egypt.

Although hidden in his illustrious father's shadow for almost 800 years, Rabbi Avraham Maimuni has recently begun to be recognized for his own unique contributions to Jewish spirituality—contributions which are clearly influenced by the teachings and practice of medieval Sufism.[1] While such influence is not without precedent in Judaism, nowhere is it more openly expressed, or by a religious leader with more temporal authority than Avraham Maimuni, the acknowledged leader *(nagid)* of Egyptian Jewry in his time. In his *magnum opus*, the *Kifayat al-'Abidin*, or 'Guide to the Servants of God,' he goes

* Edited from "The Merging of Two Oceans: Sufism and Hasidism I," a talk given in New Lebanon, New York, on April 28th, 2017, at the Abode of the Message, and *"Khalwah Batinah,"* given in 2018 or 2019 in Boulder, Colorado to Inayati-Maimuni murids.

so far as to say that the Sufis of Islam walk in the footsteps of the prophets of Israel, and that some of the practices of the prophets have now been transferred to the same.[2]

This declaration of admiration for Muslim Sufi practices and values in a time of conflict between the Abrahamic religions (in both the political and doctrinal spheres), coupled with an obvious embrace of Sufi ideals, is what first brought Avraham Maimuni to the attention of a few serious academic scholars early in the 20th-century, as well as a growing number of Sufi-influenced Jewish spiritual seekers since the late 1970s.[3]

But even as interest in and studies of Avraham Maimuni's life and works have increased, one thing has remained elusive—a clear and unambiguous picture of his own Jewish-Sufi meditation practice, or more specifically, a direct link to that most characteristic of Sufi practices, *zikr* or 'remembrance' of God, as understood by the sect.[4]

To many Jewish-Sufi enthusiasts and scholars of the medieval Jewish-Sufi sect, the omission is puzzling. There is a general feeling that the sect must have practiced some form of *zikr*, but no description of it has yet been found. There are of course tantalizing references to those who "repeat the name of God," or who "delight in God's recollection *(zikr)* and holy names,"[5] but no explicit description of *zikr* as a practice of the Jewish-Sufis.

In discussing this omission with Reb Zalman, we both felt that the sect would have used Hebrew, and would, for obvious reasons, have avoided the Muslim creedal statement, *La 'ilaha 'illa llah*, the anchor of *zikr* for Muslim Sufis.[6] He was himself of the opinion that they would likely have used a parallel phrase more strongly identified with the Jewish liturgy, such as *ain keloheynu*, 'nothing like our God,' possibly followed by *ain kadoneynu*, 'nothing like our lord.'[7] However, this is only speculation.

Nevertheless, I felt sure there was something still to be learned from the *Kifayat* of Avraham Maimuni. Thus, I took the book into retreat with me in the summer of 2008, intending to study the chapter on *khalwah* between periods of my own *zikr* and meditation.

One day, sitting on my mattress in the Maqbara Hut, pouring over the text once again in the light from my window as a storm passed over the Rio Grande Gorge, I saw it—right in the place that had drawn the attention of others through the years—a meditation practice, described in what some traditions might call 'twilight language.' That is to say, gently disguised in a series of biblical quotations to conceal it from the eyes of those who might condemn the sect for such practices.

The Politics of Concealment

In Aryeh Kaplan's *Meditation and the Bible*, the late 20th-century proponent of Jewish meditation gave many readers their first glimpse of Avraham Maimuni, devoting an entire chapter to a cryptic passage in the *Kifayat*, largely composed of verses from the Hebrew Bible, which he believed referenced the "meditative state." In describing the practice which leads to this state, Kaplan quotes from the most explicit part of the passage, which speaks in the broadest terms of withdrawing the senses from worldly things and focusing them instead upon God, using the imagination and scenes from the natural world to contemplate the grandeur and majesty of God . . .

> The main method of meditation as outlined by Rabbi Abraham, thus involves the contemplation of nature. A person can contemplate the greatness of the sea, marveling at the many creatures that live in it. One can gaze at a clear night sky, allowing his mind to be completely absorbed by the glory of the stars. Through

such intense contemplation, one can attain a meditative state directed toward the Divine.[8]

While Rabbeynu Avraham—'our teacher Abraham'—does indeed suggest the use of such imagery, I believe this imagery is only one licit or easily acknowledged part of a still concealed practice encoded in seemingly harmless (if somewhat cryptic) biblical quotes. Read in a particular light, however, I believe these carefully selected and arranged verses might be seen as instructions, a key to unlocking the secret of what Rabbeynu Avraham calls *khalwah batinah,* 'internal seclusion.'[9]

But why should he conceal the practice at all? Why should it be necessary to bury a practice of your own community in biblical verses that are more likely to obscure than reveal? This was likely done by design, both as a way of proving a biblical precedent for the practice, and in order to disguise it from the uninitiated; for through this practice, he says, "the prophets *(anbiya)* achieved union *(wusul)* with God."[10]

In our culture of information easily accessed, where nearly every kind of knowledge is available at one's fingertips—unrestricted, unfiltered, and unrefined—it is difficult to fathom why someone would want to conceal a spiritual practice considered to be of benefit to the practitioner. But in the 13th-century, esoteric instructions were not so openly discussed; they were considered sacred in themselves, and often preserved and protected by the rite of initiation. The more potentially potent a practice, the more dangerous it was considered for those who were not properly prepared; therefore, it was all the more zealously guarded. Thus, in explanation, Rabbeynu Avraham quotes, "It is the glory of God to conceal a matter." (Prov. 25:2)[11]

What was the nature of the danger? The problem then as now has to do with those who would try to do such practices in a vacuum, without the support of the teachers, teachings, and context that make them safe and meaningful. In the absence

of these safeguards, the practitioner can often draw erroneous conclusions from their experiences, distorting the message with the ego's narrow interpretations, sometimes causing harm to oneself or others. Thus, practices were carefully guarded and usually given over orally from master to disciple.

But there were other, more worldly reasons for Rabbeynu Avraham to conceal this practice. For even though he was the leader of Egyptian Jewry in his time, it is well known that he faced strong opposition from rival claimants for that leadership,[12] and that this opposition was focused on his so-called "reforms" in the liturgical rite of the Egyptian Jews, which included numerous prostrations and praying in orderly rows while facing the *'aron kodesh* or 'holy ark.'[13] In this opposition, his rivals actually complained to the Muslim Ayyubid government, coming just short of accusing Rabbeynu Avraham of *bid'ah*, or unlawful religious innovation (something which carried very serious consequences among Muslims).[14] In this, they felt justified, as many of Rabbeynu Avraham's reforms bore an unmistakable resemblance to Muslim religious practices and customs that could be seen everyday in the culture around them.

In response to these charges, Rabbeynu Avraham was forced to write a personal letter to the sultan, signed by some 200 witnesses, explaining that these practices were in no way unlawful, and were, in any event, confined to his personal *majlis* or private salon and not imposed upon others.[15] Nevertheless, he was still motivated to justify their inclusion in the rite and to explain the truth of their origins in the *Kifayat* . . .

> Take heed, in this respect, not to confuse innovated doctrines and practices with ancient ones, which, after having been neglected and forgotten, have been revived and restored, such as the question of prostration under discussion. Indeed, prostration is a halakhic obligation and an ancient Jewish rite, which [because of the tribulations] of the Exile, has been abandoned for

> numerous years. Now that its obligatory nature has been realized and adopted by some, it appears to the unversed and ignorant as a new *(mustagadd)* religious practice, whereas in fact it is a renewal only in respect of the intermediate period [when it was neglected], and not in relation to the time of the original Jewish rite.[16]

This is no mere justification; Rabbeynu Avraham is actually pointing to a historical reality. Prostration was indeed a part of the original Jewish prayer rite and was only modified when it became a prominent feature of Christian (and later Muslim) worship. In some ways, he is being bold enough to assert that Jews should not have abandoned this practice for fear of comparisons with their Abrahamic siblings. He wants to emphasize the ancient origins of the practice, and to make the point that this is not an *innovation,* but a *restoration.*

However, he was also only too aware of the part that the politics of comparison were playing in this debate; so as certain as he was of their ancient origins in Judaism, he could not afford to overemphasize the similarities with Muslim practice. As the *nagid* of his people, Rabbeynu Avraham was forced to walk a fine line, speaking openly of the superiority of some Muslim Sufi practices while carefully emphasizing their indebtedness to the Hebrew prophets.[17]

This was also likely the case with regard to the Sufi practice of *zikr* and what he calls 'internal seclusion.' It is probable that Rabbeynu Avraham was personally convinced that the origins of *zikr* practice were firmly rooted in the way of the Hebrew prophets; and even though he could point to verses suggestive of *zikr* in Torah, he was on nowhere near as sure ground as he was with prostration (for which he could find clear references in the Mishnah).[18] Thus, in this case, the practice needed to be disguised, so as not to bring further condemnation down upon

his disciples and fellow-seekers. *Zikr* practices, if indeed they existed, would be among the most closely guarded secrets of the Jewish-Sufi community.

The Jewish-Sufi Practice of Internal Seclusion

With all of this in mind, let us take a look at the unusual *zikr*-like meditation practice Rabbeynu Avraham seems to be suggesting in the opening section of his chapter on *khalwah*—the traditional Sufi term for 'retreat.' Here he makes a distinction between *khalwah zahirah*, 'external seclusion' (in the Judeo-Arabic of the book), and *khalwah batinah*, 'internal seclusion', saying: "The sole purpose of external seclusion is the attainment of internal seclusion, which is the final rung on the ladder to God, and itself constitutes union with God."[19] That is to say, the outer seclusion achieved in retreat is only a precondition for cultivating an interior seclusion, which leads to, and indeed is itself an 'encounter' or 'union' *(wusul)* with God.[20] Thus, as is the case with most discussions of meditation, both the practice and the result are described using the same terms, in this case *khalwah batinah*, or 'internal seclusion,' the name of the practice and its goal.

Now Rabbeynu Avraham goes on to make what are perhaps his most explicit statements about *khalwah batinah* . . .

> Internal seclusion refers to the complete sincerity of heart for which David prayed, saying, "God, create in me a pure heart, and renew my spirit *(ru'aḥ)* within me" (Ps. 51:12), and as Assaf attained, saying, "My body and my heart are emptied; God is the rock of my heart and my eternal portion." (73:26) Thus, we empty the heart and the mind of everything except God, allowing them to fill with God's exalted divinity.

> We accomplish this through a partial withdrawal of our senses, the detachment of our impulses from worldly things, reorienting them instead toward God alone, filling the mind with God, and using the imagination to support its observation of God's majestic existence in such things as the awesomeness of the sea, encompassing an abundance of life, and the magnificent movement of the heavens and the stars of the sphere![21]

The fact that these statements are fairly explicit suggests that these are not the aspects of the practice that he needs to conceal from the uninitiated. Nevertheless, we can still learn a number of important details from them.

First of all, "internal seclusion," he tells us, is a state that is equivalent to the "complete sincerity of heart" for which King David prayed in Psalm 51:12. The verse itself may be seen as an oblique reference to the practice of internal seclusion being the means of creating "a pure heart" and renewing the spirit. The second verse, attributed to Assaf in the Psalms, points to the desired state this practice is meant to produce, likely a reference to what later Hasidic masters will call *bittul ha-yesh*, and Sufis, *fana*—the complete effacement of the ego before God. Thus, 'purity of heart' refers to a heart emptied of everything but God, God becoming "the rock" or foundation of that heart.[22]

This is accomplished, says Rabbeynu Avraham, "through a partial withdrawal of our senses, the detachment of our impulses from worldly things, reorienting them instead toward God alone." This itself is a good definition of a meditation practice. We withdraw our senses from the outside world and its distractions, allowing the mind to take the shape of nature's vast expanses and great terrains, its oceans and fields of stars, creating peace inside of us.

> Now, with regard to the clearing of the heart and mind of everything other than God, Assaf has said, "My body and my heart are emptied"; and with regard to withdrawing the impulses from everything other than God, he has said, "Whom have I in heaven but you? And beside you, I desire nothing upon the earth" (Ps. 73:25); and with regard to directing all our impulses to God alone, Yesha'ayahu has said, "To your name *(shem)* and your remembrance *(zekher)* is the desire of my soul. My soul *(nefesh)* desires you in the night, and my breath *(ru'aḥ)* seeks you in earnest." (Isa. 26:8-9) Furthermore, David has said, "My soul thirsts for you; my body yearns for you," (Ps. 63:2) and he later adds, "My soul *clings* to you." (63:9)
>
> With regard to the quieting of the senses, it is written, "I have made a covenant with my eyes"[23] (Job 31:1) and the righteous "shut their eyes to evil." (Isa. 33:15) As David says, "Turn my eyes away from seeing what is false." (Ps. 119:37) And concerning the need to restrain the senses and desires for the sake of keeping the mind on God, Elisha said to [his disciple] Gehazi, "If you meet anyone, do not greet them; and if anyone greets you, do not respond." (2 Kings 4:29) *Understand this well.*

Now, as Rabbeynu Avraham prefaces each verse with statements such as, "With regard to the quieting of the senses," and "with regard to withdrawing the impulses," and "with regard to directing all our impulses to God alone," it is obvious that the verses which follow are meant to serve as implied instructions, or at the very least, veiled references to the practical aspects of internal seclusion.

Reading these biblical quotes as references to aspects of a meditation practice, it is not hard for someone experienced with

different forms of meditation to discern various well-known techniques for withdrawing the senses, curbing mental chatter, and replacing this chatter with a specific object of meditation.

Rabbeynu Avraham addresses the "quieting of the senses" through a number of different verses dealing with the senses most necessary to control during meditation—touch, sight, and hearing. He begins by repeating the words of Psalm 73:26, "My body and my heart are emptied" or "fail." This 'failure' of the body would seem to suggest 'inactivity,' or the relative stillness of body necessary to quiet awareness of it during meditation. In a surviving fragment of the *Kifayat* on the structure of the Jewish liturgy, Rabbeynu Avraham writes:

> One might sit before God in a way that inspires inward focus. This is done by sitting with the limbs gathered together, facing the Temple in Jerusalem—ideally, with no separation between them and the wall.[24]

This would seem to indicate at least the possibility of a seated meditation posture used to promote stillness in the body.

However, the most obvious references Rabbeynu Avraham makes to a withdrawal of the senses are with regard to the faculty of sight. In this instance, he gives us three biblical verses, suggesting that one should make "a covenant" with one's eyes, shutting one's "eyes to evil," and turning them "away from seeing what is false." From these references, it seems clear that one is to close one's eyes during the practice of internal seclusion. But it also suggests a common worldview among Sufis and other mystics of the period, i.e., that the world is a trap filled with tantalizing illusions which one should try to escape.

Last is an apparent reference to the faculties of hearing and speech: "If you meet anyone, do not greet them; and if anyone greets you, do not respond." (2 Kings 4:29) However, Rabbeynu Avraham also says that this verse concerns the need to restrain one's "desires for the sake of keeping one's mind on

God." Much discussion in meditation and prayer manuals is devoted to the control of impulses and 'distracting thoughts'—*maḥshavot zarot.* It is common to find excuses for abandoning one's meditation, and even more common and difficult to deal with the endless mind-chatter that constantly threatens to dominate the period. Most often, these thoughts and impulses are treated like unwelcome guests acting autonomously in the mind or heart. Sometimes they are labeled as they arise—'thoughts,' 'feelings,' 'sensations'—before one returns to the object of meditation, or simply ignored in favor of the object of meditation. With regard to the practice of internal seclusion, Rabbeynu Avraham seems to suggest the latter, that we do not allow ourselves to run off after our thoughts, saying, "do not greet them," "do not respond." This interpretation would seem to be confirmed by a passage in the *Maqala al-Ḥawdiyya* of Rabbeynu Avraham's son, Ovadyah . . .

> My son, if you desire to achieve the state of [internal] seclusion *[khalwah]*, and a worldly thought crosses your mind while you are seated in contemplation, I urge you to expel and banish it from your 'house' and 'bar the door' against it. "Above all that you guard, guard your heart." (Pr. 4:23)[25]

The instruction is clear: the practitioner is not to engage the different thoughts, feelings, or sensations that arise during the practice of internal seclusion.

What do we engage instead? After all, the act of meditating is not about *not*-thinking, *not*-feeling, or *not*-sensing; it is about re-orienting awareness to another more helpful or desirable object, in this case, as Rabbeynu Avraham tells us, "directing all our impulses to God alone." Thus, he quotes from Isaiah, "To your name *(shem)* and your remembrance *(zekher)* is the desire of my soul. My soul *(nefesh)* desires you in the night, and my breath *(ru'aḥ)* seeks you in earnest." (Isa. 26:8-9) And from King David,

"My soul thirsts for you; my body yearns for you," (Ps. 63:2) "My soul *clings* to you." (63:9)

Here are the key instructions of the practice, and in many ways, the most 'encoded,' dependent as they are on the meaning of key words in Hebrew and a knowledge of key concepts in Sufism. Put simply, the *zekher* or 'remembrance' of God is accomplished through the placing of God's 'name' *(shem)*—the object of the meditation—on the *ru'aḥ* or 'breath,' held in 'intimacy,' *d'veykut,* in the darkness of the senses. This is an excellent description of the Sufi practice of *zikr khafi,* 'silent' or 'hidden remembrance.'

At the end of the passage, Rabbeynu Avraham shifts suddenly (or seems to) and begins to speak of how "the prophets and their disciples also used musical instruments and melodies to achieve internal seclusion, to awaken their desire for God, and to purify their interior from everything other than God." This may be a reference to the Sufi practice of *sama*, courting ecstasy in *zikr* with music and the recitation of love poetry.

From this, I believe we can infer a general knowledge and practice of *zikr* among the Jewish Sufis of Egypt. But when I run these clues through the filter of my own meditation experience and interpret the words strictly (without assuming that they conform to conventional forms of *zikr),* I actually come up with an unusual form of *zikr khafi.*[26]

Because there are no explicit references to repetition of the divine name in these 'instructions' (if they be such), I have left open the possibility that the name is actually held loosely, as it is in Centering Prayer, and perhaps used only to 'wash over,' 'scrub,' or 'absorb' thoughts, feelings, or sensations as they arise. This would make it a more 'receptive' or apophatic form of *zikr,* creating a distinctively spacious 'presence' and awareness.[27] Of course, this is only my own interpretation.[28]

Nevertheless, I offer it here as I have come to understand it, and as I have practiced it (with my own emphases and additions) for many years.

The Practice of Khalwah Batinah

1. Carry out the proper ablutions,
Washing the hands and feet before beginning.

Although the common practice is to wash the hands alone before prayer, Rabbeynu Avraham Maimuni suggests washing both the hands and the feet.[29] This custom is based on the passage in Exodus 30:18-21, which speaks of the requirement for the priests to wash their hands and feet in a basin before entering the Tabernacle. The purpose of this is explained by his son, Rabbi Ovadyah Maimuni in his *Maqala al-Ḥawdiyya*—"it is fitting to prepare oneself [for prayer] through the ablution of one's hands and feet, thus restoring and arousing the soul,"[30] and "one must carry out the ablution of the hands and feet in order to circulate the natural heat of the body, thus arousing the soul."[31] Thus, we make the ablution in the following way . . .

> Pour water from a cup over the hands and feet into a basin. The hands are washed in the traditional manner, pouring water from the cup three times over the entire right hand and then the left. Then one lifts the hands, pronounces the blessing and dries them. After this, one takes the cup in the left hand and pours water over the right foot three times, then taking the cup in the right hand, over the left foot three times. After which the feet may be dried without a blessing.

If the washing of the feet is difficult for any reason, this step may be omitted or fulfilled in intention. It is also the custom of some to swish water in the mouth before prayer, or to wash the face and wet one's hair, but these customs are not obligatory.[32]

2. Sit down facing Jerusalem and whisper:
Lev tahor b'ra-li Elohim, v'ru'aḥ nakhon ḥaddeysh b'kirbi.
"Create in me a pure heart, God, and renew my spirit within me."
(Ps. 51:12)[33]

In the *Kifayat al-'Abidin,* Rabbeynu Avraham writes—"One should sit before God in a way that inspires an inward focus, with the limbs gathered together, facing the Temple in Jerusalem,[34] ideally with no separation between one and the wall."[35] Likewise, we read, "King David came and sat before God" (2 Sam. 7:18), and "When Sh'lomoh (Solomon) finished offering to *Yah* all his prayer and supplication, he rose from where he had been kneeling in front of the altar of *Yah.*"[36] (1 Kings 8:54) Thus, we might take the following posture . . .

> Sit with your calves and ankles folded under the knees and buttocks, ideally with the great toe of the right foot over that of the left. The palm of the right hand is then placed on the left thigh, and the right wrist is taken hold of by the left hand.

In this posture, both the legs and the arms form two different ways of writing the Arabic word, *la,* meaning 'no' or 'not,' suggesting one's nothingness before God, and the intention to release the ego during one's seclusion.[37]

Again, if this posture is not possible for some reason, one may take a posture more suitable to one's particular needs. Likewise, if one cannot discern the direction of Jerusalem, or if it is not preferable to face in that direction in a given place, at

least make clear the intention to do so before sitting down upon the *sajjada* (prayer carpet) in the posture described.

3. Close your eyes and find a quiet and natural breathing rhythm,
Allowing yourself to attune to its peaceful movements.

In the *Kifayat*, Rabbeynu Avraham tells us—"With regard to the quieting of the senses, it is written, 'I have made a covenant with my eyes' (Job 31:1) and the righteous 'shut their eyes to evil.' (Isa. 33:15) As David says, 'Turn my eyes away from seeing what is false.' (Ps. 119:37)" Closing our eyes, we remove ourselves from the distraction of our sense of sight and open to an 'internal seclusion' where we may meet God in the darkness.

Rabbeynu Avraham also seems to be making reference to both the shutting of the eyes and paying attention to the breath when he quotes the prophet Isaiah, who says, "My soul desires You in the night, and my breath seeks You in earnest." (26:9) Thus, we close the eyes and establish a stable and even breathing pattern, always breathing gently and easily through the nose.[38]

4. Take a moment and allow your heart to imagine
God's majestic existence in such things as the awesomeness
Of the sea, the magnificent vault of the heavens,
Or some other inspiring vista in nature.

As we begin to quiet our senses, turning our eyes and our thoughts away from the mundane world, we open them to an interior world of holiness. We replace the mundane with the awe-inspiring, readying our hearts for an experience of the presence of God. To do this, Rabbeynu Avraham recommends a short journey into the imagination, using it to observe "God's majestic existence in such things as the awesomeness of the sea,

and the magnificent movement of the heavens and the stars of the sphere."[39] But we are not limited to these examples. We might just as well imagine some other grand or awe-inspiring vista in nature, for "The whole earth is filled with God's glory." (Isa. 6:3) But the imagery need not be grand or majestic, as long as it suggests the sacred or holy for you.

5. Then, in the darkness of your senses,
Silently introduce one of the divine names
Into your heart on the in-breath.

Rabbeynu Avraham tells us that "we empty the heart and the mind of everything except God, allowing them to fill with God's exalted divinity."[40] Thus, into that emptiness, we allow one of the divine names to fill our awareness, and we bring it gently into the heart on the in-breath, as we are taught, "To your name *(shem)* and your remembrance *(zekher)* is the desire of my soul; my soul *(nefesh)* desires you in the night, and my breath *(ru'aḥ)* seeks you in earnest." (Isa. 26:8-9) In doing thus, we fulfill the words of King David, who says, "Create in me a pure heart, God, and renew my spirit within me." (Ps. 51:12)

6. When you become aware of other thoughts,
Feelings or sensations entering your consciousness,
Do not entertain them in any way.

However, it will not be long before different thoughts, feelings or sensations arise to draw your attention away from your remembrance of God's name. When this happens, Rabbeynu Avraham recommends that we follow the instructions of the prophet Elisha, who says, "If you meet anyone, do not greet them; and if anyone greets you, do not respond." (2 Kings 4:29)[41] To this advice, Rabbi Ovadyah Maimuni, in his *Maqala*, adds . . .

> My son, if you desire to achieve the state of [internal] seclusion *[khalwah]*, and a worldly thought crosses your mind while you are seated in contemplation, I urge you to expel and banish it from your 'house' and 'bar the door' against it. "Above all that you guard, guard your heart." (Pr. 4:23)[42]

From all this, we learn that we are not to engage these different thoughts, feelings or sensations that arise during our seclusion.

7. Simply return your attention to the divine name,
Taking hold of it as a refuge from these
Thoughts, feelings, or sensations.

But even if we do not "greet" these thoughts, feelings or sensations that arise, even if we "bar the door" against them, they will not go away of themselves. Something must be done, even if we do not engage them directly. Thus, Rabbi Ovadyah tells us, "Pursue your task, strengthening your zeal, and you will not find it difficult to remove this worldly thought from your mind; if it is [a] necessary [thought], it will return."[43] That means we simply have to re-introduce the divine name on the in-breath at this moment; we go to it as a refuge from these thoughts, feelings or sensations, as Rabbeynu Avraham reminds us, "My soul clings to You" (Ps. 63:9),[44] and as the sons of Koraḥ sing, "God is our refuge and stronghold." (Ps. 46:2) Thus, the divine name simply replaces the distraction as the pre-occupation of the mind, or is gently placed over it. We do not try to force anything out of our minds or grab hold of the divine name with violence. Returning to the divine name is done gently and with sacred intention.

8. At the end of your period of seclusion, whisper:
Kalah sh'eyri u'l'vavi; tzur-l'vavi v'ḥel'ki Elohim l'olam,
"My body and my heart are emptied; God is the rock
Of my heart and my eternal portion." (Ps. 73:26)[45]
Then remain in silence with your eyes closed
For a few moments more.

The period of seclusion should be maintained for at least five to ten minutes, though twenty to thirty are preferable. When this period is complete, one should whisper the words of Psalm 73:26 and then remain in silence for a few moments (or even minutes) more before rising. It is better to transition slowly than to rise and re-enter the world of mundane concerns too quickly.

Suggestions for Practice: It is not necessary to repeat the divine name continuously as one generally does in *zikr;* simply introduce it whenever you feel a stirring in your heart to do so, or when some other distracting thought, feeling, or sensation arises. Repeat it gently for as long as you feel it necessary to do so. Do not be surprised if it becomes vague or disappears altogether at some point, leaving you in silence. If it does, just allow your mind and heart to settle into the silence you have made to accommodate God's presence. As Rabbeynu Avraham writes, "we empty the heart and the mind of everything except God, allowing them to fill with God's exalted divinity."

Try to avoid creating goals and expectations for your period of seclusion, such as achieving a sense of God's presence or *wusul,* or of having no thoughts. The thoughts, feelings, and sensations that arise are a natural part of the process and should not cause you any anxiety or worry, even if you spend an entire period of seclusion replacing them with the divine name.

That, in itself, is a successful period of seclusion. Likewise, if you should fall asleep, it is not a problem; simply return to the divine name upon waking.

ma'asiot

A Hidden Dialogue

Hasidism's Secret Dialogue with Sufism *

A Ḥasid once met an army returning from a great battle. He stopped them and said, "Praise God, I see you have returned from the lesser battle carrying your reward; now you must go and prepare for the greater battle."

The soldiers asked, "And what is the greater battle?"

The Ḥasid replied, "That is the battle with our instincts and their armies!"[1]

This beautiful Hasidic anecdote is found in the *Toldot Ya'akov Yosef* of Rabbi Ya'akov Yosef of Polonoyye (d.1782), an early disciple of the holy Ba'al Shem Tov, the founder of the Hasidic movement in 18th-century Ukraine. And yet, it is not actually a 'Hasidic' anecdote at all; it is an anecdote repeated from the medieval Hebrew translation of Rabbi Baḥya ibn Paquda's Judeo-Arabic work *Al-Hidayah ila-Fara'id al-Qulub*, or 'Duties of the Heart,' which is itself drawing on a *ḥadith* or 'report' of the prophet Muḥammad from Sufi sources. Thus, the "Ḥasid" is

* Edited from "The Merging of Two Oceans: Sufism and Hasidism I," a talk given in New Lebanon, New York, on April 28th, 2017, at the Abode of the Message, and "Sufism and Hasidism," given on November 1st, 2016 at the Abode of the Message.

none other than the Prophet.[2] For when Muḥammad and the early Muslims were returning from a battle, we are told that he turned to his companions and said, "Now we are leaving behind the lesser struggle *(jihad al-asghar)* and proceeding to the greater struggle *(jihad al-akbar)*. The exhausted and wounded warriors were stunned at his words and asked him, "What is the greater struggle?" The Prophet replied, "The greater struggle is with the self *(mujahadat an-nafs)*."[3]

For many of the Ḥasidim of the Ba'al Shem Tov, the *Ḥovot ha-Levavot*—the translation of Baḥya ibn Paquda's Sufi-influenced work into Hebrew—served as a foundational text for the life of the spirit. Thus, a hidden dialogue ensued between Sufis and Hasidim, neither aware of the other.

The Eastern European Hasidic movement formed around Rabbi Yisra'el ben Eliezer (1698-1760), called the Ba'al Shem Tov, from whom all latter-day Hasidic lineages stem. The Ba'al Shem Tov taught that God could be served joyfully through the body in ecstatic prayer, in song and dance, instead of the harsh ascetic disciplines commonly practiced among mystics of the time. He taught that 'worlds,' 'souls,' and 'divinity' were all overlapping, interpenetrating realities, ultimately reducible to one divine reality, as it says in Isaiah 6:3, "the whole earth is filled with God's glory." Thus, the step between us and the divine is only a matter of perspective, overcome through a powerful intentionality *(kavanah)* and cleaving *(d'veykut)* to God.

In the 18th-century, various Hasidic masters or *rebbe'im* began to emigrate to *eretz Yisra'el*, the 'land of Israel' (then a part of the Turkish empire) intending to fulfill the commandment to dwell in the land. (Num. 33:53) Companions of the Ba'al Shem Tov like Gershon of Kittov and Naḥman of Horodenka, as well as prominent Hasidic masters of the next generation like Menaḥem Mendel of Vitebsk and Avraham of Kalisk, all settled in the Holy Land in the latter half of the 18th-century.

Still others came for pilgrimage, "to walk four ells" there, according to the Talmud, assuring them of a place in the world-to-come *('olam ha-ba)*. (Ketubot 111a)

Suffice it to say, these journeys brought East European Jews into contact with Muslim civilization, with Turks and Palestinian Arabs. Ḥasidim traveled by ship over the Black Sea to Istanbul, and from Istanbul over the Mediterranean to Palestine, often at the risk of their lives. The Ba'al Shem Tov himself tried unsuccessfully to make the journey on three occasions, once being prevented by shipwreck. His older contemporary, Rabbi Naḥman of Horodenka (1680-ca.1766), who ultimately settled in Palestine, tells of one journey in which they ran out of provisions on the ship, forcing him to seek help in an Arab city where there were no Jews . . .

> An Arab took me in and offered me food. I had not eaten for several days and quickly washed my hands and said the blessing for bread. I was just about to take a bite, when a thought entered my mind: "Do not eat the bread of one with a mean eye." [Prov. 23:6]
>
> A random thought is not without meaning, and I did not know what to do. I had already said the blessing, but I realized the significance of this thought, and was determined not to eat anything of this Arab. Just then another thought entered my mind. "I have commanded the Arabs to feed you."[4] [1 Kings 17:4]

The last quotation actually reads, "I have commanded the ravens to feed you." But the Hebrew word for 'ravens,' *orvin*, owing to a similarity of sounds, was sometimes used to refer to Arabs. Thus, when the verse in Hebrew occurs in his mind, Rabbi Naḥman of Horodenka interprets it as a reference to the Arabs feeding him, just as the ravens fed the prophet Elijah in his time of need.

For a Hasidic Jew of this or any other period, accepting food from a non-Jew is a dilemma: food must be kosher. Muslim *ḥalal* is not kosher for a Jew. So Rabbi Naḥman would have been on guard not to transgress this law, even in his desperation. Accepting bread, of course, is allowed; but his thoughts continued to warn him against being tempted by his own desperation. So it is only after checking his desire and receiving a second consoling thought that he is able to eat.[5]

It is an interesting anecdote, and gives us some insight into the types of encounter that these Hasidic pilgrims would have had with Muslims along the way.

A more famous and far more mysterious episode occurs in the life of Rabbi Naḥman's grandson and namesake, Rebbe Naḥman of Bratzlav (1772-1810), who makes a journey to the Holy Land in 1798. For Rebbe Naḥman and his Ḥasidim, every step of this pilgrimage is interpreted in mystical terms, and thus his puzzling encounter with a young "Ishmaelite" is the subject of much speculation.

While the Rebbe was still in Haifa, a strange and mysterious event occurred.

One day, a young Turk (Ishmaelite) came to see the Rebbe, speaking to him at length in Turkish. But the Rebbe didn't understand a word of Turkish.

Still, the Turk was there for every meal, day and night. To all appearances, he seemed very fond of the Rebbe.

Then, one day, the Turk came in to see the Rebbe, apparently enraged and armed to the teeth. He yelled at the Rebbe in Turkish and the Rebbe appeared stunned and confused. When the Turk left, a woman from Wallachia (a region in Romania,

near Turkey) who had overheard told the Rebbe: "For God's sake! Flee this house! That Turk has just challenged you to a duel!" Hearing this, the Rebbe left immediately and took refuge with Reb Ze'ev Wolf, who concealed him in an inner room.

The Turk soon returned to the house where the Rebbe had been staying and asked: "Where is the man who was staying here? Please tell him I am very fond of him. If he still wishes to go with the caravan to T'veryah [Tiberias], I will give him the donkeys. I'll even give him my own horse! He has nothing to fear from me anymore!"

The Turk was telling the truth. The Rebbe returned to the house and, once again, the Turk came to the house and sat down, smiling and saying nothing to the Rebbe. Then he became very friendly and showed the Rebbe great affection.

This whole episode was very strange, and the Rebbe's comments did little to clear it up. However, he did say, "I suffered more from that Turk's love than his hatred and anger."[6]

Thinking about this episode over the years (though not wanting to be carried away with too much mystical speculation of my own) I have wondered if there might actually be a reasonable—though still spiritual—explanation for what happened. My one indulgence is that I like to believe, as my own teacher before me, that the "Ishmaelite" was a Sufi.

Now, we must understand that Muslim Sufis in that region enjoyed the luxury of a certain liberal-mindedness and freedom unknown to Rebbe Naḥman. For Rebbe Naḥman was a Jew from the Christian dominated Ukraine, relatively untraveled up to that point, and likely unfamiliar with people of other spiritual trajectories and different cultures. Unlike Islam, Christianity

had no concept of a 'people of the book' *(ahl al-kitab)* respecting the rights of other 'children of Abraham.' Thus, a Jew from the Ukraine, having suffered endless persecution by Christians, had good reason to be cautious about all overtures from the 'enemy camp,' and was not likely to feel anything but suspicion in encounters with non-Jews.

Muslim Sufis of the region, on the other hand, enjoyed the privilege of belonging to the dominant culture in a meeting place of cultures, where Jews and Christians came and went regularly. And coming from such a place, Sufis at least were often far more friendly toward their Abrahamic siblings.

Now I can imagine that a Sufi adept might be 'sensitive' to the presence of such a soul as Rebbe Naḥman possessed, recognizing the 'fragrance' *('attar)* of holiness about him, and wish to meet with him. However, being ignorant of both Hebrew and Yiddish, he shows him affection in every other way possible, as he might do with his Sufi brethren. But Rebbe Naḥman, even if he *too* recognized a 'fragrance' of holiness about this young man, would have no context for accepting such a possibility from a Muslim. For unlike Baḥya ibn Paquda or Avraham Maimuni, he was not raised in a Muslim country, nor exposed to the genuine piety of devout Muslims. Thus, Rebbe Naḥman is polite, but generally unresponsive to his Muslim companion.

After a day or two, the Muslim Sufi of my imagination realizes the true nature of the impediment and decides to resort to a kind of 'display' of dervish wisdom that will certainly communicate. If the impediment is mistrust, then it should be brought out into the open. Thus, it is as if the young Muslim said to Rebbe Naḥman, "So, you don't understand my affection? This you'll certainly understand! And now that what you've expected is out in the open, I can make an apology for it and perhaps we can start again!"

After this, they sit in peaceful silence together and the Sufi gives Rebbe Naḥman a gift that will allow him to travel to his destination in peace.

From this perspective, I can easily understand why Rebbe Naḥman might say, "I suffered more from his love than his anger." For the anger was only what was expected from a non-Jew, but the love was troubling, possibly raising disturbing questions for him about the exclusive truth of Judaism.

I cannot say for certain that this is what happened, but I want to offer it as a possible, hopeful explanation.

Interestingly enough, this story has a kind of postscript. For a few years before my own *mushid* and *rebbe* died, an Israeli professor who had written several works on Rebbe Naḥman, told him something that seemed a kind of confirmation of the friendliness of this encounter. He was visiting someone in a two-bed hospital room in Haifa. In the other bed was an old Palestinian man who overheard them discussing Rebbe Naḥman. After a moment, he begged their pardon, and said, "It was my great-great-grandfather who met with that rabbi."[7]

Souvenirs from the Journey

Apart from the interest these rare accounts provide, the journeys of these Ḥasidim through Muslim lands also offer us a wonderful ancillary benefit, or at least an explanation for a tantalizing mystery. There are a number of classic Hasidic stories *(ma'asiot)* and parables *(meshalim)* told in the tradition that probably have their origins in Sufism or Islamic civilization, the Ḥasidim who tell them in complete ignorance of the fact.

The most famous is 'The Parable of the Hidden Treasure,' perhaps best known from Paulo Coelho's *The Alchemist.* In the Hasidic tradition, it is attributed to both Rabbi Simḥah Bunem of P'shyskha (ca.1765-1827) and Rabbi Naḥman of Bratzlav,

whose encounter with the "Ishmaelite" we have just described. The story, as I tell it, is a fusion of both versions.

Somewhere in the Ukraine, in a little *shtetl*—a small Jewish settlement—lived a poor man named Eisik the son of Yehkel. Now Eisik lived in a little shack—almost a hovel—with a door falling off the hinges; and each night he dreamed in his hovel the same dream. It was a dream of a treasure. The treasure was hidden under a bridge in Vienna outside the royal palace. In the dream, Eisik knew, if he could only get to that spot under the bridge, he could dig and uncover the treasure.

The first night that Eisik dreamed of the treasure he thought little of it. After all, a poor man *would* dream of treasure, wouldn't he? But when he began to dream the same dream night after night, exact in every detail, he started to wonder if it might actually mean something.

Finally, after weeks of dreaming of the treasure under the bridge, almost crazed with curiosity, he felt it *must* mean something! So he packed some provisions and tied them in a cloth to a stick and set out on the long journey from his little *shetl* in the Ukraine to the great city of Vienna in Austria, a journey of more than two weeks and a thousand miles.

After a long and exhausting journey, walking for days on end, occasionally getting a ride on a hay cart, sleeping in barns and under bushes on the hard earth, Eisik finally makes it to Vienna.

There, before his very eyes—magnificent in all its grandeur—is the bridge outside the royal palace, just as it had appeared in his dream. And there too is the palace, just as he had seen it in the dream; everything is exactly the same! Now he

knew he would find the treasure, for he had never seen pictures of any of these things before.

In his excitement, Eisik began to run for the bridge, the older man transformed into a child hurtling toward the object of his desire—*running, running*—until suddenly, he saw something that had not been in his dream, and he came to an almost catastrophic stop!

There, stationed at the end of the bridge, were two large and intimidating soldiers of the royal guard.

Eisik, still panting, gulped hard. He had no idea what to do. The treasure was *right there,* just under the bridge, and he knew exactly where to dig. *But the guards!* How could he get passed the guards?!

After an hour of pacing back and forth in anxious indecision, Eisik is suddenly shaken from his deliberations by a harsh voice.

"Jew! What are you doing there? Come over here—*Now!"*

It was one of the soldiers. What should he do? *Run?* No, they would certainly catch him. So, terrified, he did as he was ordered, and walked trembling to where the soldiers stood at the end of the bridge.

"What the hell are you doing?" asked the soldier who had called him. "You've been walking back and forth and talking to yourself for over an hour now. Do you have some idea of trying to beg money from the royal family when they pass?"

Eisik was in a bind. Knowing that he was about to be rousted and forced to move on, he broke down and began to tell the soldiers the truth—a desperate, rambling tale of the dream, the long journey, the privations he had suffered, and of his certainty that the treasure was there, just a few yards away!

A grim silence followed this outburst, the soldiers staring at Eisik with hard eyes. Finally, they burst out laughing!

"That's the stupidest thing I've ever heard!" said the soldier who had called him over. "What an idiot! You traveled over a

thousand miles because you had a dream about a treasure?! This is what comes of following your dreams! If I followed my dreams, where would I be? I had a dream just last night that I had traveled all the way to your home country in the Ukraine, to some pathetic little village full of Jews, and entered some little shack—a hovel really—with a door falling off the hinges, belonging to 'Eisik the son of Yehkel'! I go to the back of the shack, just behind a little black stove there is a loose floorboard, which I lift, and beneath it is a fabulous treasure, just like yours! Ridiculous! Do you know how many Jews are named 'Eisik' in the Ukraine? And the ones that aren't called 'Eisik' are called 'Yehkel'!"

The soldiers laughed harshly.

Eisik the son of Yehkel, hearing a perfect description of his own home, down to the smallest detail, including the loose floorboard behind the stove that he had never bothered to lift, enthusiastically reached out and shook the guard's hand, saying, "Thank you very much! I have to go now!"

Thus he began the long journey back to the Ukraine, walking rough roads through sun and rain, catching rides in hay wagons whenever possible, sleeping in barns and under bushes on the hard earth until, finally, he made it home to his little shack. Rushing in, he swung the door so hard that it finally fell off its hinges, and he ran straight to the stove, behind which he found the loose floorboard, which he then lifted. There, just as the soldier had described, was a treasure!

Sometimes you have to go very far to find what you had all along.

In Reb Simḥah Bunem's version, the city is "Krakow." Rebbe Naḥman says "Vienna." He tells us that in everyone there is a "treasure," but they must find a *tzaddik*, a 'righteous' person, a *rebbe*, to help them uncover it. Reb Simḥah Bunem says, take this story to heart, for there is a treasure you cannot find anywhere else in the world, not even with the *tzaddik*.[8]

From Martin Buber's telling in his German collection of Hasidic tales—*Die Chassidischen Bücher*—it is picked up by the great German Indologist Heinrich Zimmer, who gives a wonderful version of it in, of all places, his *Myths and Symbols in Indian Art and Civilization*.[9] But we must circle back before the venerable Hasidic masters picked it up to find its deeper origins.

In the 9th-century, we find the first references to the *Kitab Alf Laylah wa-Laylah*, 'the book of the thousand and one nights,' popularly known as *The Arabian Nights* in English. In the Egyptian recension, on Nights 351 and 352, we find the same basic motif of two dreamers—one in Baghdad and one in Cairo—and a treasure at the end. The man from Baghdad is arrested for vagrancy in Cairo as he wanders like a madman looking for a treasure of which he has dreamed. The judge before whom he is brought laughs at him, and tells him of his own dream in which a treasure is to be found in Baghdad beneath a fountain! The first man returns to Baghdad and finds his treasure beneath the fountain as described.[10]

Inspired by this tale in *The Arabian Nights*, the Argentinian writer Jorge Luis Borges wrote "The Story of the Two Dreamers," which later inspired the Brazilian author, Paulo Coelho, to write *The Alchemist*.[11]

However, there is also a Sufi version of the tale, which puts the two dreamers in Rey and Damascus, and adds new details.

A dervish who lives in Rey, near Tehran, dreams night after night of a treasure in Damascus. Finally, unable to shake the dream, he sets off for Damascus, more than a month's journey from Rey.

Once there, he begins to wander the city, having no idea of where to search for the treasure. Just as he is ready to give up, he bumps into a man who says, "Friend, you look bewildered; how can I help you?"

The dervish replies in frustration—"It's stupid . . . I've been plagued by these dreams that I would find a treasure in Damascus, and fool that I am, I'm here searching."

The man laughs out loud and claps the dervish on the back, "That's so funny; I've dreamt for years of a house in Rey with a treasure buried in the courtyard near a tree."

The dervish, with sudden recognition, thanks the man and returns to Rey. Entering the courtyard of his house, he proceeds to dig near the tree and finds a solid gold mortar.[12]

Did Rebbe Naḥman of Bratzlav or other Hasidic travelers hear these stories on their journeys to Palestine, perhaps during prolonged stays in Istanbul waiting for a ship? It is easy to imagine; after all, stories are the common coin of travelers, passed from one to another in the companionship of the road. Perhaps this is what is behind Rebbe Naḥman's teaching that "each faith has a special 'tune' and 'song,'" the divine 'note' ringing through all.[13]

Rebbe Naḥman also tells 'The Parable of the Poisoned Grain,' which in Sufism is 'The Parable of the Waters of Sanity.'

It happened once that Khwaja Khizr, the teacher of Moses, came with a warning for humanity—"Gather water while you may, for a great earthquake is soon to come that will cause the waters of the earth to disappear; and when they are renewed, the new waters will cause insanity."

In the end, only one person heeded the warning of Khwaja Khizr. They gathered water in great cisterns on a mountaintop, and when the earthquake came and the waters disappeared, they had enough and were sated.

Just as Khwaja Khizr had foretold, after a time, the waters were renewed in the rivers and lakes of the land. Curious, the mountain-dweller went down the mountain to observe the people in the cities below. As Khawja Khizr had said, they now thought and spoke in a confused manner that made no sense, and there was much strife and misery among them. Worse, they were hostile, thinking the sanity of the mountain-dweller was madness! Thus, the mountain-dweller departed quickly in fear, returning to their mountain abode to drink from the waters of sanity.

But, as time passed, the mountain-dweller became unbearably lonely. It no longer seemed worth it to be a sane hermit in solitude; so the mountain-dweller went down to the cities and drank the waters of insanity to live among the people, who now considered him restored to sanity.[14]

The modern Sufi anthologist, Idries Shah, attributes this version of the story to the Indian Chishti Sufi master, Sayyid

Sabir Ali-Shah (d. 1818), but suggests that it is actually far older, perhaps being a tale of the early Sufi master, Dhu an-Nun al-Misri (d. ca. 859).[15] Whatever its origins, it seems intimately connected to Rebbe Naḥman's 'Parable of the Poisoned Grain,' which gives the motif of the madness-inducing poison a slightly different slant.

One night, in the stars, the king of the land sees that the next grain harvest will be poisoned, and that whoever eats of it, will become crazy. So the king calls his prime minister, who is also his close companion, and asks, "What do you advise?"

The prime minister suggests that they gather great stores of this year's grain to live off for as long as the madness lasts.

But the king asks thoughtfully, "Is it really worth it to be the sane rulers of a crazy people? . . . The people will only think us crazy and themselves sane."

"What do you suggest we do then, my king?" asked the prime minister.

"We must eat the poisoned grain, too, just as the people of the land. But we will each mark our foreheads with a sign, a reminder to each other that we are both mad. Thus, when we see the mark on one another, we may say, 'Don't forget you're crazy!'"[16]

Here, the basic spiritual conundrum of whether it is better to live a sane life in isolation, or to live in the insanity of the

world among people, is given a new twist. We must live in the world's insanity, but we must not forget that both *we* and *it* are insane. Indeed, we must make a pact with one another in order to keep from being entirely lost in it.

It is also a parable about us and God, and God in us. God is the king who becomes mad, like us. As my *rebbe*, Reb Zalman, used to say, "God is an atheist, because God doesn't have a God to worship." Being deprived of the experience of discovering and delighting in God, God gets intentionally lost in ignorance, pulling the wool over the divine eyes and descending into our world of deluded consciousness and obscuration, until God's own divinity is forgotten. Knowing this would happen, God seeded our consciousness with a sign, a clue, to remind us, "Don't forget you're crazy!"[17]

The third parallel story that comes to mind is already described as such by Martin Buber in a wonderful essay comparing Hasidic tales to similar Zen and Sufi tales.

A Ḥasid, who has been studying with the Great Maggid in Mezritch, stops in Karlin on his journey back home to see his elder companion on the path, Rabbi Ahron of Karlin. Hurrying to Reb Ahron's door in the early evening, he knocks eagerly, seeing a light in the window.

From behind the door, he hears Reb Ahron call, "Who is it?"

The Ḥasid, certain that he will recognize his voice, calls back, "It is *I!*"

Silence.

The Ḥasid knocks again.

No answer.

“Ahron?” the Ḥasid calls out, desperately. “Why aren’t you opening the door?”

Finally, Reb Ahron’s voice calls back, “Who is it that presumes to say ‘*I*’ in the presence of God?”

The Ḥasid is taken aback; he then mutters under his breath, “I have not yet begun to learn.”

He turns around and returns to Mezritch.[18]

As Buber points out, the story is known in a fuller version in the *Mesnavi* of the Sufi master, Jalal ad-Din Rumi, possibly derived from an older tradition of Mansur al-Hallaj reported by al-Sulami.[19]

A friend knocks at a door of a friend.

The friend answers, “Who is it?”

The knocker says, “It is *I!*”

The friend does not open the door.

For a year, the knocker wanders, suffering in separation from the friend, before returning to knock again.

The friend asks, “Who is it?”

The knocker answers, “*You.*”

The door opens.[20]

Among Sufis, God is always the *wali*, the 'friend' or 'beloved.' But whether friend or beloved, the message is clear to both Sufis and Ḥasidim—in the house of either, there is no room for two I's.

Buber speculates that this may be a story that was picked up by travelers through Turkey in the Sabbatean period; but it really does not matter; for we have before us an obvious 'inner link' between Sufism and Hasidism, a link of values and parallel teachings.[21]

The Inner Link

Of the dialogue of values and parallel teachings, there is much to be said. For instance, and perhaps reflecting a knowledge of Baḥya ibn Paquda's retelling of the *ḥadith* on *jihad*, of which we have already spoken, Rabbi Nosson of Nemirov (1780-1844) teaches in his *Likkutey Halakhot* that . . .

> All the wars in the world are really only reflections of the one war against the *yetzer ha-ra*, the 'impulse to negativity' in us. Even the conflicts one has with enemies in the material world are nothing but the war against one's own negative impulse. Thus, the real war to be fought is the war against the *yetzer ha-ra*. This is why the priests would speak to the people of Yisra'el before they went out to war with their 'enemies,' reminding them that these combatants really represented their own obstacles to a life of holiness. For our sages have said, "Corresponding to a person's enemies in the lower world are also enemies in the worlds above." (Sanhedrin 44b, 103b) And when a person begins to battle the 'enemies above,' 'enemies below' rise up to assail them and prevent them from serving God. But this is precisely when one must stand firm and hold the

> line against the enemy, fighting with all one's strength in the service of God![22]

Likewise, in Baḥya ibn Paquda's *Duties of the Heart*, we find the Sufi notion of "learned ignorance,"[23] which is elegantly expressed in the *Kimiya-yi Sa'adat* of Abu Ḥamid Ghazzali . . .

> No created being is aware of the perfection of God's majesty. God alone knows the reality of God and God's knowledge. The declaration of our inability to know this is the very limit of knowledge and truly righteous. Indeed, the confession of our ignorance is praise to God. The ultimate end of the spiritual journey and the traveler's search for intimacy with God is astonishment, the limit of human reason, and sublime bewilderment.[24]

In the teachings of the Ba'al Shem Tov, we find this same notion: the supreme knowledge, and the end of our search for knowledge, especially of God, is to know that we do not know. So he asks the question: why then should we make the attempt to know God? As part of his answer, he offers us a parable . . .

> There are two commoners who wish to know the king, and who are thus invited into the palace. The first enters the palace and explores every hall, every chamber, every room, and every cabinet, delighting in becoming acquainted with every detail of the king's palace; nevertheless, in the end, they find that the king is not in any of the rooms or truly known through them. The second commoner, hearing that the king is not in any of the rooms, does not even bother to explore the palace.[25]

Rabbi Nehemia Polen explains this parable with a lovely illustration of his own. He says, imagine you have a child, and while you are out one day, you meet someone and ask them out of curiosity, "Hey, do you know my child?" The person answers honestly, "No, I don't think so." That, Reb Nehemia says, is simple ignorance. Now, imagine someone turns and asks the parent, "Do *you* know *your* child?" Well, the parent might say, "Yes, of course I know my child." Or, if they are a little more thoughtful, they might also look aside for a moment and then answer, "*No* . . . I don't know my child; every day, I look at them and find myself amazed. Everytime I think I know them, I am surprised to discover that I don't know them at all!"

This, he explains, is what the Ba'al Shem Tov wants us to understand about our so-called 'knowledge of God.' At the end of the day, you are honestly going to say, 'I don't know God.' But the whole spiritual journey is to go from the first ignorant unknowing to the humble, awe-inspired unknowing of the second example, which is filled with a rich depth and intimacy.[26]

Another parallel between Sufism and Hasidism was discerned by my teacher, Reb Zalman, who saw a connection between the "Toward the One" prayer of the 20th-century Sufi master, Hazrat Inayat Khan (1882-1927), and an 18th-century teaching of Rabbi Pinḥas of Koretz (1726-1791). The famous prayer of Inayat Khan says . . .

Toward the One
The Perfection of Love, Harmony, and Beauty,
The only Being,
United with all the Illuminated Souls,
Who form the embodiment of the Master,
The Spirit of Guidance

And Reb Pinḥas is reported as saying . . .

> What is God? *The totality of souls.* Whatever exists in the whole must also exist in the part. Therefore, in any one soul, all souls are contained.

For Reb Zalman, the "totality of souls," was very close to Inayat Khan's "the only being" who is "united with all the illuminated souls," forming the "embodiment of the master, the spirit of guidance." From this, he believed, we can understand from whence the great rebbes and shaykhs derive their remarkable insight; for whatever insight we receive—whether through the external master or the internal one—derives from "the spirit of guidance," or the 'great master,' if you will, a collective superconscious of illuminated beings producing a greater awareness than any individual is able to contain in themselves alone.[27]

In the last years of his life, Reb Zalman also excitedly shared with me another teaching of Rabbi Zvi Hirsh of Nadverna (d. 1802) which he had recently come across, and which he also interpreted in terms of the "Toward the One" of Inayat Khan . . .

> The *tzaddikim* (the 'righteous') are one unified whole, each *tzaddik* ('righteous leader') is connected to all *tzaddikim*, so that together they make one great *tzaddik*. This is what the sages meant when they said, "There is one pillar rising from earth to heaven, and its name is '*tzaddik*.' Who is this pillar? A *tzaddik* who feels completely unified and integrated with all the *tzaddikim* until they become truly one. Therefore, when a Ḥasid learns from *tzaddikim* other than their own *tzaddik*, it does not feel as if it is wisdom from 'another,' because it comes from the one great *tzaddik* connecting heaven and earth.[28]

This is consistent with the teaching of Reb Zalman's friend, the Jerrahi Sufi master, Shaykh Muzzafer Ozak (1916-1985), who says with regard to the prophets, "The sincere love that any Jew feels for the noble Abraham and the noble Moses will likewise be counted as love for Muḥammad, the Seal of Prophecy. Why? Because Allah Most High teaches clearly in His glorious Quran that all the Divine Messengers share a single essence."[29]

With regard to the Sufi practice of *zikr,* the repetition of divine names, there are a few references in the Hasidic corpus which bear some similarity. Again, in the teachings of Rebbe Naḥman of Bratzlav, we read . . .

> Although it is important to do *hitbodedut,* expressing your intimate thoughts to God each day, sometimes you find that you simply cannot do it, and you must be content to say a single word before God, and this is also very good. If you can only say one word, you should say it with concentration, and repeat it over and over again, countless times. You might even make this your prayer for a number of days, which is also a good practice. If you persist in repeating this word countless times, God will certainly have mercy on you and open your mouth, allowing you to express your thoughts freely![30]

Here, the comparisons to *zikr* are obvious; but Rebbe Naḥman mostly offers it as an option for getting unstuck when your *hitbodedut* (extemporaneous prayer) is not working—repeating one word over and over will eventually "open your mouth."

For the later Polish Hasidic master, Kalonymous Kalmish of Piasetzno (1889-1943), the repetition of divine names in a *zikr*-like fashion was actually about 'calming the thoughts' and

not about 'opening the mouth.' A disciple recorded the rebbe's advice in this regard . . .

> He then gave us practical advice on how to calm the thoughts: . . . One should look at one's thoughts for a small amount of time—say a few minutes—and then begin to see how slowly the mind is emptying, and how the thoughts stop rushing in their usual manner. Then, one should begin to say a phrase, such as *Ribbono shel Olam*, in order to connect the now empty mind with one thought of holiness. Then, one can begin to request in prayer what is needed, or in which way one needs to be made whole, or strengthened—as in faith, or in love.[31]

So, among these Hasidic masters, *zikr* of this sort was less a technique in itself than a means to cultivating prayer, the true art of Hasidism.

In the end, there is no necessity of finding precise parallels between Sufism and Hasidism, nor is it entirely desirable to do so. For those of us with connections to both traditions, the parallels themselves suggest an inner complementarity that is itself gratifying, and the nuanced differences only add dimensionality to our understanding and appreciation of both traditions.

Likrat ha-ehad

Reb Zalman's Journey
"Toward the One"
Translating Sufism into the Language of Hasidism *

Sometime in the mid-to-late 70s, my teacher, Rabbi Zalman Schachter-Shalomi—better known as 'Reb Zalman'—took it upon himself to translate the universalist Sufi prayer "Toward the One" into the traditional Hebrew of Ḥasidic Jews in Eastern Europe. The prayer itself was composed in English by the first Sufi master to bring Sufism to the West, Hazrat Inayat Khan (1882-1927), and is arguably one of the most popular prayers in the world today. But some might ask, why would a traditionally trained rabbi from Eastern Europe be interested in translating a Sufi prayer into Hebrew in the first place? That requires an explanation.

* Edited from "The Merging of Two Oceans: Sufism and Hasidism II," a talk given in New Lebanon, New York, on April 29th, 2017, at the Abode of the Message, as well as "Hasidism, Sufism, and a Universal Priesthood," a talk given at the Abode on September 17th, 2015, and a conversation with Rabbi Zalman Schachter-Shalomi, *z"l*, on the "Toward the One" after I discovered a copy of his Hebrew translation in his files. This conversation was later turned into an article for *Seven Pillars House of Wisdom*.

A Ḥasid Among the Sufis

Born in Zholkiew, Poland, in 1924, Reb Zalman was raised in Vienna, Austria, where his parents ran a small store. At fourteen, after the Nazi annexation of Austria in 1938, he fled with his family to Belgium where, in Antwerp, he first encountered Ḥasidim of the now extinct Niezhiner lineage of Ḥabad Hasidism. Disillusioned with Judaism (amid the realities of Nazi Europe), he found new perspectives and a living prayer-life among this radical group of Hasidic contemplatives. Unfortunately, Antwerp was bombed only a few months later, and he and his family were forced to flee in a coal train heading into France.

After a period of internment as refugees in Vichy France, the family made their way to Marseille, where Reb Zalman met Ḥasidim of the related Lubavitcher lineage of Ḥabad Hasidism. So, when he finally arrived in the United States in 1941, after a long journey, he presented himself at the court of Rabbi Yosef Yitzhak Schneersohn (1880-1950), the sixth *rebbe* or leader of the Ḥabad-Lubavitch lineage of Hasidism, to whom he then attached himself.[1]

The sixth Lubavitcher Rebbe, himself a refugee from the Holocaust, had recently established his headquarters at 770 Eastern Parkway in Crown Heights, Brooklyn. Reb Zalman entered the *yeshiva* (seminary) there, training to become a Hasidic rabbi. In 1947, he was ordained and sent out by his *rebbe* to college campuses to bring young Jews back to the traditional fold. A naturally talented and charismatic young teacher with broad interests, he went on to study pastoral psychology at Boston University, and eventually (after a short period as a pulpit rabbi) became a college professor at the University of Manitoba in Winnipeg, Canada, teaching psychology of religion and Jewish mysticism.

By the late '50s and early '60s, Reb Zalman had noticed a generational shift among his Jewish students. Passionate in his

desire to serve them, he sought to understand where they were coming from, exploring their questions as his own. It was clear that there was a deep spiritual impulse in them that was not being fed in the synagogues of the time. Though thoroughly grounded in the mystically-oriented tradition of Hasidism, he could see how the Jewish tradition in general was failing to meet Jewish needs in the wake of the Holocaust. Thus, many young Jews were finding their paths outside of Judaism in so-called 'Eastern religions.'

Already curious about other religious traditions, in the mid -1950s—in a move that separated him from many traditional Ḥasidim—he began to read deeply in mystical traditions at Boston University under the famous African-American Christian mystic, Rev. Dr. Howard Thurman (1899-1981), and soon began to seek out encounters with their practitioners. Before long, his knowledge of other traditions was considerable and became an integral part of the courses he taught in the psychology of religion.[2]

By the late 1960s, Reb Zalman was familiar with traditional Sufism through the writings of Idries Shah. He had also read the universalist Sufi writings of Hazrat Inayat Khan. But it was not until the early 1970s that he made his first real connections with Sufis.[3] These were the disciples of the Jewish-American Sufi master, Murshid Samuel or S.A.M. (Sufi Ahmed Murad) Lewis (1896-1971), a direct disciple of Hazrat Inayat Khan, who had become the leader of a new generation of universalist or Inayati Sufis, mostly "flower children" who had found their way to San Francisco. Contrary to common belief, Reb Zalman never met Murshid S.A.M., but first became acquainted with his successor, Pir Moineddin Jablonski (1942-2001), after being invited to teach in the Bay Area and connecting with "The Sufi Choir."

As most of Murshid S.A.M.'s students were still in their twenties when he passed, they naturally looked to Reb Zalman, then approaching fifty, as an elder mentor. Many also wanted

"a Jewish connection" through him and reciprocated by introducing the Hasidic master to Murshid S.A.M.'s 'Sufi dances' and walking practices, as well as *wazifa* practices using the ninety-nine 'beautiful names' of Allah. Thus, Reb Zalman began to study Inayati Sufism and to practice *zikr*, the repetition of the divine names on his own.

During one visit to the Bay Area, Reb Zalman was invited to a "holy man jam" (as these early interfaith gatherings were sometimes called) organized by Pir Vilayat Inayat-Khan in Santa Rosa, at which the Sufi Choir would be performing. This was his first meeting with the charismatic son and successor of Hazrat Inayat Khan.

The two men hugged, then Pir Vilayat looked Reb Zalman in the eyes and exclaimed, *"majzub!"*—'drunk'—recognizing Reb Zalman's God-intoxicated state. It was a Sufi compliment, and Reb Zalman said that he felt a clear heart attraction to Pir Vilayat at that time.[4]

In 1975, Reb Zalman was invited to teach for a semester at the University of California at Santa Cruz, allowing him to deepen his connections to the Bay Area Sufis. By now, he loved the teachings of Hazrat Inayat Khan and the practices of the Sufis. Of all the traditions to which he was exposed through the years, he said, "I was most at home among Sufis."[5] Thus, he decided to take initiation in the Inayati lineage of Sufism. As the lineage was universalist (and not confessionally bound to Islam), he felt this was not in conflict with his own commitments as a Jew and a rabbi. So he approached Pir Moineddin and asked him for initiation. Perhaps not surprisingly, Pir Moineddin demurred, feeling it was not his place to initiate an older and more accomplished master from another tradition. Instead, he suggested that Reb Zalman take initiation with Pir Vilayat.[6] Reb Zalman agreed to the suggestion, but only if Pir Moineddin would confirm the initiation afterward.

As it turned out, Pir Vilayat and Reb Zalman were both to participate in another 'holy man jam' soon after, and thus the initiation was arranged to take place during the break. In preparation, Reb Zalman wished to go to a *mikveh* in order to do a ritual immersion. But, unable to find a kosher *mikveh* anywhere nearby, he immersed in a local pool. He then dressed to honor the occasion in a black silk caftan, a black silk belt, and a large fur hat, the traditional clothing of a Ḥasid. He would go to his Sufi initiation as a Jew. It was a statement.

After the first half of the program led by Pir Vilayat was finished, and a beautiful performance by Pandit Pran Nath, the Sufi *pir* and Hasidic *rebbe*—dressed in the robes of their respective traditions—went aside to do a thing rarely seen in the history of religions, to unite two esoteric traditions born from different religions.

Pir Vilayat closed his eyes for a long time and then proceeded with the initiation. When it came to the moment of "taking hand"—initiation is often referred to as 'taking hand' in Sufism, as one takes the right hand of the master—at the moment when one would expect to be called a *murid* or disciple, Pir Vilayat called Reb Zalman "a *shaykh,*" a master.

Afterward, surprised by the turn the initiation had taken, Reb Zalman asked Pir Vilayat why he had called him a *shaykh* and not a *murid.*

Pir Vilayat answered, "As I was attuning to your presence, I found that I could not utter the word, *'murid'* . . . You are already a master."

Of course, it is well known that one of the great gifts of Pir Vilayat was his ability to attune and respond to the consciousness of the person before him. Thus, it seems that, somehow sensing Reb Zalman's 'state and station' within his own tradition—being already a Hasidic *rebbe*—he found that he could only acknowledge him as a *shaykh* in the Sufi tradition.

Reb Zalman asked, "What are my duties then?"

Pir Vilayat responded, "Treat it as a degree *honoris causa* until you know."[7]

In the years to come, Reb Zalman continued to study Sufism, eventually taking initiation into the Qadiri-Rufai *tariqah* under Shaykh Sidi Hasan al-Moumani of Balata who empowered him to lead *zikr,* and the Halveti-Jerrahi *tariqah* under his friend, Shaykh Muzaffer Ozak. He also formed important connections and friendships with Bektashi and Melami Sufis.

Nevertheless, his closest relationships continued to be with Inayati Sufis. He and Pir Vilayat would remain friends until the latter's passing in 2004, after which Reb Zalman would take a special interest in Pir Vilayat's sons, Zia and Mirza. Pir Moineddin, too, would remain a valued friend and colleague until his passing in 2001. Reb Zalman also maintained close ties with Pir Moineddin's successors, Pir Shabda Kahn and Murshid Wali Ali Meyer. But it was with two of Pir Vilayat's seniormost disciples that Reb Zalman would develop special relationships: Puran Bair would become a colleague, sometimes leading Sufi retreats for Reb Zalman, who in turn served as his rabbi and counselor (even conducting his son's *bar mitzvah* in green Sufi robes and a turban). Still closer was Thomas Atum O'Kane, former Secretary General of the Sufi Order, and Pir Vilayat's 'second' for many years. Atum would form a close spiritual bond with Reb Zalman, seeking his guidance on spiritual matters and working directly with him as his academic advisor on both his master's thesis and doctoral dissertation.

For Reb Zalman, the initiation into Inayati Sufism was also connected with the function of the Sufi *'cherag'* and the idea of a 'universal priesthood.' The non-denominational priestly function of the *cherag* allowed him a freedom that was not possible for him as a rabbi. It allowed him to perform non-Jewish weddings and other rituals for which he could not find a basis under Jewish law *(halakhah),* i.e., to function as a priest

of a universalist spirituality. Thus, the universalist "Toward the One" prayer of Hazrat Inayat Khan held particular significance for him.

Toward the One,
The Perfection of Love, Harmony, and Beauty,
The Only Being,
United with All the Illuminated Souls,
Who Form the Embodiment of the Master,
The Spirit of Guidance.

Translating the Toward the One into Hebrew

Once, as we discussed the "Toward the One," Reb Zalman told me that he initially had trouble getting through a single recitation of the prayer, saying . . .

> For even as I was speaking, I would be lifted "Toward the One" to regions of "Love, Harmony, and Beauty" where my feet no longer touched the ground of materiality, but instead were grounded in "The Only Being." I was overwhelmed by the energetic *qurb*—'proximity' to the One—in the words themselves. There was such holy precision in them and manifest spiritual energy that my heart could not fail to respond to them. And, as with other things that touched me powerfully from outside of the Jewish tradition, I immediately wanted to translate it into Hebrew, the language of my spiritual upbringing.[8]

For similar reasons, he had translated a number of the Indian devotional songs of the Baul singers into Hebrew,

and was even once at work on a translation of the Buddhist *Dhammapada* into Hebrew.[9]

The function of a translation, of course, is to give speakers of one language access to a message originally given in another. And yet, that translation is always an interpretation of that message and not the message itself; for each language has a beauty and sophistication of its own which resists translation; there are no one-to-one equivalencies for the cultural understandings of words translated from one language to another.

When Muslims speak of the miraculous *'i'jaz*, or 'inimitability' of the Arabic Qur'an, they are right. There is something about its content and form that cannot be reproduced. Thus, the Qur'an in translation is not considered *the* Qur'an by Muslims; it is an 'interpretation' or 'approximation' of it. That fact being acknowledged, the question is, how well does that translation convey the original message—with what accuracy and precision—and does it create a parallel effect in the consciousness of readers and listeners from other cultures?

In the decades since Reb Zalman made his own private translation of the "Toward the One" in the mid-to-late 1970s, other Hebrew translations have appeared in various places. All of them, however, are interpretations of the original English into Modern Hebrew. Whereas, Reb Zalman had rendered the "Toward the One" in the traditional Hebrew of the Hasidic *beyt midrash*, or 'house of study,' where the Jews of pre-Holocaust Eastern Europe had prayed and explored Torah together. That is to say, he had rendered it in the language of Hasidism and Hasidic texts.

As many have noted, the Hebrew of early Hasidic texts is often "poor in vocabulary, syntax, and grammar, but rich in history, symbolism, and allusion."[10] It was precisely these latter qualities, which Reb Zalman, by his own admission, wished to invoke by mirroring the former.[11]

Today, there is a traditional Hebrew of Judaism and a secular Hebrew of social discourse. For Israelis raised with it, Modern Hebrew is more fluid and syntactically elegant; but for others, for whom liturgical Hebrew is primary and traditional texts fire the imagination, there are words and phrases in Modern Hebrew that do not come across as 'authentically Jewish,' as odd as that may sound. Thus, Reb Zalman labored to translate the "Toward the One" in such a way that those who have a solid footing in traditional Judaism may add it to their prayers without feeling it is something foreign.

This is the translation into traditional Hebrew as he gave it to me . . .

לִקְרַאת הָאֶחָד
הַיָּחִיד, הָאֶחָד וְהַמְּיוּחָד
שְׁלֵמוּת הַאֱמֶת, הַצֶּדֶק וְהַתִּפְאֶרֶת,
הַנִּמְצָא הַיָּחִיד,
הַכּוֹלֵל כָּל הַנְּשָׁמוֹת הַנְּאוֹרוֹת-
יוֹצְרֵי הַגְּשָׁמַת הָרַבִּי-
הַרוּחַ הַקּוֹדֶשׁ

A printed version from Reb Zalman's files
with vowel points added to my copy.

Transliterated from Hebrew into English characters, it would appear something like this . . .

(Ashkenazi Pronunciation)

Likros ha-eḥod,
Ha-yoḥid ho-eḥod v'ha-m'yuḥod,
Shleymus ha-emes, ha-tzedek v'ha-tif'eres,
Ha-nimtzo ha-yoḥid,
Ha-kolel kol ha-n'shamos ha-ne'oros,
Yotzrey hag'shammas ha-rabbi,
Ha-ru'aḥ ha-kodesh.

(Sefardi Pronunciation)

Likrat hā-eḥād,
Ha-yāḥid ha-eḥad v'ha-m'yuḥād,
Sh'leymūt ha-emet, ha-tzedek v'ha-tif'eret,
Ha-nimtzā ha-yāḥīd,
Ha-kōlel kōl ha-n'shāmōt ha-ne'ōrōt,
Yōtzrey hag'shāmmat hā-rabbī,
Ha-rū'āḥ ha-kodesh.

Some of the words, of course, will be the same in nearly all translations into Hebrew; but there will also be critical differences, and in this case, even additional words.

The phrase *Likrat ha-eḥad* is a fairly direct translation of 'Toward the One' into Hebrew. But wanting it to impart more of the sense of non-duality intended by Hazrat Inayat Khan, Reb Zalman felt it was necessary to include a supplementary phrase from the Jewish tradition. In Hasidism, a distinction is made between *eḥad ha-manuy*, the number one, and *eḥad v'ain sheyni*, the one for whom there is no other, no two or three.

The phrase in traditional Hebrew that best expresses this notion comes from the Italian kabbalist, Rabbi Moshe Ḥayyim Luzzatto (1707-1747), the author of the *Mesillat Yesharim,* who gives us the phrase—*Eḥad, yaḥid, u'meyuḥad,* 'One uniquely simple unity.' (This of course parallels the Arabic phrase used by Sufis, *Aḥad, waḥid, wa-samad.)* But since this Hebrew phrase cannot follow *Likrat ha-eḥad* in a natural manner, Reb Zalman created an echo of it with *ha-yaḥid ha-eḥad v'ha-m'yuḥad.*

In the next line, we have *shleymut ha-emet, ha-tzedek v'ha-tif'eret,* which is quite different from what we have in the English "Toward the One" and requires some explanation. *Shleymut,* or 'wholeness,' is simply the word that best conveys the notion of 'perfection' in Hebrew;[12] but *ha-emet, ha-tzedek v'ha-tif'eret* actually translates to 'truth, righteousness, and beauty.' Somehow, *emet,* 'truth,' struck him as a better choice from within the Jewish tradition to put in this trilogy of words.[13] Nevertheless, he believed *ahavah,* 'love,' *(ha-ahavah* if put into the whole phrase) would still be acceptable here. He likewise chose to use *tzedek,* 'righteousness' for 'harmony' because 'righteousness' in Hebrew carries with it the sense of harmoniously balanced scales.[14] *Tif'eret* is indeed the Hebrew for 'beauty,' but it is also a word loaded with meaning in the world of Jewish mysticism. In a very simple sense, *tif'eret* is what balances and completes the forces of love and justice in the universe, so often opposed to one another.

The next three lines are fairly straightforward. *Ha-nimtza ha-yaḥid* is basically, 'the only one who can be found,' 'the only existent.' *Yaḥid* is also the 'one infinite being,' the 'simple unity' without separation or parts, God without limits. *Ha-kolel kol ha-n'shamot ha-ne'orot* is 'who contains all the souls that have been illuminated.' And *Yotzrey hag'shammat ha-rabbi* is 'forming the actualization of the master,'[15] or *'rebbe'* in Hasidic parlance.

Finally, in the last line, Reb Zalman chose not to translate the words, "The Spirit of Guidance," but to replace them with the parallel concept from the Jewish tradition, *ha-ru'aḥ ha-kodesh,*

'the spirit of holiness' or 'Holy Spirit.' This is the phrase most often used in the talmudic and midrashic literature to denote prophetic inspiration. And while there are statements in the tradition that say that *ru'aḥ ha-kodesh* departed after the passing of the prophets Haggai, Zachariah, and Malachi, Ḥasidim clearly believe that it is still available, even today.

Now, if one were to translate this more traditional Hebrew version of the "Toward the One" back into English, it would probably come out something like this . . .

Toward the One,
Unique, Alone, Unified,
The Completion of Truth, Righteousness, and Beauty,
The only One in existence,
Who contains all the Illuminated Souls,
Forming the actualization of the Master,
The Spirit of Holiness.

While there is a clear variation in the sense of the words, Hazrat Inayat Khan's "message" of the unity of all being is still available in them.

Without a doubt, Inayat Khan's "Toward the One" is so precise and beautiful in English that all attempts at translation will continue to fail in one way or another; for it has its own miraculous *'i'jaz,* and will likely stand among the great prayer-creations of the English language forever. Nevertheless, Reb Zalman offers those of us who might consider ourselves 'Jewish-Sufis' an opportunity to add this prayer to our other Hebrew prayers in a way that feels natural in the prayer-space of Judaism.

ani ma'amin

Hyphenating Sufism and Hasidism

The Formation of the Inayati-Maimuni Order*

"In Sufism, I'm an 'uncle' and not a 'papa.'"

This is how my *murshid*, Rabbi Zalman Schachter-Shalomi, or 'Reb Zalman' as he is generally known, used to answer people about his own status within Sufism before I came along.

In August of 1998, shortly after my 26th birthday, I moved to Boulder, Colorado, in order to meet him. He was then 74 years old and the holder of the World Wisdom Chair at the Naropa Institute, a Buddhist-inspired ecumenical institution founded in 1974 by Chögyam Trungpa Rinpoche. I had been a History of Religions student at Michigan State University up to that point, and had enrolled in the Indo-Tibetan Buddhist Studies master's program at Naropa to continue my education. However, my primary objective was to learn with Reb Zalman. So, for the next two years, in addition to my studies of Buddhism and Buddhist philosophy, I took classes with him in "Judaism as a Civilization," "Jewish Ethical Literature," and attended his popular "World Wisdom Lectures" on Wednesday afternoons, in addition to any other public talks or events he was offering around Boulder.

---

* Edited from "The Merging of Two Oceans: Sufism and Hasidism II," a talk given in New Lebanon, New York, on April 29th, 2017, at the Abode of the Message, and "Hasidism, Sufism, and a Universal Priesthood," a talk given at the Abode, September 17th, 2015, and other talks.

As graduation approached in April of 2000, Reb Zalman called me into his office at what had now become Naropa University.[1] I think he believed that I might be leaving Boulder with graduation and wanted to talk about my future.[2]

He sat me down in his office in the main building at Naropa and said: "I'm not sure what to do with you; I could make you a rabbi, but I don't think it would serve your soul well to do that. And the truth is, I probably use less than ten percent of what I learned in *yeshiva* ('seminary') to become a rabbi."

He was silent for a moment, looking at me discerningly. He then closed his eyes and began to rock gently back and forth. With his eyes still closed, he said: "I can see in what worlds your soul is Jewish; but it is not necessarily for you to represent Judaism in *this* world. But if you can stand to exist at the crossroads of religion—in that uncomfortable place—you will help a lot of people." Then he opened his eyes and said, almost casually, "What do you know about Sufism?"

I was caught off guard by the whole conversation, but managed to respond that I was familiar with Sufism from my studies of comparative religion, and had done some study of the writings of Abu Ḥamid al-Ghazzali as an undergrad while working with my earlier mentor, the Qur'an scholar, Alford T. Welch.

He then told me the story of his own involvement with Sufism over the years, adding that he had been made a *shaykh* in the Inayati lineage of Hazrat Inayat Khan in the mid-1970s by his friend, Pir Vilayat Inayat-Khan.

"Up 'till now," he said, "I have been an 'uncle' and not a 'papa' in Sufism. This is the answer I have given over the years when people have asked me for initiation. I have been happy to give a little advice, maybe a practice or two; but I did not want to take responsibility for anyone else's spiritual life as a Sufi. However, I am going to initiate *you.* We will continue to study *ḥasidus* (Hasidism) together; but I also want you to study Sufism

with two senior students of Pir Vilayat with whom I have had a special relationship over the years—Puran Bair and Atum O'Kane—studying meditation with one and the teachings with the other."

So began my journey with Sufism, and my future work at the "crossroads of religion."

Initiating a Sufi Path

The year before—mid-way through my graduate studies—I had begun working on a writing project with Reb Zalman, exploring the kabbalistic concept of *tzimtzum,* based on a talk he had given to B'nai Or students in 1985. Now, as I approached graduation, I had begun a much larger book project on the teachings of the Hasidic masters, as much to feed my own interest in *ḥasidut,* as to be of service to my *rebbe.*[3] I remember taking an early draft of a chapter on the Maggid of Mezritch to his house that summer after graduation. He was ill at the time—set up in a special *chaise longue* in his living room by his wife with a canopy of netting over him. He read the chapter as I sat by his side and commented on it, talking to me about the subtle differences in how Muslims and Jews viewed themselves in relation to God (as exemplified in the roles of Eliezer the servant of Avraham, and Yitzhak, his son). It was the beginning of a long dialogue about Islam and Judaism, as well as the nature of religion and ecumenism.

For much of the rest of that year, I worked at transcribing lectures he had given on the "Hasidic Masters" at Naropa in the spring of 1998, producing edited drafts of chapters for him to review every few weeks. I also worked as a gardener and groundskeeper at a local condominium complex, a trade I had cultivated since starting college in Michigan. At the same time, I began to study Sufism on my own, reading what I could,

and reaching out to Murshid Thomas Atum O'Kane, as Reb Zalman had recommended.

As it turned out, Atum was coming to lead a retreat in Boulder that fall at the old Rolf Institute building on Canyon Boulevard. I attended the retreat and arranged to meet with him in private. Atum was about six feet tall, fifty-ish, with a bright Irish-American face and elegant silver streaks at his temples. He was very soft-spoken, but had a discerning eye. As he considered Reb Zalman one of his primary teachers, he was generous with his time and took seriously the latter's desire that he mentor me in the basics of Inayati Sufism. He offered me a simplified initiation and gave me a *wazifa*, a divine name with which to work for the time being. I remember his insightfulness as he explained the name to me over breakfast—"*Qahhar*, pronounced 'kuh-hahr,' is the deep foundational center; it is the majestic one-pointed lion whose heart is calm, clear, and centered."[4] It was exactly what I needed.[5]

Atum lived in Seattle, but rarely missed an opportunity to come teach in Boulder, mostly because it afforded him the chance to visit Reb Zalman. Because of this, I also benefitted, getting to take walks with him (often near Reb Zalman's house or my own apartment on the same side of town), during which I asked him the deeper questions I could not easily communicate on the phone, or in writing. This was a precious opportunity, as I had heard that Atum had once been the Secretary General of the Sufi Order (the former name of the Inayati Order) and Pir Vilayat's designated successor should he pass on before his son Pir Zia had come of age.[6] Thus, he was able to get me access to the Sufi Order practice manuals that he had assembled in his time as Secretary General, and also his own master's thesis and doctoral dissertation (for which Reb Zalman had been his advisor), both dealing with psychology and the training of Inayati Sufism.[7] These practice manuals and Atum's dissertation became the primary texts of my early studies of Inayati Sufism.

On our walks and phone calls through those first years, Atum offered me guidance in practice, refining my understanding of *zikr,* and gave me an insider's perspective (as well as some historical background) on the aspects of Inayati Sufism about which I was most curious. He was also a wonderful storyteller, often illustrating a teaching with a poignant anecdote related to someone he had known. Thus, it was Atum, more than anyone else, who shaped my early understanding of Sufism.

It was not until July of 2001, more than a year later, that Reb Zalman again brought up initiation. We were standing at the island in his kitchen when he told me that he would give me the name "Mu'in ad-Din," as Sufis often receive a *laqab* or initiatory 'nickname.' He explained that Mu'in ad-Din was the name of the founder of the Chishti lineage in India, and also the name of his friend, Moineddin Jablonski (1942-2001), the former *pir* of the Sufi Ruhaniat Order, who had died earlier that year. "You remind me a little of him." He had said this about Atum, as well, so I took this as a kind of recommendation.

My *bay'ah,* or 'initiation,' took place on Tuesday, July 24th, 2001. Reb Zalman asked me to go "prepare" in his library while he went into his prayer room. I seated myself in meditation in the library for about a half-hour until he called me into the prayer room. Motioning for me to take a seat next to him, he reached into a white *mala* bag—the kind Vaishnava sannyasins carry—from which he took two Sufi tesbiḥs of ninety-nine beads each. He gave me a rich reddish-brown *tesbiḥ* with wooden beads, probably acquired on one of his trips to India. He then took out two conical cream-colored felt hats, flattened on top like a fez, and gave me one to wear, donning the other himself.

Taking out a tablet, he outlined a set of practices for me to do daily, using a different *wazifa* or divine name in Arabic for each day of the week, corresponding to the seven lower *s'firot* or divine qualities in Kabbalah.

He then asked me what I felt my particular "work" in Sufism might be.

I answered him to the best of my ability, and he offered me some perspective and a practice related to "Ibrahim (Abraham), who was called *khalil Allah* in Sufism, the 'friend of God'" to do before I entered into "my work." I was to recite *Ya Khalil,* 'O Friend,' seven times, concentrating on that work.

He then kissed his palm and offered me his right hand, palm up. I took it with my own right hand, and he explained that this was the hand that had held the hand of the masters who had initiated him into Sufism. He told me how he had been initiated into the Chishti lineage by his friend Pir Vilayat Inayat-Khan, into the Qadiri-Rufai lineage by Shaykh Sidi Hasan al-Moumani, and the Halveti-Jerrahi lineage by Shaykh Muzaffer Ozak. "And now," he said meaningfully, "those hands have touched yours." After a moment, however, he added, "But the Chishti lineage of Hazrat Inayat Khan is primary for us."

Then, while still holding hands, we recited together . . .

Toward the One
The Perfection of Love, Harmony, and Beauty
The Only Being
United with all the Illuminated Souls
Who form the Embodiment of the Master
The Spirit of Guidance.

"Now," he said, "let's do a round of *zikr* on the *mala* together—*La 'ilaha 'illa llah* ninety-nine times, with *Bi-smi-llah ar-Raḥman ar-Raḥim* and *Al-ḥamdu lillah* at the breaks."

We did not do the *zikr* in the Chishti manner, as I had learned it from Murshid Atum. Instead, we repeated *La 'ilaha,* 'there is no God,' as we moved from the left shoulder to the right, and *'illa llah,* 'nevertheless God,' as we came back to the left shoulder. After each section of thirty-three beads, we stopped

and, hinging at the waist, began a circle, dropping down on the left side and moving right, saying, *Bi-smi-llah ar-Raḥman ar-Raḥim,* 'in the name of God, the merciful, the compassionate,' and *Al-ḥamdu lillah*, 'praise be to God,' as we arched over the right shoulder, before beginning the next thirty-three of *La 'ilaha 'illa llah*—doing this until we had recited a full round of ninety-nine.

With that, the initiation was complete. Reb Zalman embraced me and sent me off with the *tesbiḥ* he had given me to use.

An Ordination and Unexpected Investiture

After my initiation, I deepened my understanding of *zikr*, reading transcriptions of the oral teachings of Pir Vilayat on the practice, and experimenting with different versions of it based on suggestions from Atum.[8] I added to this basic practice the kabbalistically-oriented Sufi practices I had received from Reb Zalman.

That fall (or the previous one), I began to serve as Reb Zalman's teaching assistant at Naropa, creating his syllabi and attending classes with him. I would continue in this role until his retirement in 2004, assisting him in classes like "Rituals for People Helpers," "Issues in Spiritual Direction," and "Contemporary American Religions." I also began to travel with him as his attendant, driving him where he needed to go and carrying his bags.

In the spring of 2002, a brilliant young student, recently graduated from Harvard, came to Naropa to learn with Reb Zalman, asking him to be his teacher. Reb Zalman referred him to me, authorizing me on the spot to act as a *"mashpiyya,"* a mentor instructing him in basic *ḥasidut* in his stead. He would do this again with a second equally brilliant young man from

Montreal later that year. These were my first students.

Not long after, in late May or early June, Pir Puran Bair—the other Sufi mentor Reb Zalman had asked me to seek out—came to Boulder to teach a seminar on meditation. "Puran," Atum had informed me, "was known in the early days as Pir Vilayat's finest student, the perfect disciple" a practitioner *par excellence* who had been the "head of the retreat activity of the Sufi Order for many years." Reb Zalman had also told me that he had performed Puran's wedding and his son's *bar mitzvah* (as Puran had married a Jewish woman) and had often asked him to design Sufi retreats for him when he would visit the Boston area in the late 1970s and early '80s. In 1988, Pir Vilayat suggested that Puran and his later wife Susanna begin teaching meditation publically without the 'Sufi wrappings,' as described in his book, *Living from the Heart* (a book which Reb Zalman had recommended to me).[9]

I attended Puran's sessions on meditation with delight that weekend and arranged to meet with him privately, as I had done with Atum. Puran was different though; about my own height, he was in his mid-fifties, his still-brown hair carefully combed straight back, his clothes simple and nicely ironed. He was precise in his manner, both in word and action, and seemed to be contained in an atmosphere of his own, as if breathing in a mystical field sensible only to him. He was less familiar and approachable than Atum, but not for lack of kindness or courtesy; he simply measured his surroundings, just as he seemed to be measuring me. But, after hearing me out and quietly meditating on the matter, he initiated me into his own lineage of Sufi meditation practice right there in a meeting room in the Marriott Hotel, confirming the name "Mu'in ad-Din" for me.

I found Puran to be a profound student of meditation, and a gifted teacher, skillfully explaining and demonstrating difficult psychological and physiological concepts with ease. The Heart Rhythm Meditation practice he taught (based on the Sufi

meditation teachings of Hazrat Inayat Khan) was perfect for me, and I quickly incorporated it into my daily practice routine. I was also interested to find that I had memorized almost everything he had taught that weekend without effort, and thus I soon abandoned almost all of the other Buddhist and Hindu meditation techniques I had been practicing. For the next several years, I would seek Puran out whenever he came to Boulder or the Denver-metro area.

Around the same time, Reb Zalman introduced me to Dr. Edward Bastian, the founder of the recently formed Spiritual Paths Foundation, suggesting that he hire me to help him develop content for his programs. Besides beginning my work in 'interspirituality,' it brought me into contact and conversation that year with Muslim Sufis like Imam Feisal Abdul Rauf, who later became nationally-known when his desire to create the "Cordoba House" in New York City, a place in which Jews, Christians, and Muslims could all pray together, was dubbed the "Ground Zero Mosque" by conservative opponents and ultimately quashed. I also met and formed a good relationship with Shaykh Kabir Helminski, said to be the first American to receive *ijazah* or 'authorization' as a Mevlevi Sufi *shaykh,* and his wife, Shaykha Camille, who have together created many important resources for American Sufis.[10]

In July of that same year, Reb Zalman told me that he planned to ordain me a "*cherag*" *(chiragh),* an Inayati Sufi ordination authorizing me to lead and perform lifecycle rituals and universalist religious services. In preparation, he asked me to study the section on "The Spiritual Hierarchy" in Hazrat Inayat Khan's *The Unity of Religious Ideals*. He also gave me one of the two conical felt hats we had worn during my initiation the year before, asking if my then wife, Jennifer, would stitch in floss a heart and wings design on the face of it. For the inside of the hat—in the place that would touch my forehead—he wrote out a phrase in Hebrew (in a special manner) for her to copy and stitch as well.

The ordination took place on Thursday, August 1st, 2002, the day before my 30th birthday. Again, Reb Zalman asked me to "prepare" in the library outside of his prayer room. I placed the felt hat on my head, wrapped in my large brown wool shawl, and sat down to meditate and do *zikr* until he called me.

When I entered the prayer room, Reb Zalman was dressed in a long dark green caftan tied with a woven fabric belt (mostly sage green with bands of fuchsia and dots of turquoise and yellow). On his head was a green turban of coarse green fabric wrapped around a green velour pillbox hat. These were the robes he often wore when he was teaching local Sufis or doing anything "ecumenical."

I believe he invited me to place the felt hat with floss embroidery on the table between us, and to sit in a chair opposite him (the large oil portrait of his *rebbe* framed behind him). In my memory, the ordination was long, but now I remember only a few elements of it. In the center of the table, he had placed his wooden *rehal*, a folding x-shaped bookstand used in the Middle East—this one in the form of two open hands with long spooky fingers. On it was a paperback copy of *The Unity of Religious Ideals*, which lay open to the section on "The Spiritual Hierarchy."[11] A copy of the *Gayan* may also have been on the table,[12] along with a set of candles and a small cobalt blue bottle of olive oil he had asked me to bring.

I remember that he directed me to stand and take up the copy of *The Unity of Religious Ideals* so as to read aloud the long passages on "The Spiritual Hierarchy" and "The Seven Grades of the Spiritual Hierarchy." When I finished, I placed the book back on the *rehal*.

Coming around the table, Reb Zalman took the small cobalt blue bottle of olive oil and removed the cork, pouring a little of the oil on the fingertips of his right hand. He then traced a symbol on my forehead, poured a little more oil on his fingertips and traced another symbol over my head. Replacing

the bottle on the table, he put both of his large hands on either side of my head and inclined it to him. He then blew gently on my forehead, whispering the name, "Mu'in ad-Din Da'ud." He did this three times, telling me that the name binds the soul to the body.

While still standing, he put his hand on my back and began to rock gently back and forth, as if praying. He talked to me in a prayerful tone about the life of a spiritual leader, the responsibilities of that life, and the nature of blessings—how they arise in response to a need, how they wait above for us to bring them down, and how they can be channeled simply, even in small moments of contact.

I don't know how long this went on; I was awed by the moment, I remember, and in tears. This was the ordination itself—the anointing with oil, the transmission of the spirit, and the laying on of hands—he explained, referencing the oft' misunderstood passage in the Gospels when Jesus ordains Peter, saying, "I give you the keys to the kingdom of heaven: whatever you bind on earth will be bound in heaven; whatever you loose on earth will be loosed in heaven." (Matt. 16:19) Finally, he said, "You will be my *khalifa.*"

This was unexpected. The *khalifa* is a 'deputy,' or successor of sorts. Throughout, I had felt something more was happening than 'just' a *cherag* ordination; but I was not entirely sure what it was until that moment, nor even after, really.

We sat down to do *zikr* together, using the divine name, *Y-H-V-H,* in a manner which he said was a special transmission from Murshid Samuel Lewis.[13]

What I remember afterward was more relaxed. We sat and discussed practical aspects of leading ritual and offering guidance. He lifted the felt hat from the table now to examine it, admiring the heart and wings that Jennifer had stitched on it at his direction, noting with delight my design (having placed a heart and wings over a circle, with a cross of the four cardinal

directions penetrating the circle, with a flame above. The colors used were those of the *s'firot* on his rainbow *tallit).*

He was still happier with what was within, the phrase *kodesh l'Eyl Eliyon*—'holy to God, Most High'—stitched in Hebrew, just as he had written it. He said that he had written the same on the *tallit* he had given to Pir Vilayat at his ordination into the priesthood of Malkhi-tzedek, explaining to me the passage in Genesis in which Malkhi-tzedek ordains Avraham (Gen. 14:19-20) as a *koheyn l'Eyl Eliyon*—'priest to God, Most High.'[14]

"You are to wear this when contemplating ritual or the work you must do," he said.

He then brought out the *ijazah* he had prepared authorizing me to act as a *cherag,* signing it and telling me to have Atum sign it the next time I saw him.[15]

He then gave over to me his *rehal,* his copy of *The Unity of Religious Ideals* (the binding of which had broken, so that it always opened to "The Spiritual Hierarchy"), a box of candles, a packet of special matches, camphor, and oil lamps—*A ritualist's tool-kit,* I thought. He also gave me a long green *dishdashah* of his own to wear on special occasions.

He asked me to call his secretary Mary to come and take a photo of us together, after which he told me to remove my hat and my wool shawl. He then took off his green caftan and put it on me, tying the woven belt around my waist, and placing the green turban on my head. I was surprised, as this was the literal act of investiture in both Sufism and Hasidism, placing the robes of the master on the disciple. I remembered again that he had said, "You will be my *khalifa,*" but I was too shy to ask him about this.

Mary then took a photo of me in the robes, a rather comic photo to my mind of me swimming in robes too large for me; it was a good metaphor, as the role would be too big for me for some time yet.

Recognizing the Inayati-Maimuni Order

After this, I pursued my studies and practices with renewed zeal, feeling that I should try to live up to being Reb Zalman's *khalifa.* Pir Shabda Kahn of the Sufi Ruhaniat Order, recognizing the beginnings of a new Inayati lineage, generously made their entire corpus of study materials available to me.[16]

In 2003, I performed two minor initiations for the first students Reb Zalman had sent me to mentor. But the first full initiation I performed was done on March 23rd, 2004, for Gavin Breeze, a lovely man from the United Kingdom I had met in my first retreat with Murshid Atum O'Kane. As Gavin was friendly with a few local Sufi Order initiates, it soon came to the attention of the Sufi Order representative of Boulder and Denver, Pamela Hakima Mumby, that I had performed an initiation.[17] A friendly person, she called me to discuss what this meant, and what her responsibilities might be to students I initiated. But the real question for everyone was—by what authority was I performing initiations in the first place?

Because Reb Zalman had been initiated by Pir Vilayat and confirmed as a *shaykh* by him, he was a *shaykh* of the Sufi Order. Moreover, he was an almost universally respected spiritual leader, allowed to act with some autonomy. However, it was unclear where I fit within the structure of the Sufi Order, not having passed through its formal grades of initiation. Also, there was the question about what I was teaching; was it *Sufism* or *Hasidism?* Although I knew the differences, I was clearly a hybrid by this time, having been equally influenced by both.

I understood the dilemma; and yet I did not see it as a dilemma for me personally, as the only authority I recognized at the time was my *murshid,* who had empowered and trusted me to act as his *khalifa.* I was initiated within the lineage of the Sufi Order by Murshid Atum, and into the practice lineage of Pir Puran, but I actually understood my initiation with Reb Zalman to be broader and more complex, as he was himself an

initiate of multiple Sufi lineages, including the Ruhaniat.[18] It was clear that he considered us Inayati Sufis (from the lineage of Hazrat Inayat Khan), but there was no sense of organizational affiliation to either the Sufi Order or the Ruhaniat. Thus, I told the Sufi Order representative that I would speak to Reb Zalman about the matter.

A little embarrassed, I apologized for causing him trouble; but he only smiled, dismissing my concern. He told me to compose a letter to Pir Zia Inayat-Khan, the new head of the Sufi Order, explaining the situation and giving him my "credentials," as Pir Vilayat was already ill at that point and had given over most of his authority to his son.[19]

I did not know what my "credentials" might be, so I composed a somewhat awkward letter outlining my education and background with various spiritual practices, and explained the situation in brief to Pir Zia. Reb Zalman signed the letter after me and we sent it off.

Truth be told, I had very little attachment to its outcome at the time, as I had that particularly fiery brand of loyalty to my *murshid* that gave me a confidence greater than that with which I was naturally endowed. I was his soldier in an army of two, which was just fine with me. Still, I was sorry to have caused him any 'political' difficulties.

I had met Pir Zia in October of 2002 when he came to Boulder to lead a weekend retreat with Reb Zalman.[20] Reb Zalman had put us on the dais together to do a paired gazing exercise, and later, we participated in a large group *zikr*. We were about the same age—he a year older—and Reb Zalman had suggested a number of times that he very much wanted us to become friends. Pir Zia struck me as a deep practitioner with a great sense of responsibility for what had been given into his hands. He also clearly had a strong regard and respect for Reb Zalman; thus, I felt some assurance that he would answer us well.

In late April, Reb Zalman informed me that Pir Zia had responded, suggesting that if we had created a significant new emphasis in Inayati Sufism—combining the streams of both Sufism and Hasidism—it should perhaps be acknowledged as a new lineage. After a brief discussion, on April 26th, 2004, I composed two letters at Reb Zalman's request: one a personal letter to Pir Zia, and the other a formal letter to him as the head of the Sufi Order, both accepting his offer to acknowledge a new Inayati lineage.

On May 5th, Pir Zia sent Reb Zalman the draft of a *khilafat-nama,* or 'deed of recognition,' for the new order, asking us to review it and to correct any details that might not be accurate. Reb Zalman dashed off a quick response, offering the approximate dates of the mutual initiations that took place between he and Pir Vilayat, and suggesting a replacement for the place-holder name—"Zalmaniyya"—which Pir Zia had given the order . . .

> Everything you have written in the *khilafat-nama* is good except the name of the *tariqah*—better be Obadiyya. This was the name of Moshe Maimonides' grandson who headed the *tariqah* in Cairo; and it was by this connection that I felt myself to be deployed in it. *Obad-yah—Abd-Allah,* and that would give it additional weight since the intent here is the devoted service of the holy one; it points to a belonging that should not be a place for spiritual 'groupies.'[21]

I had recently given Reb Zalman a copy of Ovadyah Maimuni's *Treatise of the Pool,* which had perhaps caused some momentary confusion, as we had already decided to use the name "Maimuni" (after the dynastic lineage of Jewish Sufism held among the Maimuni family in medieval Egypt).

In 1997 or '98, when I was still a student at Michigan State University—long before meeting Reb Zalman and his

suggesting that I become a Sufi—I had taken an old hardcover volume off a lonely lower shelf in the library stacks, curious that it said in faded gilt letters on the spine, "The High Ways to Perfection of Abraham Maimonides." Though a Maimonides enthusiast—a fact which brought me to that section in the first place—I had forgotten that he had a son, Avraham, and was unaware of his having written anything of significance. Thus, I took the book off the shelf to peruse, mostly as a curiosity. When I opened it in a nearby park later that day, I found to my surprise that Avraham Maimonides (or Maimuni) actually had deep ties to Sufism (though this was not yet of any particular significance to me).

Some four or five years later, I arose one day at four o'clock in the morning to do a special practice in the dark and silence of the night before my wife arose (signaling that it was time for us to get ready for work). It was a practice taught by Pir Vilayat that required great concentration, a practice for discovering one's "ideal being" and inner teacher learned from Atum. Proceeding through layers of the unconscious, I finally opened the 'door' to a 'room' that would reveal my inner teacher. There I found an elegant older man seated on the edge of a desk, looking as if he had been expecting me. Though I had hardly thought of him since discovering the book years before, I knew immediately that this—to my mind, at least—was Avraham Maimuni.

This led me to begin to investigate and study the scholarly literature regarding the unusual Jewish-Sufi sect led by Rabbeynu Avraham in Egypt. Reb Zalman was interested in my discoveries, and liked me to keep him updated on what I had found in this text or that, or in whatever article I happened to be reading at the time. Thus, I had been the one who had purchased that copy of Ovadyah Maimuni's *Treatise of the Pool* for him to read, and it took only a moment to suggest again that we should use the name "Maimuni" to honor the contributions of the entire lineage of Jewish-Sufism that had once existed

and that had died out so long ago. He agreed. But the point which he had made in his letter to Pir Zia, i.e., that it should be a devotionally-oriented practice lineage not for 'spiritual groupies' was nonetheless important.

Thus, we quickly communicated the final name choice to Pir Zia, and the next day, Thursday, May 6th, 2004, he created the final version of the *khilafat-nama* of the Inayati-Maimuni *tariqah,* given below . . .

KHILAFAT-NAMA

Toward the One, the Perfection of Love, Harmony and Beauty
The Only Being, United with All the Illuminated Souls
Who Form the Embodiment of the Master, the Spirit of Guidance.

WHEREAS the sacred traditions of the faiths of Beni Israel—Judaism, Christianity, and Islam—derive from the prophecy of Abraham, who "was the first to bring the knowledge of mysticism from Egypt, where he was initiated in the most ancient order of esotericism";

AND WHEREAS the early Sufis of Islam were deeply studied in Judaica (*isra'iliyyat*);

AND WHEREAS Rabbi Abraham Maimonides observed, "the ways of the ancient saints of Israel ... have now become the practice of the Sufis of Islam," and developed a school of Hasidic Sufism in thirteenth-century Cairo;

AND WHEREAS Hazrat Pir-o-Murshid Inayat Khan founded, in London in 1914, the Sufi Order in the West, a new order of universalist Sufism rooted in the transmission of four unbroken lineages: Chishtiyya, Suhrawardiyya, Qadiriyya, and Naqshbandiyya;

AND WHEREAS Hazrat Inayat Khan appointed Pir Vilayat Inayat Khan as his Sajjada-nishin, and Pir Vilayat has in turn appointed this faqir as his own Sajjada-nishin;

AND WHEREAS in 1975 and 1976, invoking the names of Melchizedek and Abraham, Pir Vilayat and Reb Zalman Schachter-Shalomi performed mutual initiations, bestowing the titles of Shaikh and Kohen l'el eliyon respectively;

AND WHEREAS as a duly authorized Sufi Shaikh and Hasidic Kohen ha'yisrael, Reb Zalman has masterfully integrated the authentic traditions of the Sufis and the Hasidim, in the manner of a "merging of two oceans";

NOW, THEREFORE it is with jubilation of heart that I hereby recognize the establishment, by Reb Zalman, of the Maimuniyya, as a new order of Hasidic Sufism, reviving the tradition of the Egyptian Hasidic school and bearing the initiatory transmission of the Sufi Order in the West, whereby it is vested with the *baraka* of Hazrat Inayat Khan and the fourfold chain of Pir-o-murshidan preceding him.

It is my prayer that the Maimuniyya will bring healing to the tragically divided family of Abraham and guide many sincere seekers on the path that leads to the fulfillment of life's purpose. May the Message of God reach far and wide!

IN WITNESS THEREOF I have signed this deed at The Abode of the Message on the 6th day of May, 2004.

Zia Inayat Khan

Pirzade Zia Inayat-Khan

Growing an Order

Word of a new Inayati lineage 'combining Judaism and Sufism,' or 'connecting Sufism and Hasidism'—however each person chose to interpret the news—spread quickly in Inayati Sufi and Jewish Renewal circles, and we soon began to receive a number of inquiries.

In response, Reb Zalman said to me one day, "I guess we will have to 'open the gates.' "

I was quiet for a moment, thinking about the situation. Finally, I responded, "I'm not so sure we should do that."

"Nu?" he asked, using the Yiddish expression.

I told him that it seemed to me, we would soon face two major problems if we 'opened the gates,' as he had suggested. For there were already many Jews practicing in a variety of Sufi lineages, often having rejected, or been rejected by the Judaism of their parents. And I suspected, many of them would naturally see the Inayati-Maimuni Order—connected as it was to "Rabbi Zalman Schachter-Shalomi, founder of Jewish Renewal movement"—as an opportunity to validate their earlier choices, while at the same time reclaiming their Judaism by simply joining something else.

"While I understand the desire," I said, "I'm not sure that is a desirable role for us to play. Moreover, it isn't your intention to actively lead or develop this lineage, and the older Jewish Sufis—long-established in their own practices with their own teachers—are not likely to take guidance from me, twenty to thirty years their junior."

Reb Zalman nodded in agreement.

"In any event," I continued, "we would soon be overrun by the objectives and desires of others, losing the precious opportunity we have to grow something organically; it would soon become the 'membership organization' we wanted to avoid, instead of the devotionally-oriented practice lineage we

intended. So, actually, I think we should 'close the gates' for a while so we can do 'research and development.'"

I wasn't often so forthright, but I felt certain in this case, and Reb Zalman agreed. He said that it had become habitual to try to serve such demands, but he actually believed this lineage should stay true to its own *meshreb* ('distinctive character'), and not become "another movement."[22]

In the years to come, I initiated a few murids, often after asking for a confirming dream, or after receiving some other guidance; but most I turned away, hoping not to offend them. Thus, the years between 2004 and Reb Zalman's passing in 2014, a decade later, were mostly used for personal experimentation and careful investigation.

In that time, it became clear that there were actually two emphases for the Inayati-Maimuni *tariqah:* one, to create a simple but effective option for Jewish initiates to practice Judaism in a Sufi manner, inspired by the Jewish Sufi sect of Egypt; and a second, no less important, to create an Inayati lineage integrating the teachings and practices of both Sufism and Hasidism, in a universalist manner, for initiates both Jewish and not Jewish. While Reb Zalman was alive, we worked more on the former, coming to some clear expressions of it by the time of his death.

On January 25th, 2007, Reb Zalman gave me full *ijazah* or 'authorization' as a Sufi *murshid,* adding my name to the Chishti-Nizami-Kalimi-Inayati-Maimuni lineage tree *(shajara).* During that time, I came into a deeper relationship with my first group of murids, for whom he served as a kind of 'spiritual-grandfather.' When he died on July 3rd, 2014, I became the *pir* or head of the lineage.

s'firot

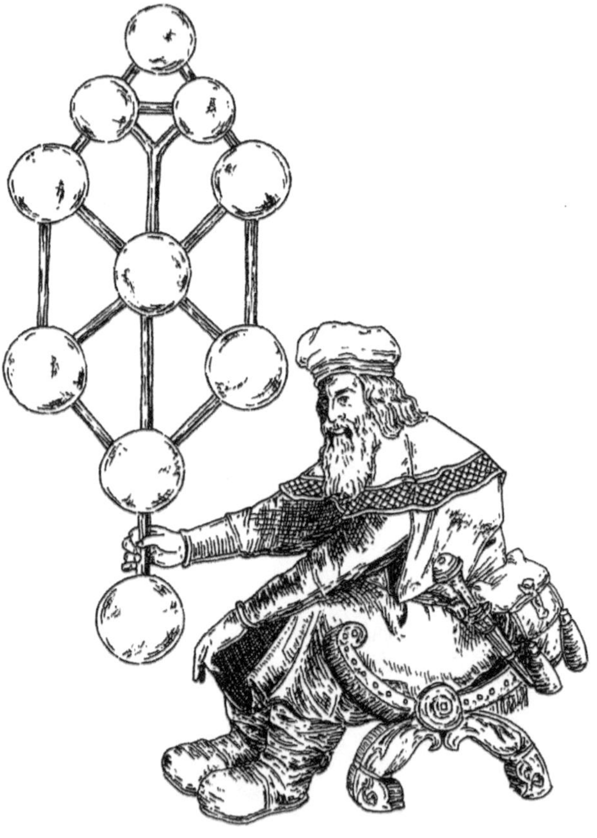

The S'firot in Sufi Zikr

Sufi Remembrance and the 'Tree of Life' *

The first practice Reb Zalman ever gave me was an integrated Jewish-Sufi practice, a practice that was his own prior to my coming to study with him. At my initiation, I was given a divine name to repeat each day of the week, one of the *asma' al-ḥusna,* the ninety-nine 'beautiful names' of God found in the Qur'an and recited by Sufis. However, the Arabic names he gave me corresponded to the seven lower *s'firot,* or 'divine qualities,' found on the *etz ḥayyim* or 'tree of life' in *kabbalah,* as well as the days of the week. Thus, the practice looked like this . . .

> SUNDAY: *Ya Raḥman* ('O Compassionate One') 10 times, concentrating on the divine quality *ḥesed,* or 'loving-kindness.'
>
> MONDAY: *Allahu 'Akbar* ('God is Greater') 10 times, concentrating on the divine quality *gevurah,* or 'strength.'
>
> TUESDAY: *Ya Raḥim* ('O Merciful One') 10 times, concentrating on the divine quality *tif'eret,* or 'beauty.'[1]
>
> WEDNESDAY: *Ya Manṣur* ('O Victorious One') 10 times, concentrating on the divine quality *netzaḥ,* or 'victory.'

---

* Edited from "The Merging of Two Oceans: Sufism and Hasidism II," a talk given in New Lebanon, New York, on April 29th, 2017, at the Abode of the Message, for the Inayati Order event, Wisdom of the Prophets: Sufism & Judaism.

THURSDAY: *Ya Jamil* ('O Beautiful One') 10 times, concentrating on the divine quality *hod*, or 'glory.'

FRIDAY: *Ya Wadud* ('O Lover') 10 times, concentrating on the divine quality *yesod*, or 'foundation.'

SATURDAY: *Ya Malik* ('O Sovereign') 10 times, concentrating on the divine quality *malkhut*, or 'sovereignty.'[2]

The exception to the assignment of divine names to the *s'firot* and the days of the week is, of course, *Allahu 'akbar*, which is not a divine name but a powerful phrase of the Islamic tradition, meaning, 'God is great.' Reb Zalman, however, insisted on the more appropriate translation, 'God is greater.' Greater than what? *Whatever* . . . Whatever you can think of, God is greater.

The Dynamics of the S'firot

But what are the *s'firot* as presented in Kabbalah, the Jewish mystical tradition? And how are they to be understood in this context?

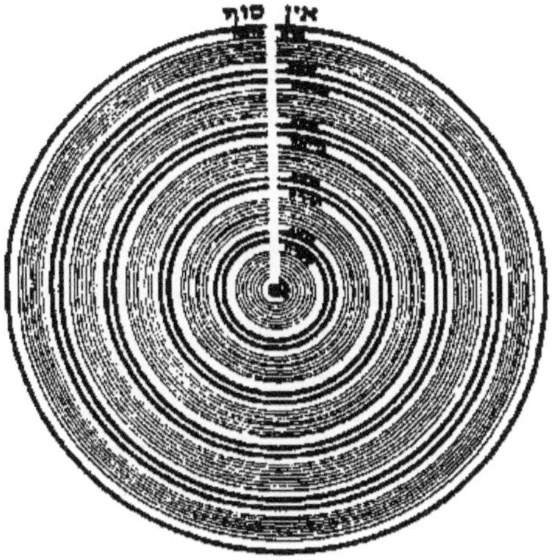

There are various ways of interpreting the *s'firot.* I tend to interpret them in relationship to one another, as archetypal dynamics in the play of the universe (especially as understood in Ḥabad Ḥasidism, and by Reb Zalman himself). From a practical perspective, they are a 'thinking tool' for the *mekubal,* or kabbalist, describing a sequence in the mind of God, as it were, from the idea of creation to its manifestation. But they can also be seen as paralleling our own process of ideation, inspiration, and action, a way of thinking through an idea and determining a right course.

There are ten successive divine emanations unfolding creation, which, like a ladder, can also be climbed back to the divine. These are sometimes depicted as concentric circles and sometimes in a tree structure called the *etz ḥayyim,* or 'tree of life,' with ten spheres on it.

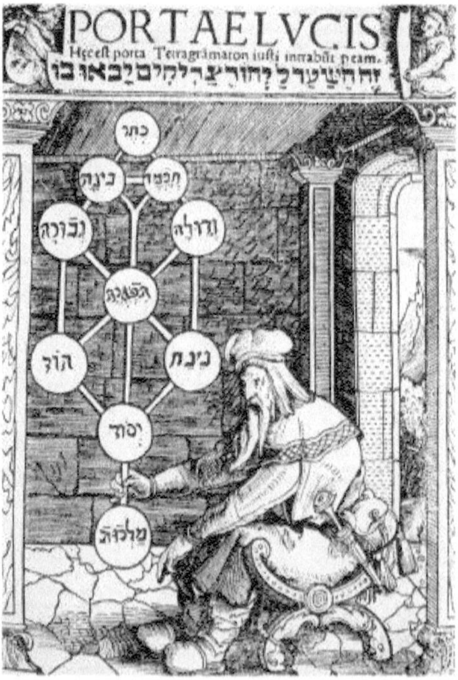

Amid the ten clearly drawn spheres of the tree structure, you will sometimes notice another more faintly drawn sphere in the upper third, a kind of hidden *s'firah*. This is *da'at*, 'knowledge.' If included in the count, it would make eleven *s'firot.* But in the classic text of Kabbalah, *Sefer Yetzirah*, we read "ten and not nine, ten and not eleven."[3] Thus, in any discussion of the *s'firot,* we either count *keter,* the 'crown' (the *s'firah* at the top of the structure), or *da'at,* 'knowledge,' a little further down; but never both at once.

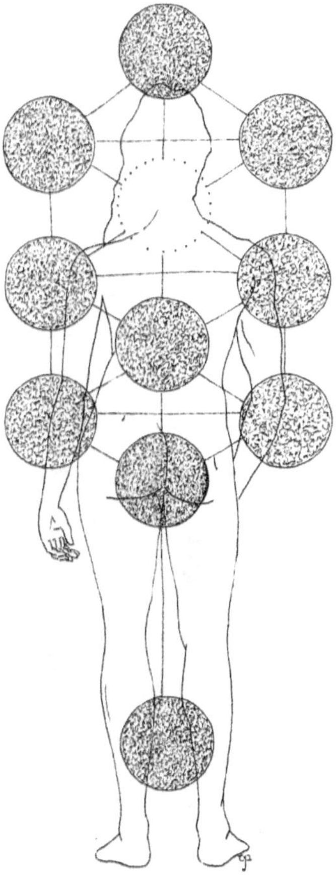

The 'Tree of Life' as depicted by the author.

For now, we will leave *keter* aside—the divine quality representing the transcendent absolute—and we will count *da'at*, 'knowledge.' Not 'head knowledge' or 'information,' but 'experiential knowledge.'[4]

It is also important to note two structural features of the 'tree of life'—its three triads and three pillars. The triads I will discuss as we go, but of the pillars, we can say, there is a 'masculine' pillar on the right, a 'feminine' pillar on the left, and a central pillar that represents their union in the middle.

The First Triad—Knowing

Starting from the top right on the 'tree of life,' the first movement of the divine thought-sequence begins with *ḥokhmah*, 'wisdom.' *Ḥokhmah* is the *'Ah-ha!'* or 'light-bulb'-moment, when we know we've 'got it,' but we don't exactly know what that is yet!

I think most of us have had the experience of struggling to find an answer to a problem, and of being forced to walk away from it for a time. Then, suddenly, often while doing something else entirely, we are seized by a kind of exultation of knowing, a pre-cognitive awareness which is more awareness and exultation than actual information.

Maimonides speaks of this experience in his *Guide to the Perplexed*, when he says . . .

> You should not think that these great secrets are fully and completely known to anyone among us. They are not. But sometimes truth flashes out to us so that we think it is day, and then nature and habit draw a veil over our perception, returning us to a darkness almost as dense as before. We are like those who, though beholding frequent flashes of lightning, still find themselves in the

> thickest darkness of the night. Though, on some the lightning flashes in rapid succession, and they seem to be in continuous light, and their night is as clear as day.[5]

When the lightning flashes, there is a glimpse of *something* illuminated by it; but it is only through subsequent flashes that we can truly discern what that *something* is. Thus Rabbi Dov Baer of Lubavitch says, "*Ḥokhmah* is a flash of insight that illuminates the mind like a bolt of lightning," and as these flashes continue, more and more is gradually revealed to us.[6]

Sometimes the letters of *ḥokhmah* are rearranged to spell *ko'aḥ mah*, the 'power of what-ness!' That is to say, *ḥokhmah* is related to 'essence'; it is essential knowledge, even if all the details are not yet understood.

From *ḥokhmah* we proceed to the left or 'feminine' side of the 'tree of life,' where begins the examination of what we think we saw in the lightning flash of *ḥokhmah,* or rather, the dawning realization of what is revealed in its flashes. This is called *binah,* 'understanding.' If you want to know how an old watch works, you have to take it apart and see how all the little gears and wheels work together. *Binah* is the 'understanding' of all the 'parts' and 'ingredients,' all the infinite potentialities of this *'Ah-ha!'*-moment—all that was, is, and might be about it.

From there, we descend to the place of *da'at,* 'knowledge,' between *ḥokhmah* and *binah. Da'at,* as I have said, is *'experiential knowledge';* but how can we speak of experiential knowledge when we are still 'in the head,' as it where, working out an idea in the 'divine mind'? Because, *da'at* is the pre-cursor to experience, the scenario-tester of the mind, akin to Einstein's "thought experiments" *(Gedankenexperiment).*

For instance, Einstein imagined a stationary observer on a train platform who witnesses two simultaneous lightning strikes equidistant from him at the same time. But he also imagines another stationary observer aboard a train moving passed

the platform at near the speed of light. For that observer, the simultaneous lightning strikes would be experienced one *after* the other—not simultaneously—because the train is moving toward one and away from the other. This is known as the 'relativity of simultaneity.' Thus, it is clear from the thought experiment that something may be *'as if'* experienced prior to a physical experience. This is *da'at*'s function on the 'tree of life,' to imagine and pre-test the idea glimpsed in *ḥokhmah* and revealed in *binah* in a thought experiment.

The Second Triad—Feeling

Having passed through the scenario-tester of *da'at,* we come into the second triad of divine qualities, coming out of the 'head' and into the 'heart,' the terrain of feeling. The *'Ah-ha!'* of *ḥokhmah,* whose potential was understood in *binah*, and which was imagined in the thought experiments of *da'at*, is now given room to breathe in *ḥesed*.

Here we experience the excitement of the idea.

Ḥesed means 'loving-kindness,' but also represents unbounded excitement—the child full of love who hugs everyone and wants to be hugged by everyone. This, too, is a stage in the process of ideation leading to action; this is where we allow our joy in possibilities to swell and expand. If it does not do so, the idea never comes to fruition.

But, as so often happens, that loving child, who only wants to hug and be hugged, at some point, receives an undeserved slap from the environment, or burns its soft hand on a pretty flame. Thus, we come to *gevurah,* 'strength,' and the need for boundaries, or limitations. Boundaries keep us safe. There are things in the world that may hurt and harm us, and boundaries are necessary to take care of us, to protect others, and even the unboundaried themselves. This is the place where the

excitement of the idea—sometimes a little inflated—gets 'a reality check' and is confronted by real-world constraints.

Many people are often confused when they learn that *gevurah* is on the feminine side of the 'tree of life,' assuming 'strength' to be a masculine quality. That assumption may explain a great deal of dysfunction in our society. But it is the feminine that knows the wisdom and need of boundaries, and *that* is also its great strength. If we interpret *ḥesed* as unbounded masculine assertiveness (even without a negative value judgment), there is a need for a feminine boundary to counterbalance it.

But *ḥesed* and *gevurah* are polarities, and *gevurah,* too, sometimes requires a corrective. If its boundaries are impermeable—so rigid that nothing gets in, or nothing gets out—they become the tomb of the divine impulse. Boundaries shape and mature love, but walls that are insurmountable can just as easily deny it. Thus, we seek the middle path between masculine *ḥesed* and feminine *gevurah,* an integration of them in the heart called *tif'eret,* 'beauty.'

Tif'eret can be compared to a mature love. When you love a child, it is easy to become permissive, wanting them to have anything they desire, simply because you love them so much. If someone asks, 'Why did you give it to them?' The answer is almost invariably, 'The child wanted it so badly that my heart wanted it for them, too!' This is *ḥesed.* But that kind of permissiveness also becomes a problem, as we all know, and the child sometimes becomes 'spoiled.' So we must correct the tendency to permissiveness with *gevurah,* which is also understood to mean, 'discipline.'

And yet, the *gevurah*-corrective can also have a tendency to become too strict—'I'm not giving them a damn thing; they need to learn discipline!' Thus, the more mature love, or balance between *ḥesed* and *gevurah,* is *tif'eret*—giving what is *needed,* not necessarily what is *wanted.* This is often the most loving thing

one can do; and for this reason, *tif'eret* is also called 'mercy' in Kabbalah.

The Third Triad—Action

Now we come into the region of action with *netzaḥ*, 'victory,' or what I tend to think of as raw efficacy. If *ḥesed* is the excitement necessary to drive one to act, *netzaḥ* is the energy necessary to make it happen. If the Incredible Hulk wants into a house, does he bother with a door, or with knocking at it? No, he breaks through the wall. That is raw efficacy—*sometimes a little too raw!*

Its corrective on the feminine side is *hod*, 'glory,' or what I tend to think of as an aesthetic-elegance. *Hod* is like the Japanese tea ceremony. The ceremony will be beautiful—an example of the art of serving—but you may be thirsty awhile. If the tea-master wishes to enter the same house that the Incredible Hulk nearly ruined, they will knock at the door with exquisite manners, likely having made a courteous appointment ahead of time. And yet, they may knock so gently on the day—not wishing to be loud or obnoxious—that no one ever hears the knock in the back of the house.

Thus, we come to a middle path with *yesod*, 'foundation,' which corresponds in my mind to efficiency. Channeling the energy of *netzaḥ* through *hod*'s beauty of manner we are left with an efficient action, efficacious in that it works, and elegant in the easy manner of its working.

The Result

We have gone from ideation in the triad of knowing (experiencing the flash of an idea in *ḥokhmah*, the unpacking of it in *binah*, and the thought experiment of *da'at)* through the triad

of feeling (the emotional excitement and energetic inflation of *ḥesed* necessary to get started, the reality-check on the inflated elements in *gevurah*, to the balanced need of *tif'eret)* through the triad of action (gathering the raw physical energy of *netzaḥ* to carry-out the action, introducing it to an ideal in *hod*, and bringing the two together in the best possible way in *yesod)*. And finally, we have the result in *malkhut*, 'kingdom' or 'sovereignty,' the union of masculine and feminine, the expression of the idea in this world, the child born of that union.

My friend, Rabbi Tirzah Firestone, likes to speak of *malkhut* as "embodiment," and the *Shabbat* or Sabbath, its day, as "the day of embodiment and occupying our full self."[7] Some interpreters conceive of *yesod* as the masculine genitalia, and *malkhut* as the feminine genitalia, though I tend to think of them as unified in the central pillar at the place of *yesod*, and *malkhut* as what is birthed from their union.[8]

The Divine Names in the 'Tree of Life'

When we look at the Arabic divine names that Reb Zalman associates with the lower seven *s'firot* in context, we discover more dimension in them, and his rationale becomes clearer.

Ya Raḥman, 'O Compassionate One' – This is clearly related to the wide-open, indulgent love of *ḥesed*. According to the Sufi view of the ninety-nine names of Allah in *Physicians of the Heart* . . .

> *Ar-Raḥman* is endless love. It is the infinite, unconditional reality of love. This is the Name said in the Qur'an to be inscribed on the heart of Allah. In other words, God's essence necessarily includes this quality of love. *Ar-Raḥman* might be imagined as the inner self of God, an infinite container that is incredibly compassionate,

> kind, and tender. It is the sun of loving compassion that is endlessly shining. *Ar-Raḥman* includes all the other divine Names. It is the source of all; it is the gate that opens onto all God's qualities, and an inner secret of each one.[9]

Allahu 'Akbar, 'God is Greater' – Here, Reb Zalman seems to want to emphasize the 'strength' aspect of *gevurah*, and even a sense of God's loving 'justice,' or *din,*[10] beyond any ordinary human conception of it.

> The oft-repeated phrase *"Allahu 'akbar"* means God is greater, not as a specific comparison, but in exactly the sense of incomparability we have just been talking about.
>
> If we think "what I am experiencing is the ultimate power," then God is a greater power. If we think "this is ultimate love," then God is a greater love. Whatever we think, in doing so we have set a boundary. So if we expand it, then we keep breaking down all the limitations that are within our mind, and that can enable our mind to be free.[11]

Ya Raḥim, 'O Merciful One' – Just as the unconditional love and compassion of *ḥesed* is brought to balance by the 'mercy' of *tif'eret*, the overwhelming compassion of *Raḥman* is differentiated from the mercy of *Raḥim*.

> *Ar-Raḥim* is the embodiment of loving mercy, and it brings the gentle touch of divine mercy. Nothing other than *ar-Raḥim* possesses the mercy that pours forth freely and fully reaches all beings and all things, without exception. It is an all-pervading infinite presence that is manifesting into a boundless number of finite things.
> Its root meaning, like that of *Ya Raḥman*, comes from the

> Arabic word for womb, *raḥma*. It carries an inner feeling that is naturally connected with childhood. *Ar-Raḥim* actively brings divine love into human relationships. It enables each and every being to more fully manifest loving mercy. Recitation of *Ya Raḥim* is an antidote for all who feel abandoned by God and who need to experience the healing activity of divine love reaching deeply within them.[12]

YA MANṢUR, 'O VICTORIOUS ONE' – Although not traditionally given in the lists of divine names, *Ya Manṣur!* was part of the battle cry of the companions of the Prophet.[13] Here Reb Zalman is obviously connecting it with the literal meaning of *netzaḥ*, 'victory,' but also the energetic power of the divine quality that overwhelms the enemy, as we see in one episode with Moses (who is also associated with *netzaḥ)* and his famous staff *(matteh)* . . .

> Now came Amalek and made war upon Israel in Refidim. And Moses said to Joshua, "Choose us men to go out and fight Amalek. On the morrow, I will stand on the hilltop with the staff of God in my hand."
>
> So Joshua did as Moses had said to him and fought with Amalek, and Moses, Aaron, and Hur went up to the top of the hill. And it came to pass, when Moses raised his hand, Israel prevailed; and when he let down his hand, Amalek prevailed. (Ex. 17:8-11)

YA JAMIL, 'O BEAUTIFUL ONE' – This is an interesting choice for the divine quality *hod*, or 'glory.' After all, Reb Zalman might also have made a simple association with the 'beauty' of *tif'eret*. Instead, he highlights hod's *aesthetic elegance*, and appeals to the relationship between *netzaḥ* and *hod*, similar to the relationship that obtains between *jalil* and *jamil*.

> As seen in the sound code, the use of the grammatical form *jalal* (rather than *jalil)* and *jamal* (rather than *jamil),* specifically points to "the only source of power and beauty." Since they specifically relate to source, *jalal* and *jamal* can be said to be closer to the essence. In contrast, in the sound code the forms *jalil* and *jamil* show the divine quality expressing itself throughout the whole of manifestation, leaving nothing out.[14]
>
> *Al-Jalil* is the omnipotent divine power and strength that manifests into each thing and everything without exception. Its opposite is *al-Jamil,* the divine beauty that likewise penetrates all.[15]

Ya Wadud, 'O Lover' – As the divine quality *yesod,* or 'foundation,' is connected with creativity and sexuality, Reb Zalman chose *Ya Wadud,* 'O Lover.'

> *Al-Wadud* is divine love's most intimate manifestation. It is the constant embrace of the affectionate, loving universe. The way we learn to love Allah is by learning how to love, and human beings especially learn how to love by learning how to be intimate. Repetition of *Ya Wadud* is an antidote for all who have difficulty achieving intimacy with others. *Al-Wadud* includes sexual intimacy.[16]

Ya Malik, 'O Sovereign' – Parallel to the divine quality *malkhut,* or 'sovereignty,' is the divine name in Arabic, *malik,* representing God as 'sovereign.' Sovereignty is to be whole in oneself, and to recite the name is to invoke that quality.

> The quality of *al-Malik* is to hold everything in the universe in the hands of the one and only being. It is an all-inclusive and majestic embrace. The word for angel, *malak,* is closely related to this name. Angels

are made of light and are held in the hands of Allah. The light of *al-Malik* holds the inner essence of each and every thing. Each thing's essence never leaves this majestic embrace and never returns to it because it is permanently rooted in it.[17]

The Forty-Nine Day Practice & Associations

After Reb Zalman passed on July 3rd, 2014, Pir Shabda Kahn, the head of the Ruhaniat lineage of Inayati Sufism, wrote me while traveling in Germany, offering his condolences, telling me that after his son, Solomon, passed two years earlier, Reb Zalman had written him, too, offering a forty-nine-day practice with these same *waza'if*. Pir Shabda now offered this practice to me for my period of mourning . . .

Ya Raḥman ('O Compassionate One'), Days 1-7;
Allahu 'Akbar ('God is Greater'), Days 8-14;
Ya Raḥim ('O Merciful One'), Days 15-21;
Ya Manṣur ('O Victorious One'), Days 22-28;
Ya Jamil ('O Beautiful One'), Days 29-35;
Ya Wadud ('O Lover'), Days 36-42;
Ya Malik ('O Sovereign'), Days 43-49.[18]

To this might be added two further associations to add dimension to the practice. For Reb Zalman, each *s'firah*, or divine quality, was also associated with a part of the color spectrum, as well as male and female exemplars from the Jewish tradition . . .

Ḥesed is associated with Miriam and Abraham, as well as the color violet of ultra-violet light;

Gevurah is associated with Leah and Isaac, as well as the color blue;

Tif'eret is associated with Hannah and Jacob-Israel, as well as the color green;

Netzaḥ is associated with Rebecca and Moses, as well as the color yellow;

Hod is associated with Sarah and Aaron, as well as the color orange;

Yesod is associated with Tamar and Joseph, as well as the color red;

Malkhut is associated with Rachel and David, as well as the color of reddish earth or infra-red.[19]

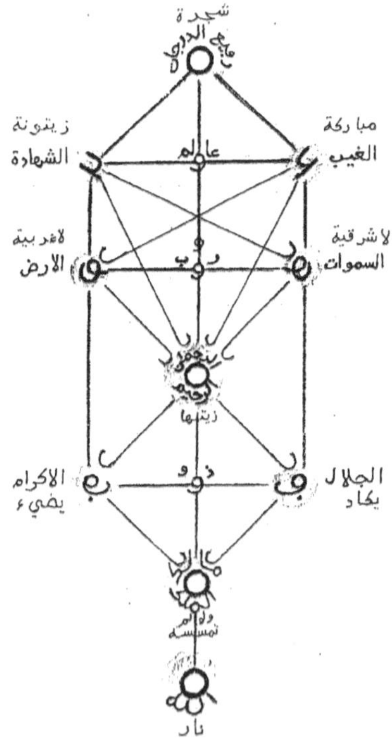

The 'Tree of Life' connected with the name Allah by Dreyfus.

olamot

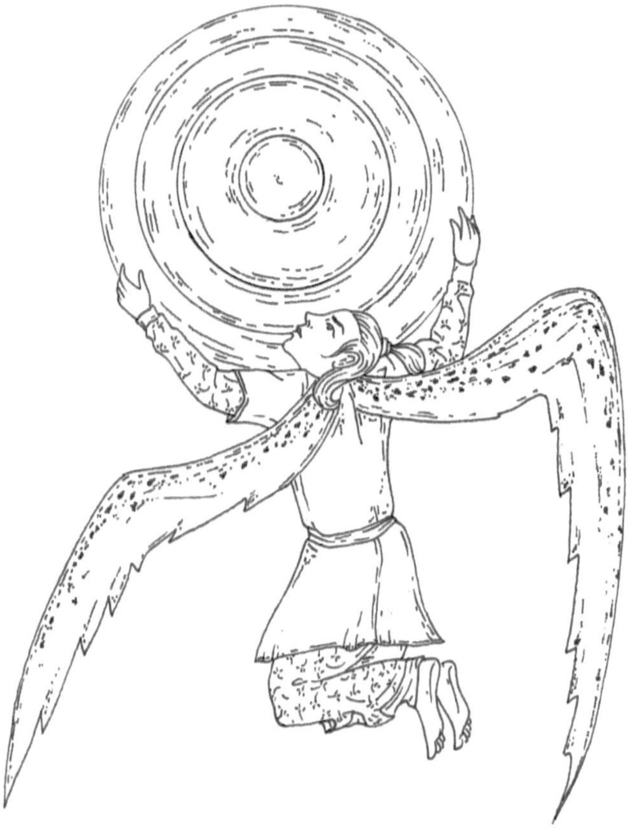

One God, Many Worlds

Living in the Four Worlds of Sufism and Hasidism *

In the summer of 1920, Rabbi Yosef Yitzhak Schneersohn, the sixth Lubavitcher Rebbe, was summoned before a Communist tribunal in Russia to account for his so-called "Godly activities." During his interrogation, one of the committee members—annoyed by his lack of cooperation—said to him, "You had better think about cooperating." The Rebbe told the committee he would not depart from his principles. The man then lifted a revolver and pointed it at the Rebbe, saying, "Many a man has changed his mind while looking down the barrel of this *'persuader.'* " The Rebbe stared back at him and replied, coolly, "Only a person who has many gods to serve, and only one world to serve them in, is frightened by your 'persuader.' But I, who have only one God to serve, and many worlds in which to serve, I am not frightened."[1]

* Edited from a talk given to a gathering of Inayati Sufis in Denver in the Spring of 2013, and reproduced in my Sufi retreat intensives from 2017-2020. It was the first subject Reb Zalman ever asked me to teach publically.

It is hard to imagine anyone having such confidence today. The lives that most of us lead are so small; we live in one highly circumscribed world with so many 'gods' to serve—love, money, sex, attention—and at whose altars we worship every day, often from moment to moment. We chase after every desire and run from every fear. How different it would be to worship just one God in all things, to worship "the only being" everywhere we go, in everything we meet, to live in realities that free us from the tyranny of such "persuasion."

But what did the Rebbe mean by "many worlds"? On one level, at least, he was referring to something we talk about everyday. We say, so and so 'belongs to the art world,' 'the world of science,' or 'politics.' And when we say this, we all understand what we mean—overlapping worlds of special significance to those who take part in them—worlds with their own rules and nomenclature, like those inhabited by artists, scientists, or politicians. In this case, however, the rules and symbols belong to the metaphysical realities described in Hasidism and *kabbalah,* the Jewish mystical tradition, whose terrain is mapped by spiritual masters like the sixth Lubavitcher Rebbe.

Nevertheless, the Jewish mystical tradition is not the only tradition to speak of other worlds. In the mystical teachings of Sufism—sometimes called the 'tasted wisdom' *(ḥikmat al-zawqiyya)*—we are also taught that there are an infinite number of worlds in existence (of which four are most useful for us to understand, just as we find in Hasidism). Though there are occasional variations and differences in their descriptions and number, there are also striking parallels between them.[2]

Knowledge and Worlds

As both Hebrew and Arabic are Semitic languages, their words for 'worlds'—*olamot* and *'alamin*—are based in the same Semitic root, *ayin-lammed-mem* or *'ayn-lam-mim*. In Hebrew, the

words derived from this root generally have to do with things hidden, as well as great, undefined distances beyond the horizon.[3] Thus, the Hebrew word, *olam*, can mean both 'eternity' and 'world,' depending on the context. In Arabic, the words derived from the same root also have to do with knowledge. So there is a relationship between knowledge *('ilm)* and the world *(al-'alamun)* in Arabic due to the boundless nature of each in Semitic thinking. For, unlike our modern tendency to think of worlds and knowledge as things contained (or containing definite constituent parts), our Semitic forbears looked out on the far horizon and thought only of how vast and undefined it was. Thus, their ideas of knowledge and worlds had these same characteristics—both being open-ended and participating in 'eternity.'

This is something that we need to keep in mind when thinking about the mystical worlds of Hasidism and Sufism. For when we attempt to talk about them in a static way (as I am doing here), what we are really talking about is "their middle," as my *rebbe* and *murshid* once reminded me. We do not know where they actually begin or end; nor is it as easy to talk about where they 'meet' and 'overlap.' Thus, we are often forced to describe an idealized 'middle zone,' where the admixture of worlds seems least evident, and where they are most 'themselves,' as it were.[4]

This, of course, is an abstracted and artificial way of talking, but at least it gives us a place to begin. And really, that is all we are doing here—making a beginning. It is important to understand that everything that I am going to say is merely heuristic, meaning that these are ways of talking about metaphysical realities that help us to understand them, but which are not to be thought of as definitive. My own understandings and descriptions will certainly differ from those of others who may see the "middle" differently, or who may have more insight and ability to describe the 'far reaches' of these worlds. But the more perspectives one gets on them, the better; each perspective adds dimension to our understanding and breaks the idols of certainty that we so often put in place of genuine experience.

The Four Worlds

For simplicity's sake, I will use my teacher Rabbi Zalman Schachter-Shalomi or 'Reb Zalman's terminology to help us grasp the more immediate parallels between the worlds in both traditions. In his teaching, he would often talk about "the four worlds" as the 'world of action,' the 'world of feeling,' the 'world of knowing,' and the 'world of being.' In these, he saw the celestial archetypes responsible for the mysterious phenomenon of 'four-foldness,' or "four-sies," as he called them, found throughout creation. Thus, he liked to draw attention to the parallels between the four elements (earth, water, fire, air); the four functions of Jungian psychology (sensation, feeling, thinking, intuition); the four yogas of Vedanta *(karma yoga, bhakti yoga, jñana yoga, raja yoga);* and the four levels of spiritual understanding in Sufism *(shari'ah, tariqah, ma'rifah, haqiqah).*

Let's consider the latter four for a moment. In Sufism, each of these four levels of understanding provides a foundation for the next. *Shari'ah* is the 'well-trodden path.' It refers to the

normative religious path of Islam and all that is required of a Muslim. This is the ground level of spiritual work, everything that a Muslim must do in the world of action. *Tariqah,* on the other hand, is "the trackless path in the desert that the Bedouin follow from oasis to oasis."[5] This is the Sufi path, requiring a spiritual guide who is intimately familiar with the landscape of the heart in the world of feeling, and who knows the way to your ultimate destination. Following such a guide's direction, we begin to experience things for ourselves, and begin to get a sense in the world of knowledge of that landscape. This is what is called *ma'rifah,* 'experiential knowledge' or *gnosis.* Beyond this is *haqiqah,* the 'truth as-it-is' in the world of being, which cannot be expressed in the ordinary world of duality.[6]

Nevertheless, Sufism also speaks of metaphysical worlds that more directly parallel the worlds of Hasidism and Kabbalah, and it is these that I would like to talk about in detail here.[7] In particular, I want to look at them from the differing perspectives of Reb Zalman, who often described the worlds from a psychological perspective, and his friend, Pir Vilayat Inayat-Khan or Pir Vilayat, who looked at them as stages in the development of consciousness in which one is incrementally freed from bondage to the ego.

The World of Action

Of course, the world with which we are most familiar, and to which we most closely relate on a daily basis, is the 'world of action' or doing. In Hasidism, this is *olam ha-assiyah,* the 'world of making,' or the world in which we make and do things.[8] In Sufism, the same world is called, *'alam an-nasut,* the 'world of humanity,' the visible world we inhabit, the material world of the senses. This is the world we all know—though we might make one distinction. Jewish sources sometimes distinguish between what could be called the *'life'* of the visible world and

its *'matter,'* often describing *assiyah* as its 'life,' its animate or living quality.[9]

Thus, in his own teaching, Reb Zalman placed "the body and its energies" in the world of action, saying . . .

> *Assiyah,* or 'doing,' is the designation for the physical world of action, which includes action for spiritual purposes. It is the world of the *guf* and *nefesh,* the body and its energies, located in the realm of sensation and behavior. The Jewish code of religious practice, the *halakhah,* operates largely in *Assiyah.* On this level, religion trains people in behaviors intended to please God by obedience to the divine law, and piety is expressed mostly through *g'millut ḥassadim,* doing 'deeds of loving-kindness' and observing the *mitzvot.*[10]

But *assiyah* is also said to be the world that conceals the light of divinity *from us,* and at the same time, reveals it *to us.* This is because it is the most dense 'contraction' *(tzimtzum)* of the divine light, allowing for the illusion of finitude and separation, and thus also our general ignorance of the divine reality. But it is also "a vessel that was made to receive God's light," being the "place where the spiritual actually interacts with the physical dimension."[11] That is to say, *assiyah* is both materiality and the energies of the material universe blinding us to more subtle dimensions, and our interface with those subtle dimensions.

Similarly, Sufism treats *nasut* as the "fruit" of the divine tree, the place where we can interact with and enjoy the divine presence: "Some call it the visible world *(shahadat)* or simply the created world *(mulk);* others call it the world of waking consciousness *(bidar)* or the world-as-believed *(pindar).*"[12] In the school of Ibn 'Arabi, *nasut* (humanity) is also understood to be the vessel which contains *lahut* (divinity).[13]

Following on his father Hazrat Inayat Khan's description, Pir Vilayat likens our experience of the 'world of action' to a

stage in the development of consciousness where one is addicted to sensory experience and caught in an egoic solipsism . . .

> *Nasut,* according to the Sufis, is the ordinary state in which we, along with most people, find ourselves. We think of ourselves as the subject who is observing the world as the object. We are in a state of dependence. . . we identify with our body, our thoughts, our emotions, or our self-image . . . to evolve we need to be weaned from that attachment.[14]

This is the trick of the senses, allowing us to identify with the body as separate from the rest of reality. Thus, for Pir Vilayat, *nasut* represents the generally limited state of consciousness which the world of action engenders. And yet, this very tendency also creates the dissatisfaction with limited consciousness that drives one to seek a world beyond.

The World of Feeling

Beyond the energy of life in the 'world of action' is the 'world of feeling.' In Hasidism, this is *olam ha-yetzirah,* the 'world of formation.' The sense here is of a sculptor forming and shaping soft clay with their hands. It has not yet reached the stage of drying and being baked in a kiln. It is still a plastic, malleable world. In Sufism, it is called, *'alam al-malakut,* the 'world of angels,' the invisible world, perceivable only through the spiritual-senses.[15] This is the world made up of emotion, qualities, intentions, forms, and spiritual energies, often related to the faculty of speech—all the aspects of experience that 'feel' tangible to us, but which are not quite that in the world of action.

Reb Zalman writes of *yetzirah* mostly from the point-of-view of emotion . . .

> The inner experience of feeling or deep emotion is in the world of *yetzirah,* where we find *ru'aḥ,* the 'breath-spirit.' *Yetzirah,* which means 'formation,' also involves images, values and myths. On this level, piety is measured in terms of devoutness: the sincere feeling one invests in prayer and worship. Purification of emotions is one of the central tasks to be accomplished on this level, and is a prerequisite for full entry into the world of the Kabbalah.[16]

Likewise, *malakut* in Sufism is often discussed as the essential entry-point into deeper spiritual realities. A number of terms in Sufism are merely synonyms for *malakut*, it being called "the world of spirits *('arwaḥ)*" or "the unseen *(ghayb),*" "the subtle world *(latif)* or the world of dreaming *(khwab).*"[17] Moreover, some of these—according to one source, at least—are described differently merely to facilitate access to this world. For instance, the often-discussed 'world of the imagination' *('alam al-mithal)* is really, according to Dara Shikuh, the means to opening *malakut*, and to "make this opening clear, it is described as different from the spiritual world and is called the imaginative world; but in reality the imaginative world is part and parcel of the spiritual world *[malakut].*"[18]

Interestingly, in both traditions, the 'world of feeling' is associated with angels: "The living creatures of the world of formation, the beings who function in it as we function in the world of action, are called, in a general way, 'angels.'"[19] Pir Vilayat suggests that it is necessary for one to enter into the angelic consciousness in order to experience *malakut.*[20] But this is perhaps better discussed in relation to the *soul's* experience of this world later.

The World of Knowing

Above this 'world of feeling' is the 'world of knowing' or thought. Among Ḥasidim, it is called *olam ha-b'riyah,* the 'world of creation.' Among Sufis, *'alam al-jabarut,* the 'world of power.' This is the heavenly world of divine names and characteristics, the world of souls[21] where divine decrees are made and everything is planned before it descends into form and matter (feeling and action). Here is where the 'architectural plans' are made for creation, or maybe the sketch for the aforementioned sculpture to be worked on in the world of feeling.

Of the world of knowing, Reb Zalman writes in terms of 'understanding' . . .

> The third level of reality is the world of *b'riyah,* or 'creation,' the world of thinking and philosophy, thought or contemplation, where we seek to understand the blueprint of the universe. This is where the *neshamah* [soul] is rooted. *B'riyah* also includes the faculties of concept, idea, hypothesis and theory. On this level, piety expresses itself in how one invests time and awareness in the study of Torah and the esoteric teachings.[22]

Just as *yetzirah* below it is described as a 'world of feeling' or emotion, filled with beings of pure emotion (angels), *b'riyah* above it is described as a 'world of knowing, 'or "pure mind." It is said, "This mind quality of the world of creation is not a merely intellectual essence but rather expresses itself as the power and capacity to grasp things with a genuine, inner understanding; in other words, it is the mind as creator, as well as that which registers and absorbs knowledge."[23]

Among Sufis, there is some debate about how this world is to be described. Dara Shikuh writes that *'alam al-jabarut* is called "the causal realm *('alam-i lazim),*" but says that many Sufis err in calling it "the realm of names and attributes" *(asma o sifat),*[24] a description which would generally coincide with the world of knowing as the locus of divine archetypes. Nevertheless, this is how we are dealing with it here.

Pir Vilayat steers a middle course between the two views, staying close to the knowing aspect of *jabarut*, while not forgetting Dara Shikuh's description of it as "a state of being in which one sees nothing that exists in the human realm or the spiritual realm."[25]

> The breakthrough that marks access to what the Sufis call the *[jabarut]* level is triggered off by grasping meaningfulness, which is not based upon an interpretation of existential experience or a search for causality or retrocausality.[26] If consciousness is voided of any perception or conception, being reabsorbed in its ground, which is intelligence, then a meaningfulness is revealed that makes sense of what we could not figure out with our mind . . . That is not the kind of knowledge we acquire but the kind of knowledge that is written right into our intelligence.[27]

The World of Being

Finally, we come to the 'world of being.' In Hasidism, this is called *olam ha-atzilut,* the 'world of nearness,' being so close to the divine as to be almost indistinguishable from it.[27] Likewise, in Sufism, it is *'alam al-lahut,* the 'world of divinity,' where there is no separation, everything being merged in the divine essence. If the world of knowing is where the 'plans' are made, or the 'sketch' is drawn, the world of being is where the pre-formative

idea exists. There is no idea there yet, as such, but it is the source of the *'Ah-ha!'* moment in which you know 'something' which you cannot yet describe. Here, it is as if the whole idea of the unfolding of creation is still in God's 'mind' or 'belly,' as it were; it has not yet been 'outer-ed' in any way. This is why it is called the 'world of nearness.'

In his psychological presentation of the 'world of being,' Reb Zalman explains *atzilut* in terms of intuition derived from the undifferentiated source . . .

> The fourth level of reality is *atzilut,* or 'emanation.' This is the world of being, intuition, inner teaching, the 'secret' and 'mystery' of *sod,* and the anagogical level of interpretation. *Atzilut* is a deep, divine intuition—a state of 'beingness' with God in the soul's aspects of *ḥayyah* and *yeḥidah (yeḥidah,* actually, is what is 'touching' *Adam Kadmon).* It is the source of inspiration . . .[29]

According to Hasidism and the Kabbalah, *olam ha-atzilut* is a world "of such absolute clarity and transparency that no concealment of any essence whatsoever is possible . . . consequently essences do not exhibit any particular separate self at all." For this reason, it is characterized simply as 'being,' and is seen as nearly identical with divinity or the Godhead.[30]

From the Sufi perspective, *'alam al-lahut* is similarly described as "the uncreated universe, present and existing in divine knowledge. Nothing in it has free will, everything there being subject to absolute dominion."[31] In Pir Vilayat's teaching (because he is using an expanded schema of worlds and values), this 'world of being' is described using the term *hahut,* 'is-ness,' or literally, 'he-ness,' instead. Again, he explains the world in terms of consciousness . . .

> The *[hahut]* level is exactly the same as *samadhi.* We have lost sight of the multiplicity because we have

> downplayed the multiplicity in unity. All we are aware of is the unity behind it all.[32]

So here we have a sense of undifferentiated consciousness, "where all sense of multiplicity has disappeared. You cannot say you see the unity because you merge into this unity. This is articulated in the words of Al-Hallaj: *An al-Haqq!* (I am the Truth!)"[33] That is to say, it is experienced by the spiritual adept as union or identity with divinity.

The Ladder of Creation

Often, these worlds are described as rungs on "a ladder of intersecting reality-patterns through which we (and all the universe) ascend and descend, physically and spiritually."[34] Above, I have listed them in order of ascent—moving from the world of materiality to the affective world, from the affective world to the world of the mind, from the world of the mind to that of undifferentiated being beyond—the journey we all must make back to the source. But in their descriptions from top to bottom, it is clear that they also describe an evolutionary process of metaphysical unfolding—from the pre-formative idea of creation existing in inchoate being to the actual idea and plan of creation, from the shaping of the subtle form of it (where everything is plastic and changes are still possible) to the solidified reality of creation as-we-know-it.

Or, again, the process might also be compared to the journey from the pot in the potter's mind to the design and drawing of the pot, from the clay spinning on the potter's wheel, shaped by their hands, to the finished pot taken baked and dry from the kiln.

The Four Souls

Interesting as these descriptions might be in themselves, there would not be a lot of point in talking about such metaphysical worlds if we did not have a means of experiencing them. Thus, we are also taught about the corresponding souls of action, feeling, knowing, and being, through which we are continually in contact with these various metaphysical realities.

Qualities	Has. Worlds	Suf. Worlds	Has. Souls	Suf. Souls
Action	*Assiyah*	*Nasut*	*Nefesh*	*Nafs*
Feeling	*Yetzirah*	*Malakut*	*Ru'aḥ*	*Nafas*
Knowing	*B'riyah*	*Jabarut*	*Neshamah*	*Ruḥ*
Being	*Atzilut*	*Lahut*	*Ḥayyah*	*Izn*

The Active Soul in Relation to the Body

Just as we distinguished between the *matter* of the visible world and its *life,* we also distinguish between the substance of the body—called *guf* or *jasad* (meaning 'flesh' in Hebrew and Arabic, respectively)—and the 'active soul,' called *nefesh* or *nafs.*[35] This is the vital or animating soul in the body, its very life and energy. This is the soul you can feel in a handshake, the glow in a pregnant mother's skin, the very pulse and vibration of all life. It is what is so evidently missing when we look at the body of a friend or loved one who has passed on. It is present in all organic life, from plants to animals to human beings, and perhaps even at lower levels in a way that is difficult to perceive.[36]

It is through the agency of the 'active soul' that we do our work in the 'world of action.' We do not need to say a lot about

this, as almost all of our awareness is already given over to it. Nevertheless, it is worth noting that this 'active soul' can be 'charged' and 'cultivated' through various kinds of meditative breathing, as well as the breath-coordinated movements of Sufi *zikr,* Hasidic *davvenen,* Hatha Yoga, and T'ai Chi.[37]

The Feeling Soul and the Angelic Realm

Now the soul through which we do our work in the 'world of feeling' is called *ru'aḥ* or *nafas,* 'wind' or 'spirit' in both Hasidism and Sufism. It is related to wind because it is always in motion. This 'feeling soul' is sensitive to and conveyed through presence, quality, attitude, intention, and emotion. While the 'active soul' is sensitive to sound, sight, touch, taste, and smell, the 'feeling soul' assigns values to these ordinary senses. It is 'stirred' by them in one way or another. It knows whether something has *'heart,'* whether music is 'soulful' or 'vacuous,' or whether a prayer is 'deep' or 'empty.' It knows whether there is tension or friendliness in a room, as we have all experienced at one time or another. You see, we forget how much we are in touch with these different souls, and how much we are actually living through them. We do not think about *why* we know these things; but the esoteric tradition is telling us that we are continually reaching-out with this soul.

But the 'feeling soul' is more than just a *receiver* of subtle information; it is also the means through which we *communicate* presence, qualities, attitudes, intentions, and emotions to the 'world of feeling.' This is why it is also called the 'world of angels' among Sufis.

The Hebrew and Arabic words for angel, *malakh* or *malak,* both mean 'messenger.' Angels, according to the esoteric theosophical teachings, are not compound beings like us (made up of different elements and filled with complex motivations),

but simple essences which convey their own essence as a message.[38] Marshall McLuhan used to say, "the medium is the message," the object is its own message.[39] Well, an angel is very much like that. A feeling of love or hate in a specific context, in a particular moment, becomes an angel that carries that message to the 'world of knowing,' which receives it and sends back a response in another angelic messenger.[40]

This is actually a description of "Jacob's Ladder." In Genesis 28:12, it says that Jacob dreamed of "a ladder set upon the earth which extended to heaven," on which the angels of God were ascending and descending. This is what angels do—they go up and down. Why do they go up and not just down? Because *we* create angels, too. For example, if I am walking through the park one day and see a child on a swing, smiling with delight, and my heart is moved with joy, that moment births an angel. Likewise, if I have a particular kind of frustration with someone at work, or a difficult encounter with my partner, an angel is birthed which conveys that frustration as a message to the higher worlds also.

But it is not only emotions. If I have an intention to quit drinking, or an intention to live a life of integrity, an angelic messenger is birthed from that intention, too.

Therefore, the types of emotions we feel, and the types of intentions we cultivate, are extremely important. They do not actually stop at the borders of our skin. They travel on through the 'feeling soul' to the 'knowing soul,' which exists in the 'world of knowing,' and which conveys that message to a 'council of souls' or a 'heavenly court' which crafts a response, or a 'decree' for us. So we have to take responsibility for our emotions and intentions; we have to cultivate better intentions, a higher quality of feeling, and be careful about what kinds of emotions and intentions we let loose in the worlds.

The Knowing Soul in the Heavenly Court

The 'knowing soul' is called *neshamah* or *ruḥ*, 'soul' or 'spirit' in Hebrew and Arabic. As you might expect, this is the soul that thinks and plans in the 'world of knowing,' also known as the 'world of souls.' Now, we have seen that the 'feeling soul' is really about conveying emotion and intentions as messages; but where are those messages received, and what is done with them? The 'world of knowing' is where the archetypes of our personalities, the reflections of our consciousness, our 'knowing souls' congregate and conceive together (as a collective) what needs to happen in the 'world of action' (based on the intentions coming up from our 'feeling souls').[41]

This is why the Kabbalah also speaks of it in terms of a 'heavenly court,' where judgments are created and decrees are made with regard to the 'world of action.'[42] Moreover, it might also be seen as the place where souls 'rub elbows' and create alliances to make new things, where the soul of Shakespeare may collaborate with the soul of Rumi to create a certain effect in the world.[43]

I personally tend to think of the work of the 'knowing souls' as a collective discernment process, a 'feedback mechanism' of the Morphogenetic Field, if you will. It collects messages from below, about which it makes a decision, and then sends a response back 'down' into the 'world of action.' If so many messages of love or hate from the 'world of action' reach a critical mass in the 'world of knowing,' a response of a certain type, meant to act as a corrective in the universe, is created. But it is not a simple, one-to-one, mechanistic response; there is an aggregate or cooperative intelligence shaping the responses, a cosmic balancing system.[44]

The thing to remember about the 'world of knowing' is that it does not view 'good and evil' the way we do down here. The knowing faculty is, by definition, intellectual and dispassionate, and only looks for healthy, long-term solutions. Thus, when the

more elevated, collective consciousness of the 'knowing souls' conceive of a corrective for our world, we are often unhappy with the short-term results, which we might even consider 'evil.'

There is an interesting anecdote in the Hasidic tradition which precisely illustrates this disparity in perspective . . .

Once, Reb Elimelekh of Lizhensk saw great trouble approaching the Jewish people and he began to pray very hard for God's help. Later, when he was asleep, he saw the Maggid of Mezritch in his dream, and he asked him, "Rebbe, why are you silent? Why don't you cry out against this terrible catastrophe?"

The Maggid answered him, saying, "In heaven, we do not see any evil—we see only the goodness and the kindness of judgments. You who are on Earth see the good as well as the evil, therefore, you must insist and pray very hard to move the heavens in these matters."[45]

That is to say, the angel created by our intentions must be 'big' enough to move the 'heavenly court' to an action that is as helpful and as satisfying to us in the short-term as it will be in the long-term.

The Inseparable Soul of Being

Beyond the 'knowing soul' is the 'being soul,' called *ḥayyah* and *izn,* 'living essence' and 'permission' in Hasidism and

Sufism. This soul is beyond thinking; it has more to do with intuition and flashes of insight. It is less about process, because it is connected to the 'world of being,' where everything is intermingled and undifferentiated. There is no real separation between one thing and another. Everything is direct, and thus we get flashes of insight and intuition, making connections that seem spectacular or miraculous.

In the 'world of knowing,' there is a clear intellectual process. For instance, if I want to start a business, I have to consider a number of factors and tasks. I have to develop the basic idea, consider how I might produce and deliver my product, research how to obtain a business license and pay my quarterly taxes, etc. You put all this information together and go through a process of building an idea into a plan. But with intuition, there is no obvious process.

Think about it this way. Here in the 'world of action,' many famous discoveries have come about through intuitions: in a flash of insight, John Nash makes a connection between Game Theory and Economics; or August Kekulé makes a connection in a dream between a serpent swallowing its own tail *(ouroboros)* and the arrangement of carbon atoms in Benzene. In our world, there is no apparent or necessary connection between A (representing Game Theory) and C (representing Economics); but, three levels up, in the 'world of being,' everything is intermingled and intimately connected. That is why an intuition that turns out to be correct seems so amazing; it makes a connection we cannot see in the world of separation.

This is one of the most difficult concepts to understand because we are mostly trying to understand it from 'below,' as it were.

Living and Working in the Worlds

It is important to know something about these worlds because we can be empowered in our spiritual work by remembering that we exist in all of them simultaneously. For in each successive world we are less affected by the limits of time, space, and matter. Those limits belong to the 'world of action.' But in the 'worlds of feeling,' 'knowing' and 'being,' the limits are increasingly irrelevant; so much so, that in 'being,' there is no 'distance' between anything. What is impossible or improbable because of the limits of the 'world of action' are possible, and can be more easily accomplished, in the 'world of being.' This has important implications for the way we live, the intentions we cultivate, the thoughts we create, and how we respond to our intuition every day—at home and at work, with strangers and friends, family and acquaintances—and especially in how we put it all together in our prayers and meditations.

In the 'world of action,' there is only so much money you can give to a cause, or so much help you can offer to anyone owing to the limits of time, energy, and opportunity. But these limitations fall away in the other worlds, where we can more freely offer our love, our knowledge, and our insights. In our prayer-life, we can direct all of these to a definite end. Even more importantly, we can work on *ourselves* through these souls. We can ask, 'Am I feeding my body right to give it energy, cultivating and directing my intentions and thoughts in the right way, or responding bravely to my intuitions?' By acting accordingly, we can live more consciously in all four worlds, filling-out the most profound dimensions of our being, and doing our best for the health of the planet as a whole.

beynoni

Between the Animal and Divine Souls

Hasidic and Sufi Models of Spiritual Development *

It is taught *(tanya)*—"An oath is administered to us before birth—'Be righteous, and be not wicked; but even if the whole world tells you that you are righteous, regard yourself as if you were wicked.'" *(Niddah* 30b)

This requires an explanation, for in the *Mishnah* it says, "Be not wicked in your own estimation." *(Avot* 2:13) Furthermore, people who consider themselves wicked are often heart-sick and depressed; consequently, they are not able to serve God as they should with a joyful and contented heart. On the other hand, if they are not bothered by this thought, they may be led into irreverent behavior by it, God forbid. So obviously this matter needs to be discussed further.

In the *Gemara,* we find that there are five distinct types: the righteous who prosper, the righteous who suffer, the wicked who prosper, the wicked who suffer, and those in-between—*beynonim.* *(B'rakhot* 7b, 66a) It is explained, "the righteous who prosper" are the complete *tzaddikim,* and "the righteous who suffer" are the incomplete *tzaddikim.*

---

* Edited from "Between the Animal and Divine Souls," a talk given in New Lebanon, New York, on October 18th, 2016, at the Abode of the Message, while serving as its resident teacher in the fall of 2016. Also represented in chapter 2 of my book, *A Hidden Light: Stories and Teachings of Ḥ̣aBaD and Bratzlav Hasidism* (2011).

> In the *Zohar*, it is further explained that "the righteous who suffer" are those whose evil nature is subservient to their good nature. (II: 117b) According to the *Gemara*, the righteous are ruled by their good nature, the wicked by their evil nature, and those in-between by both their good and their evil nature. *(B'rakhot* 61b) Rabbah said, "I, for example, am in-between"—a *beynoni*. But Abbaye objected, "Master, you make it impossible for anyone else to live."
>
> — Shneur Zalman of Liadi, *Tanya*, *"Sefer Shel Beynonim"*[1]

In the Jewish tradition, we are taught that an oath is administered to us by an angel before we are born. That angel says to us, "Be righteous and not wicked; but even if the whole world tells you *'You are righteous,'* do not think of yourself as *'righteous,'* but as wicked." We are asked to agree to this before we are allowed to pass into this world; and we all do, apparently, and then we all break our oath.

On the other hand, the tradition also says, "Do not think of yourself as wicked." For, if we see ourselves as wicked, it is often indicative of a problem that prevents us from serving God and our own potential fully.

So what are we to do? And how are we to know if we are 'righteous' or 'wicked'?

Righteousness and Prosperity

In the Talmud, we are told that there are five types of people in the world, each defined by the aggregate of their known behavior, and their material status . . .

- The Righteous One Who Prospers *(tzaddik v'tov lo)*
- The Righteous One Who Suffers *(tzaddik v'ra lo)*
- The Average Person 'In-Between' *(beynoni)*
- The Wicked One Who Prospers *(rasha v'tov lo)*
- The Wicked One Who Suffers *(rasha v'ra lo)*

That is to say, a person who behaves 'righteously' more often than not is considered 'righteous,' and one who behaves 'wickedly' more often than not is considered 'wicked.' It is basically a tally system for good and bad deeds, qualified by whether one is prospering or not.

On the highest end of the scale, we have 'the righteous who prosper,' or who have it good in the material sense because their righteous actions allow for no wickedness. Below them are 'the righteous who suffer' because some wickedness has crept into their actions. We then have 'the wicked who prosper' because they have some good deeds to their credit. And on the bottom of the scale are 'the wicked who suffer,' having it bad materially because their sins allow for no righteousness. In the middle of the scale is the person 'in-between'—the *beynoni*—being neither very righteous, nor very wicked, their good and bad deeds being fairly evenly divided.

Obviously, if left unqualified, this system leads to a number of logical contradictions. Thus, the Hasidic master, Rabbi Shneur Zalman of Liadi (1745-1812) brings up an example that forces us to rethink this oversimplified explanation. He quotes the famous saying of Rabbah bar Naḥmani (ca. 270-330), "I, for example, am a *beynoni*," to which his nephew, Abbaye (ca. 280-340) objects, "Master, you make it impossible for anyone else to live." By this he means, 'If *you*, with all your holiness, are only a *beynoni*—having a roughly equal number of sins and good deeds—then the rest of us must be so wicked that we are liable for the death penalty!'

This indicates that the tradition itself is not so unsophisticated as it might at first seem, this exchange calling into question the assumptions on which the system seems to be based. Namely, the more good deeds you have to your credit, the more you prosper; and if you suffer, it is on account of your sins. It is a simplistic formula, frequently contradicted by the evidence; and yet, many still cling to this naïve theology of 'righteous reward' and 'wicked punishment.'

Realizing the contradiction, Reb Shneur Zalman agrees—someone as holy as Rabbah could *not* be a *beynoni* according to this simple definition . . .

> We must understand the essence of the one 'in-between,' for surely the *beynoni* is *not* one whose deeds are equally divided between good and evil; if this were the case, how could Rabbah make the mistake of classifying himself as a *beynoni?* Especially as it is known that his lips never ceased reciting Torah, so that even the Angel of Death had no dominion over him. *(Bava Metzia* 86a) God forbid that half of his deeds were sinful![2]

He goes on to point out that this tally system does not account for one's interior reality or intentions. For instance, a person may give to charity and be thought very righteous for the act; but their motivation might actually be to be *seen* giving charity, and thus to be thought 'very righteous,' which is not very righteous at all. Thus he writes . . .

> As for the well-known saying that *beynonim* are those whose deeds and misdeeds are equally balanced, while *tzaddikim* are those whose virtues outweigh their sins, this is only a generalization used to make a point with regard to reward and punishment, because we are judged according to the majority of our deeds, and one

who is acquitted in a trial is called 'righteous.' But if we truly seek to define the distinctive qualities of *tzaddikim* and *beynonim,* we must look to our sages who have remarked that the righteous are ruled by their good nature, as it is written, "And my heart is slain within me," (Ps. 109:22) meaning that David had overcome his evil nature through fasting. But whoever has not achieved this mastery—even if their virtues outnumber their sins—is not at the level of a *tzaddik.*[3]

Righteousness, Behavior, and Intention

Thus Reb Shneur Zalman gives a new interpretation of these five categories, describing them as five clear spiritual identities, each defined by their engagement with natural impulses, as well as by the behaviors that result from them . . .

- The Completely Righteous *(tzaddik gamur)*
- The Conditionally Righteous *(tzaddik sh'eino gamur)*
- The In-Betweener *(beynoni)*
- The Conditionally Wicked *(rasha sh'eino gamur)*
- The Completely Wicked *(rasha gamur)*

The strength of his model is that it emphasizes *kavanah,* the 'intentionality' and struggle behind our righteous and wicked deeds. But to the surprise of many—both then and now—it also prices 'righteousness' out of the market for most of us. For, according to Reb Shneur Zalman, the *tzaddik gamur*, or 'completely righteous person,' like King David, has entirely overcome their evil nature. They have so subdued and transformed their own demons that there is not even so much as an unconscious inclination to invest energy in a negative behavior—all fascination with sin and wickedness has been

completely eliminated. The *tzaddik gamur* cannot even conceive of a sin anymore!

On the other hand, the *tzaddik sh'eino gamur*, or 'conditionally righteous person,' *might* have a negative thought, or an unconscious inclination to invest in negative behavior, but does not even come close to acting on it; the fascination with wickedness in them is just a murmur in the deep unconscious. But because these residual negative impulses still exist in them, the conditionally righteous are subject to *karma* and the reciprocal effects of that negativity, whereas the completely righteous are not.

Now, keeping this in mind, let us see what he has to say about the *beynoni* . . .

> The *beynoni* is the one in whom evil never attains enough power to capture the 'little city,' to clothe itself in the body and make it sin. That is to say, the three garments of the animal nature *(nefesh ha-behamit)*—thought, word, and deed—originating in the shell of materiality *(k'lippah)* do not prevail over the divine nature *(nefesh ha-elohit)* within one to the extent of clothing themselves in the body—in the mind, the mouth, and the other 248 organs—thereby causing them to sin and defile themselves, God forbid.[4]

The "little city" is the body, which, like a medieval city, needs to be fortified and defended against forces that would overrun it and bring it to ruin. It is disputed territory in a 'holy war' waged between two opposing forces: the *nefesh ha-behamit*, the 'animal nature,' which would bring it to ruin, and the *nefesh ha-elohit*, the 'divine nature,' which would elevate it to holiness. For Reb Shneur Zalman teaches us that there is within us a basic duality—almost a schism—caused by these two magnetic poles.

Both the *nefesh ha-elohit*, our 'divine nature, and the *nefesh ha-behamit*, the 'animal nature,' are whispering to us continually. But we tend to live on the animal end of our potential. This is because the divine nature is light, immaterial, and transcendent; whereas the animal is immanent and heavy, having the kind of gravity-pull we associate with matter. Being in bodies, it is thus easier for us to lean into our material, animal nature.

Because the 'animal nature' is associated with the left chamber of the heart (and the left side of the body), we get an amusing story of a sincere and enthusiastic young Ḥasid introducing himself to Reb Shneur Zalman in an odd manner . . .

Overcome with zeal on his first visit to Liozhna, Reb Yekusiel of Lieple climbed up on the roof of Reb Shneur Zalman's house and pressed himself against the window of the attic where the *rebbe* had his study. When he was sure the *rebbe* had seen him, he called out with great anguish in his voice, "Rebbe, cut off my left side!" Feeling compassion for him, Reb Shneur Zalman motioned for him to come in and he blessed him.[5]

Reb Yekusiel was trying to say, 'Rebbe, please relieve me of these disturbing urges from my animal nature!' So perplexed was he at that very moment, that he just wanted to be rid of them; he wanted to be all 'right side,' completely in the service of his divine nature.

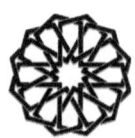

Of Animals, Angels, and Humans

Although the 'animal nature' is often equated with negativity in these discussions, it is not actually 'negative' at all—it is merely animal. And though the 'divine nature' is equated with all that is good and positive, it is not necessarily 'good' for us to try to be angels (as we are something between animal and angel, with the qualities of both).

If a lion on the Savannah kills a rival for the leadership of the pride, do we think of the lion as 'wicked,' or as having 'broken the law'? No, it is a lion living according to the law of its species. But if I kill my co-worker for a perceived threat to my livelihood in New York, or 'my manhood,' I am probably going to prison; for this action is almost universally judged 'wrong' among human beings. *Why?* Because what is 'good' for lions is not necessarily 'good' for human beings.

We may be part animal, but we are not the *same* animal as a lion. And though it is important to acknowledge our animal nature, it is equally important to know that *this* 'animal' has different standards based on our different capacities and context.

On occasion, our animal nature compels us in ways that prove troublesome. We have 'biological imperatives' or 'drives' that steer us in directions we might not go otherwise. We have survival drives, drives for sex and procreation, drives for security, and power drives, each of which, if left unchecked, can prove problematic or damaging for our lives as human beings: the biological urge to have a child may prove inconvenient to a person just beginning to establish their career; a desire for material security may sabotage a relationship with the right person with whom material security does not seem assured; or a moment of anger and violence over a slight in a bar may cost us our freedom.

We cannot afford to ignore these drives; but we cannot afford to obey them unreservedly, either.

Still, it is not our 'animal nature' and its drives that are *'wrong'* or *'bad'* according to this system. Most of them are neutral in themselves. What is 'wrong' or 'negative' for us is to live below the capacity of our humanity, to allow the human animal to act as if the rules of the Savannah are appropriate in New York.

When we apply the Yiddish word *mentch* to someone, it is a high compliment; but the word only means, *'human.'* This implies that 'human'—at least in the context of Ashkenzi Yiddish culture—is conceived of as something extraordinary, something to which we must aspire; and sadly, that most of us are not yet living up to it, acting 'like animals,' meaning, 'like *other* animals.'

To be 'human' is actually the goal of our lives.

In some ways, the *nefesh ha-behamit*, the 'animal nature,' as it is discussed in the *Tanya* of Reb Shneur Zalman, really stands for 'materiality'—specifically, materiality on a spectrum opposite to the 'immaterial.'

Most of the spiritual systems of antiquity (up through the medieval period) tell us that we must 'mortify the flesh' to release the pure spirit. It is a judgment based on an ascetic separation of 'matter and spirit.' Matter was assigned a negative value for seeming to 'imprison the spirit,' which was associated with everything immaterial, and therefore 'positive.' Thus, spiritual practitioners were often known to go to extremes in denying themselves food, sex, or a life in the world, giving rise to the image of the spiritual aspirant as an emaciated figure seated on a mountaintop or a platform above the world (apparently awaiting a reunion with God). It was an attempt at starving the animal in order to give birth to an angel.

But this kind of dualism comes at a terrible cost, to our bodies and the earth, and to our relationship with self; it requires us to believe that God made the world to be used and discarded, a belief for which we continue to suffer the

consequences. Thus, the holy Ba'al Shem Tov, the founder of Hasidism, taught *M'lo khol ha-aretz k'vodo,* 'The whole Earth is filled with God's Glory.' (Isa. 6:3) We must serve God with our bodies and souls united. It is not for us to seek to be other than we are, to be either 'angels' or 'animals.' We must be *exactly what we are* in our unique hybridity! The material of the earth is sacred, the vessel of the body no less sacred than the spirit, the angelic *anima* no more sacred than the animal.

Five Responses to Two Poles

Now, all five of Reb Shneur Zalman's spiritual identities hear the 'whispers' of both their divine and animal natures, but they respond very differently to them. The *tzaddik gamur*, the 'completely righteous person,' responds only to the whispers of the divine nature and the neutral aspects of the animal nature; they do not have the slightest inclination to respond to its negative aspects. These are silenced in them. Whereas the *tzaddik sh'eino gamur,* the 'conditionally righteous person,' likewise responds to the whispers of their divine nature and the neutral aspects of their animal nature; but, unlike the *tzaddik gamur*, *does* have some desire to respond to its negative aspects. They do not; but there is a murmur in the depths to do so.

The *rasha sh'eino gamur,* the 'conditionally wicked person,' responds to the whispers of their animal nature, both neutral and wicked; but they also feel a desire to respond to their divine nature, even if they generally do not. The *rasha gamur,* the 'completely wicked person,' on the other hand, responds exclusively to the neutral and wicked aspects of their animal nature; they feel no desire to respond to the whispers of their divine nature, as if it has been silenced in them.

When Reb Shneur Zalman was asked, 'And what are you?" He answered, like Rabbah, "I am a *beynoni.*"[36] But what does he mean by *beynoni?*

Here is where things get really interesting; for while the Talmud seems to suggest that the *beynoni*, the 'in-betweener,' is just 'average'—neither very good, nor very wicked—we see that Reb Shneur Zalman's *beynoni* is something far more than average . . .

> Now, the level of the *beynoni* is one that is possible for everyone to attain; and let everyone aspire to it. For anyone can become a *beynoni* at any time. The *beynoni* does not abhor evil altogether, for a battle rages in the heart, and does not go the same at all times; but to "turn away from evil and do good" (Ps. 34:15) in actual behavior—in thought, word, and deed—is something we may choose for ourselves. For even when one's heart craves and desires a physical pleasure—whether permitted or forbidden—one can prevail over this craving with a counter-desire, saying to the heart: "I don't want to be wicked, even for one moment! Under no circumstances do I wish to be severed and separated from God, Heaven forbid! As it says, 'Your iniquities separate you from God.' (Isa. 59:2)"[7]
>
> The *beynoni* has not committed, nor will commit a transgression; the name *rasha*, 'wicked,' cannot be applied to the *beynoni*, even momentarily.[8]

If this is true, then who among us would not call the *beynoni* extraordinary? For Reb Shneur Zalman tells us explicitly that, while the *beynoni* still struggles with desire and the urge toward the negative aspects of the animal nature, the *beynoni* is *never* guilty of succumbing to the temptation in behavior!

This is a long way from our understanding of 'average' or 'in-between.' When this is considered 'average'—between righteous and wicked—most of us, like Abbaye, have to come to terms with the reality of being classified as 'conditionally

wicked,' at best! Or, as my teacher, Reb Zalman, used to say, "By this system, most of us are just *reshayim* (wicked people) in-recovery!"[9] For even one negative act brings a person into the category of the *rasha sh'eino gamur,* or the 'conditionally wicked.' Thus, it appears that most of humankind—from those who 'sin' only rarely to those who 'sin' fairly often—can be classed under the category of the conditionally wicked.

Nevertheless, Reb Shneur Zalman seems to suggest that it is indeed possible to hold the course through our struggles, and to refrain from committing the transgressions which bring us into the category of the 'wicked.'

How is this accomplished? He tells us that there is a kind of fulcrum between the poles of the divine and animal nature—like the lever railroad switchmen pull to shift the tracks and change the course of a train. It is called the *nefesh ha-sikhlit*, the 'rational nature,' which can shift the balance one way or the other. The rational nature in human beings can *'give reason'* to the impulses and whispers that come from the animal or the divine nature.

As we have already said, we usually give in to the wishes of our animal nature more readily than we do to those of the divine nature. Often, we do this by default, moving from impulse to action almost without a thought. At other times, we do it by an interesting 'rationalization' process; for instance, justifying another piece of apple pie as if it were just as healthy for us as an apple!

But our rational nature can also weigh the potential and probable consequences of our actions, making good decisions based on this process of reasoning. In the war between competing impulses—animal and divine—it might reason: 'Really, I *could* have that piece of pie; after all it is kosher and certainly not forbidden. But I also know that I'm pretty full already, and have to wonder if it is 'good for me'—either physically or spiritually—to give into the wishes of my animal nature in this

particular case. Will I lose the weight I am trying to lose? Will I have taken a step toward releasing myself from the hold of my animal impulses? *Surely not.* If I can be self-disciplined now, I'll find greater freedom afterward. Therefore, I'll abstain.'

The Beynoni—A Realistic Hero

This is why we emphasize the *nefesh ha-sikhlit*, the 'rational nature,' which can be used in the service of either righteousness or wickedness. It is the central feature of our humanity, through which we make decisions about our thoughts, words, and deeds, the "three garments" in which we 'clothe ourselves' in any given moment.

Now, we can wear the 'clean clothes' of our divine nature, or the 'dirty clothes' of the negative aspects of our animal nature; it is up to us. So the rational nature should be asking, "How should I 'dress' for this moment?" i.e. what is the etiquette appropriate for this moment: if I allow myself to lose my temper or drift into some prurient thought, what will be the outcome?

For Reb Shneur Zalman, this is the battleground of the soul—the place in which the "little city" is lost or won—and the hero is the *beynoni*.

After all, what merit is there for the *tzaddik* who feels no real compulsion to sin? Is not the *beynoni*'s victory the greater one?

There is a wonderfully good-natured character in Charles Dickens' *Martin Chuzzlewit*—Mark Tapley—who works in the Blue Dragon tavern, and who is always ready to help with a good attitude, no matter how difficult the task. He is so genial and good-natured that nothing seems to get him down. Even amid the hardest work and most difficult situations, he utters no complaints. But he is also discontented and disappointed in himself, because he thinks there is "no merit" in his good nature, as it is *just his nature.* Others praise him for his exemplary

attitude, but he cannot accept their praise, because he has not personally experienced his conditions in life as either 'bad' or 'hard.' Even when he deals with a difficult or particularly irascible personality, he does so with grace and ease; it is just so easy for him, as it is his nature to be genial. Thus, he feels there is no merit in anything that he has done in life. Merit comes from struggling and overcoming adversity. Eventually he travels to America—which is seen as a backwater swamp, full of flies and all manner of foulness—thinking that the hardships of America will be so great, and the people so intolerable, that he will finally earn some merit though his patient endurance![10]

From this Dickensian perspective, there is no merit in being a *tzaddik gamur*, a 'completely righteous person,' who is never even tempted by the negative whispers of the animal nature. It is easy for them; thus there is no real temptation.

The *tzaddik gamur*, or 'completely righteous person,' is no more realistic than the *rasha gamur*, or 'completely wicked person.' Voldemort was once Tom Riddle, an orphan like Harry Potter. Darth Vader was once Anakin Skywalker, and suffered losses not unlike his son, Luke. It is only that they made very different decisions around their similar circumstances. It all comes down to the fulcrum of decision: what do we do with the 'whispers' of our divine and animal natures?

Righteousness and Wholeness

The *tzaddik gamur*, or 'completely righteous person,' creates no *karma*, no negative reciprocal effects because, in intentionality, they have no conflict to dilute and modify the purity of their actions. Thus, the *tzaddik gamur* is also the *tzaddik v'tov lo*, the 'righteous one who prospers.' The *tzaddik sh'eino gamur*, the 'conditionally righteous person' on the other hand is the *tzaddik v'ra lo*, the 'righteous one who suffers,' experiencing

some negative reciprocal effects due to the remnants of desire still active in them.

In a similar manner, the *rasha sh'eino gamur*, the 'conditionally wicked person' is the *rasha v'tov lo*, the 'wicked one who prospers,' because there is a little good in them to modify their actions. The *rasha gamur*, the 'completely wicked person,' is the *rasha v'ra lo*, the 'wicked one who suffers,' meaning that their *karma*, or the negative reciprocal effects of their actions, is severe and unmodified by any admixture of good.

Thus, the *karma* of the *beynoni* is the most complex (and apparently mysterious to the onlooker) due to the remarkable internal conflict they experience, regardless of how disciplined their actions.

The major remaining problem with the five categories is the sense of a 'locked' or 'static' identity: in the talmudic paradigm, it is a *quantitative* identity—the aggregate of one's deeds at any given point in one's lifetime defining whether a person is righteous or wicked; in Reb Shneur Zalman's model, it appears to be a *qualitative* identity in a rigid hierarchy which, while theoretically scalable, seems unrealistic with regard to human frailty.

I would not say that these categories are wrong, just *inaccurate* when projected as rigid identities on the human being who is always in transition. But I do not actually believe that Reb Shneur Zalman was truly suggesting such a static model, as is sometimes supposed.

With regard to the statement, "The *beynoni* has not committed, nor will commit a transgression," my rebbe's *rebbe*, Rabbi Menachem Mendel Schneerson (1902-1994) has said that this does not mean that the *person* has not committed a transgression and will not, but that the *beynoni* has not and will not.[11] What does this mean? It means that a person is a '*beynoni*' only as long as they are *being* a *beynoni*; while one is in that 'mode,' as it were, one is so distant from one's past sins—and potential

future sins—that it is as if they don't exist!

So let us go back and re-examine these five categories from a new perspective. Let's try to think of our participation in the world at any given moment as characterized by one of five different states of consciousness, with the aggregate of these momentary-modes—during any given period of time—determining the *relative wholeness* or *health* of the individual for that period, *not one's identity.*

Now, each of these five states of consciousness expresses a particular quality of being in a specific moment of decision (the moment in which we decide which 'voice' to listen to), and might be re-cast in terms of how much of the divine nature can penetrate them in that moment. Thus, we might think of them in the following terms . . .

- *Luminous Transparency*
- *Relative Transparency*
- *Translucence*
- *Relative Opacity*
- *Absolute Opacity*

Again, these are not rigid *identities*, but temporary *states of consciousness* in a moment of decision. In any given moment, when we need to make a decision, we participate in one of these five states of consciousness. So, for instance, 'luminous transparency' would be a state of consciousness in which there is not the slightest inclination to invest energy in negativity or a negative act. In some moments of decision, it is absolutely clear what we must do and we do not hesitate to act, no matter how difficult the situation. It is a pure, momentary expression of divinity in the human being, the ego having become transparent to a *hierophany*, a divine manifestation, free of personal agenda. Those moments, when they occur on the spiritual path, feel like pure grace. It is absolutely clear what we must do and we do it.

'Relative transparency' then is a state of consciousness in which there may yet be a mild inclination to invest energy in ego-driven agendas, but one succeeds fairly easily in making the ego transparent to the need of the moment, and behaves according to that need. These are those moments that are 'pretty clear'; there may be small reservations in us, but they do not really get in the way.

In both the 'luminous' and the 'relative' states of consciousness, it is still the divine nature (sharing a common ontology with God) that dominates. In these states of 'transparency,' one *cannot* act against the desire of the 'divine nature' or the pure will of the moment, for it would be tantamount to acting against one's own nature.

But if we happen to notice that our relative wholeness or spiritual health is poor, we may suspect that the balance of our decisions has shifted into the realm of 'relative opacity.' In this state of consciousness, the inclination toward negativity dominates the moment of decision, and the battle for transparency-in-action is lost. The moment is pretty dark; it is hard to see, and there is only a little light to guide our way. The light of the divine nature comes as "through a glass darkly" (1 Cor. 13:12), dimmed and distorted by the opacity of one's egoic desires. In behavior, 'relative opacity' may appear fully opaque, or may seem an admixture, minutely 'warped' for the good by the pull of the divine nature.

Then there are moments of complete darkness, in which we seem to be entirely cut off from the light. This is 'absolute opacity,' a momentary eclipse of the light of the divine nature by a negative impulse. The critical difference here between 'relative' and 'absolute opacity' is the absence of conscience. It is a momentary malevolence—whatever the particular act—absent of goodness. Again, this does not speak to one's identity, but to one's relative health and wholeness, or the lack thereof in that moment. 'Absolute opacity' is utter separation from God in consciousness.

Most of life, however, happens somewhere in the middle. Therefore, just below 'relative transparency' on this scale is the state of *'translucence,'* corresponding to the *beynoni*. 'Translucence' refers to the diffusion of light as it passes through an object, making objects on the other side appear less distinct; this refers to the state in which one consciously *struggles* with negative, ego-based impulses, but does not succumb to them in actual behavior. Again, it is the fulcrum of the five states, the place of conscious 'turning,' and is thus the state most advantageous to the spiritual practitioner.

In terms of behavior, 'translucence' is the same as 'transparency,' because *in action* at least, one has succeeded in overcoming the negative impulse. Choice is critical for the person in the state of 'translucence,' and this is what makes this state most human. 'Translucence' is a conscious choice not to draw energy from negativity, but rather from the pure well of the divine will. And this decision makes an impression on general consciousness that may, in time, create a positive pattern, opening one to deeper levels of 'transparency.' It is this mode, says Reb Shneur Zalman, that is available to all of us, all the time.

In this way, we can see that these five states represent a spectrum of human consciousness and potential integration, as Reb Shneur Zalman describes in the *Tanya* . . .

> However, the essence and being of the divine nature, which is to say, its ten faculties (i.e., the ten *s'firot),* do not hold a constant and undisputed sway over the "little city," except at very specific times, such as during the recitation of the *Sh'ma* or the *Amidah.* At these times—when the celestial mind is in a sublime state—here below, it is a propitious time for the *beynoni* to bind their *Ḥ aBaD (ḥokhmah, binah, da'at,* i.e., higher spiritual faculties) to God, contemplating the greatness of the blessed *Ain Sof,* the 'infinite one,' arousing a burning

> love in the right chamber of the heart, and adhering to God through the fulfillment of the Torah and its *mitzvot* as acts of love. . . . At such times, the evil contained in the left chamber of the heart is subdued and nullified by the goodness that suffuses the right chamber from the *Ḥ̣aBaD* (higher spiritual faculties) of the mind, which are bound to the greatness of the blessed *Ain Sof.*
>
> Nevertheless, after prayer, when this sublime state of the blessed *Ain Sof* recedes, the evil in the left chamber reawakens, and the *beynoni* begins to feel desire for the world and its delights once again.[12]

So here we see that some situations have a greater potential for introducing the light of the divine nature into our consciousness than others. At these times, we are best able to touch the place of the *tzaddik*, opening to the infinite dimension of God as *Ain Sof.* But, as Reb Shneur Zalman says, this situation cannot last, and the pull of the animal nature begins to reassert itself fairly quickly. Nevertheless, this description of a period in which a particular consciousness—in this case, that of the *tzaddik*—holds sway, brings up the issue of identity again.

Sufi States and Stations

Now the Sufi tradition has particularly good language for dealing with the difference between states of consciousness and spiritual identities, speaking of the difference between a *ḥal* and a *maqam*. A *ḥal* is understood to be a temporary 'state,' such as ecstasy, while a *maqam* is a 'station,' or a 'level' of sustained spiritual integration. Thus, it is understood in Sufism that while a person may have an ecstatic or illuminating experience in prayer, that does not necessarily indicate any change in their spiritual identity. It is an 'experience,' not a promotion to the rank of 'enlightened being.' There is a clear recognition in

Sufism that those spiritual epiphanies, of which we are often so proud, and which we are certain have changed us permanently, are only passing 'states.' So it is somewhat less shocking then the next day when we discover that we are largely the same person we were the day before!

The *maqam*, however, is more difficult to describe; for it is both solid and fluid at the same time. That is to say, it is a general state. For instance, a person might conceivably reach a certain level of maturity on the spiritual path—let us say—acting mostly like a *beynoni*, while still falling into occasional foolishness, and occasionally reaching higher states. But neither the 'reaching higher,' nor the 'falling lower,' really has much of an effect on their spiritual station in general.

It is as if they are standing on a large platform: from that platform, they may leap up and feel assured of landing safely and solidly on the platform again; and if they happen to fall down, they are only falling on the platform itself. That is to say, people who have reached a certain level of sustained spiritual integration do fall, but they do not often fall off the platform entirely and tend to get up without too much difficulty. It is this tendency to get up, or the consistency of their getting up, that keeps them at that level.

Thus, we can see the relationship between the five 'states' of consciousness—'luminous transparency,' 'relative transparency,' 'translucence,' 'relative opacity,' and 'absolute opacity'—and our relative wholeness or health at any given point in our lives as a *'station.'*

Now what happened to the original statement that Reb Shneur Zalman set out to clarify in the beginning? "Be righteous, and be not wicked; but even if the whole world tells you that you are righteous, regard yourself as if you were wicked." This paradox—as Reb Shneur Zalman presents it—is left open. Nevertheless, the explanation is there for the careful

aspirant to discover. It is the basic teaching of the Ba'al Shem Tov—"one must never be satisfied with one's humility before God, from the higher to the lower and the lower to the higher, there is always room for repentance."[13] According to Hasidism, there is no righteousness without sincere humility and heartfelt *t'shuvah*, 'reprentance.'

We make the attempt to be righteous; but we cannot afford to tell ourselves that we are *'righteous,'* because once we do that, we are probably not. The ego becomes inflated and we step right off the *maqam* of righteousness. And so we have to remain in the tension of *not* thinking of ourselves as *'wicked'*—because we then fail to act, having not the strength and motivation to do what we should—and *not* thinking of ourselves as *'righteous.'* Thus, we are left with the admonition—'Be righteous, and be not wicked, but do not regard yourself as if you were righteous or wicked.'

Amen.

hakim

Threads of Connection

Questions and Answers with Pir Netanel Mu'in ad-Din Miles-Yépez *

Question: Rumi says, "Moses and Pharaoh are both within you; find them in yourself is what you must do." The Exodus story is obviously not just a story about a distant past; it is a story about ourselves. Is this perspective reflected in Kabbalah or in Judaism generally?

Pir Netanel: In re-telling the Passover narrative during the *seder*—remembering the going out of Egypt into freedom—we always look for how the story is reflected in our lives today. Thus, whenever I lead a Passover *seder*, I say—"Just as in a dream, when we re-tell and re-live the myth of Passover, *we* are playing all the parts. Thus, we are both Moses and Pharaoh. And if we are going to be truly free, we have to acknowledge how we enslave ourselves."

So, based upon something my *rebbe*, Reb Zalman, once did in an experimental ritual, I pass around a bowl into which the *seder* guests put their jewelry.[1] Because in Exodus, we are taught that the Hebrews are told by God to go to their Egyptian neighbors

* An edited and expanded version of questions and answers from the "Wisdom of the Prophets: Sufism & Judaism" event at the Abode of the Message, in New Lebanon, New York, April 27-30th, 2017, and from "Between the Animal and Divine Souls," a talk given at the Abode on October 18th, 2016.

and borrow their jewelry, their silver and gold, prior to going out of Egypt. (Ex. 3:22, 12:35) For to what were the Egyptians enslaved? *To comfort and luxury.* That 'addiction,' that 'enslavement,' necessitated the enslavement of the Hebrews. Until they were willing to yield their comforts, and their addiction to such leisure and luxury, neither they nor the Hebrew slaves could be free. So, we might ask ourselves—our inner 'Egyptians,' our inner 'pharaoh'—to what comfort and luxuries are we addicted that keep us and others enslaved. We might even put this in the language of 'privilege,' examining how our addiction to it leads to injustice in the world, or how our addictions to our comforts and luxuries of convenience are damaging the planet.[2]

Question: With regard to the Exodus narrative, Ibn 'Arabi says, "God-appearing-as-pharaoh *appears opposed to* God-appearing-as-Moses." *How do we reconcile this opposition between God and God? Ibn 'Arabi frames this as an opposition between "God's will" and "God's wish." Pharaoh appears to enact God's will, acting in the expected manner of the way of the world and its conventional laws—whatever happens; but Moses is attempting to enact God's wish for us. It seems that Moses represents this possibility for us.*

Pir Netanel: Beautiful. So a 'confrontation' between God's will and God's wish, between Pharaoh and Moses, is necessary in order to make God's wish a reality (God's will). In the tension of that confrontation, where possibility meets the situation as-it-is in that moment, something new is created that can become God's will. This is what God *wants*, apparently, but it requires our bravery and participation with the *wish*—our choosing God's wish over God's will—to make God's wish God's will. This is the knowledge we must all embrace in our sacred activism.[3]

Question: "At the very root of all motivations is love," says Ibn 'Arabi, "the root cause of every impulse." This accords with Hazrat Inayat Khan, "At the root of every impulse is a divine impulse." Does this teaching have a parallel in Hasidism?

Pir Netanel: The Ba'al Shem Tov—based on the *kabbalah* of Rabbi Yitzhak Luria—teaches that there are *nitzotzot*, 'sparks' of holiness, in all things, waiting to be recognized and uplifted. For instance, when a sexual image or persistent thoughts of attraction arise during prayer, he says, these thoughts have arisen in order to give you an opportunity to raise the sparks of holiness in them back to their divine source. How do you do this? By saying, 'Where does the attraction of that beauty come from? From whence does the attraction originate? Am I not made by God? And did not God give me this body and these impulses? Surely God must have had a reason for doing this and allowing these thoughts to come to me outside of the moment of lovemaking. Obviously they come from the source of beauty! I must take them back to their divine root!'[4]

Question: This kind of reflection in our lives is what Sufis call muḥasaba, *'accounting.' Is there an inquiry practice in Judaism that is parallel to* muḥasaba *in Sufism?*

Pir Netanel: Yes, there is a direct parallel. The practice is called *ḥeshbon ha-nefesh*, 'soul accounting.' My teacher, Reb Zalman, gave it to us as a practice to be done at night before bed. Basically, we 'walk backward' in our minds through the day we have just completed, examining each action—each interaction, each motivation—questioning the quality of our responses.

At any given point in the timeline, we might say something like . . . '*Hmmm*, I'm not so happy with how I spoke to them,' or 'with how angry or unnerved that made me,' or 'how poorly I handled that situation.' In this way, we are effectively 'flagging'

these moments in consciousness for further reflection and correction the next day.[5]

Question: In Sufism, there are the connected concepts of fana' *and* baqa', *'annihilation' and 'subsistence,' suggesting a process in which we are annihilated to this self, and then return; but it is not a return to the prior state, because the encounter with the infinite has brought about a transformation. So the separation is providential, creating a spectrum of experience in which love can grow and deepen. Is there such a concept in Judaism, too?*

Pir Netanel: According to Hasidism, God created 'existence from nothing,' *yesh mi'ain,* which is to say, God as nothing—the unity which allows no distinction—is the ground of all existence. But, having come from nothing, we seek to return to our source. Thus, the Ḥasidim speak of *bittul ha-yesh,* the 'nullification of existence,' experiencing our own 'nothingness' *(ayin)* in God.

According to the Maggid of Mezritch, the successor of the holy Ba'al Shem Tov, the *ani,* the 'I', was created from *ain,* 'nothing,' and it is our job to turn the *ani* back into *ain,* to know ourselves properly, and then return to the *ani* again. But its not the same *ani,* not the same 'I' as before.[6]

Songs of Love and Songs of Grief

Question: Would you say something about the Song of Songs? *In the ghazals or love poems of Sufism, there is an intentional ambiguity about human and divine love, evocative because they speak from the directness of the heart's experience. Is the* Song of Songs *a* ghazal *in this sense?*

Pir Netanel: The first ghazals were, of course, love poems; and in this sense, the Song of Songs *(Shir ha-Shirim)*, is very much a *ghazal.*

In my translation of the *Song of Songs—My Love Stands Behind a Wall*, a reference to the separation between lover and beloved—I wanted to make a statement about the importance of the original language and its context. By "language" and "context," I do not mean the Biblical Hebrew alone, but the fact that the *Song* is really an erotic love poem. I wanted to translate the raw immediacy of the language without the later theological overlay making God the "beloved," etc. Inasmuch as many translations assume a 'religious' meaning, adding this as an interpretive layer, the raw sexuality of the original is muted, and sometimes lost. It's not a 'bad' thing; but I do think it diminishes the impact of the poem. The fresh visceral language of the original is what inspired the mystical associations in the first place, and without it, inspiration can be lost over time. So if there are to be new insights today, new mystical associations, I believe it is necessary to translate it as a love poem.

I also believe Juan de la Cruz, who uses imagery from the *Song of Songs*, is aware of the erotic and secular nature of the original, and thus calls his own mystical poem a "Spiritual Canticle" or "Spiritual Song."

Our mystical search comes from our direct relationship to life—its pain, its joys, its beauty and ugliness. It is not a mystical *interpretation* of life that sets us on a path, but the experience of life itself.

The *Song of Songs* is really a love song, but that love is an invitation to understanding that love itself is divine.[7]

Question: In many of the Psalms of David—what are called the Zabur *among Muslims—we find bitter complaints to God, as well as violent expressions of feeling. How are we to understand this in the context of scripture?*

Pir Netanel: The Psalms make up the greater part of the Jewish liturgy and are remarkably beautiful. But they also belong

to another time and there is a primitive quality to them. But there is a primitive quality to us, too, a quality that we have not escaped in our long journey to modernity, however we may judge it when we encounter it in the Psalms.

I read the Psalms differently now than I used to, especially having gone through very difficult and painful periods in my own life. With a bitter heart, or while feeling remarkably angry at what was happening in my life, I've recited the words of the Psalms that speak to such emotions with a deep sense of kinship.

People often assume that everything in scripture is *prescriptive*, but some things are simply *expressive.* The Psalms are expressive, and allow us to express a range of emotions in the context of prayer. Just because we are uncomfortable with the feelings expressed in the Psalms, or the thoughts attached to them, does not mean that we are exempt from them, or the need to express them ourselves. It is sometimes necessary. These feelings exist, and often need to be expressed.

Think about it; is there really any better place and context to express them than in prayer to God? Is it better on the freeway? Is it better in an argument with your neighbor? Or in endless complaint to your spouse or friend? If I have to give vent to those feelings—even the worst parts of myself—maybe expressing them to God, the one who can truly hold them, is best.[8]

Question: In the Qur'an, Job (Ayyub) is depicted as the model of steadfast devotion and loyalty to God, even amid adversity and personal suffering. Unlike the Torah account, in which he discusses his travail with friends and utters a complaint in his suffering (though never abandoning God), the Qu'ran only says: "And Job, when he cried unto his sustainer, only said: 'Oh! Adversity afflicts me, and you, God, are most merciful of all who show mercy!'" *(21:83) This, to many Sufis, suggests that he took his 'affliction' as a mercy from God. Others suggest that the hint of complaint in it—i.e., that he even referred to his suffering—demonstrates*

an imperfection in his spiritual attainment. In response, some Sufis say—because a prophet's behavior is exemplary—this hint of complaint was actually a kindness to future generations, making it acceptable for them to complain a little when they too were suffering. What is your view on this?

Pir Netanel: To tell the truth, I am more than a little unhappy with such intellectual discussions of suffering, so coldly removed from a person's actual suffering, as if anyone could judge them in it.

There is a lot of high-minded talk in spirituality about suffering, much of it concerning what a person's experience of it says about their spiritual 'state of consciousness.' If they cry out to God in misery, they are somehow displaying 'disloyalty' or a 'weakness' of realization, because they should somehow know that 'all of this is for the good,' or 'that it is all divine' and 'meaningful.'

But who has the right to say this? Who has the right to judge Job's experience of suffering, and to categorize it on a scale of righteousness and perfection? There is a kind of arrogance to such an evaluation, or at least an intellectual forgetfulness that makes *Life* a plaything of the mind.

Once, I remember sitting around a table with a small group of Reb Zalman's students in his library for a *shiur*, a study session. On Friday mornings, he would give a *shiur* on the weekly Torah portion, often using a Hasidic text, and we would all learn together. I was the youngest among us and usually kept quiet, sitting next to Reb Zalman at the end of the table. A rabbi was visiting from another city on this occasion, and Reb Zalman was telling stories of Reb Levi Yitzhak of Berditchev and his arguments with God. The visiting rabbi objected to how Reb Levi Yitzhak was questioning God, and Reb Zalman told another story to illustrate (a story I have told many times) . . .

There was once a Hasidic master who sat unseen, late at night, in a dark corner of an inn before the Day of Atonement. He watched as the innkeeper sat down at a table and took out a ledger. The innkeeper opened the ledger and said, "God, these are all my offences for the year . . ." and he went on to list them one-by-one. Then, he took out a second ledger and said, "But these are all your offences against *us* . . ." and he listed all the bad things that had happened to him and the community that same year: "Malkah's child who died of a fever . . . The fire that burned Sholem's home . . . The *pogrom,* in which an entire Jewish village was destroyed, and most of its inhabitants murdered." In the end, he closed both ledgers and said, "Perhaps, God, we should call it even?"[9]

The visiting rabbi was still more troubled by this story. And, as Reb Zalman stepped away to take a phone call, she expressed her issue: "But God's actions are *perfect,* and all these things are for our own good!"

I responded, *"But* we *don't know what* God *knows."*

We can only see so much from where we stand. We don't know what is behind us. We don't know what lies down the road. We don't know what among the painful things that happen to us is 'really for our own good.' And that perspective, however incomplete, is a true perspective that must be honored. Our experiences are not invalidated by what 'may' be happening from a larger, divine perspective.

From where we stand, something is indeed 'wrong,' and it often hurts. When it does, why should we not cry out? Why should we not offer our pain to God? It is not that we are entirely right, but our experience *is* valid. Our hurt has to be expressed and heard.

There may be, or may have been, spiritual masters who sat amid the ruins with a beatific smile. I imagine that could exist. But why is Reb Levi Yitzhak no longer a 'saint' because he mourned his son's death, or implored and cajoled God to help his people? Why is Job diminished for uttering a groan in his misery? Why must it be justified? Is 'sainthood' or 'spiritual mastery' something that is supposed to opt us out of our humanity? And what would be the value in that?

We cry out to God in our distress, and sometimes curse God in our pain. Do these cries represent a rejection of God, or the spiritual path? I don't think so. There is a bitterness of heart that cries out as an expression of its pain. It is trying to register a human complaint 'from below,' as it were. But that is not a rejection of God or the spiritual path; it is actually a testimony of relationship to both.

In his *Answer to Job*, Carl Jung was interested in framing a more inclusive understanding of God. He wanted to talk about God as the totality of being, in which all things and their opposite exist. But in coming to that understanding, one has to suffer the death of the 'good God,' or rather, the God who is *'good.'* That is a painful death for us; because that is the death of our own God-ideal, and in a sense, a very personal death. But God is not good; *God is God*—the God of life and death, creation and destruction, beauty and ugliness, joy and suffering.

There is a special kind of maturation that happens over time through suffering, and perhaps *only* through suffering. It is a maturity characterized by 'patience' and 'gratitude,' *sabr* and *shukr.* The patience is born from grief, a grief that is experienced again and again. It is a kind of acceptance of life *as-it-is.* The

gratitude of this maturity does not lead to a beatific smile; but there is a smile. It is a little sad; but it is genuine. It is sad for all that it must accept in patience; but it is genuine because there is a compensation in the form of grace and beauty. For this it is grateful. And if it is not grateful, then it is willfully blind, or not paying attention.[10]

Question: When we are facing extreme suffering at the end-of-life, is there some guidance that can be offered from a spiritual point-of-view about the right to die?

Pir Netanel: There is always an element of choice in our lives, including the choice of how to feel about our lives. At the end -of-life, in situations in which we might feel most disempowered, my teacher Reb Zalman was willing to say that a person can always choose to withdraw. But I think this is a very personal choice, and is actually a choice about how we want to live, how we are going to relate to these most difficult of circumstances. In his pain, and even his complaint, Job was perhaps never more connected to God. Thus, if one is continuing the 'dialogue,' even when we are considering a withdrawal unto death, then there remains a connection to God even in that decision-making, and this might be the most important aspect of that process.[11]

Righteousness and Wickedness

Question: Does the notion of the 'divine nature' and 'animal nature' that we find in Hasidism exist in Sufism?

Pir Netanel: Yes, in the teachings around the levels of the soul in Sufism, we find the 'animal soul,' *ruḥu haiwani*, and the 'divine

soul,' *ruḥu sultani.* And between them is the 'human soul,' the *ruḥu insani.*[12]

Question: What is the purpose of the terrible conflict we experience in life, being torn—according to the Hasidic model—between our 'divine nature' and our 'animal nature'?

Pir Netanel: Well, I believe that such tensions mature us. If we simply give-in to the animal nature and its drives to avoid the tension, they will cause all manner of chaos in our lives. If we try to kill the animal in us to avoid the tension on the other side, we will be in denial of the most tangible part of our being, effectively putting it 'in shadow.' But if we bear them both, allowing the pull of each to stretch us, to mature and season us, our *human nature* grows. As we grow the capacity of our human nature, we tend to have more moments characterized by 'relative transparency' and even 'luminous transparency,' moments of grace.[13]

Question: How do we begin to befriend our 'animal nature' so that we are not controlled by it? Do any of the Sufis or Hasidim talk about this?

Pir Netanel: The story is told in Hasidism that once, when Rabbi Menahem Mendel of Kotzk was a young man, he was walking with a group of friends. Suddenly, they heard a fierce dog barking and running toward them. In those days, many non-Jews trained their dogs to attack Jews, so Reb Menahem Mendel's friends ran for their lives; but Reb Menahem Mendel stood firm. The fierce dog ran right at him and skidded to a stop. Then the dog whimpered and ran away. Reb Menahem Mendel's fleeing friends, seeing this incredible sight, were mystified and came back to ask him what had happened.

He answered, "It suddenly occurred to me, 'Do I have my inner dog under control; and have I put it in the service of God?' I made sure that it was, and then the dog in front of me recognized it—recognized that there was no enemy—and walked away."

In fact, he was the 'big dog,' because he had mastery of his dog nature.

It says in Reb Zalman's interpretation of the *Sh'ma'* prayer of Judaism, "Watch out! Don't let your cravings delude you . . . because the God-sense within you will become distorted." (Deut. 11:16)[14] The moment of decision is so important. Once I give in to my "cravings," I have diminished resolve in the future; I am running a rut in the mind that leads me to slip into that behavior more and more easily.

But if I delay the gratification, I build a certain power and strengthen my resolve and capacity around my ability to do that. Hazrat Inayat Khan gives the example of staring at a certain point on the wall, or fasting from food for periods, for the purpose of learning such "mastery."[15]

Question: Can we fall from a maqam? *If a* maqam *is a sustained 'station' or level of maturity and integration, can we actually drop a level in maturity? And if we can, what might cause us to fall?*

Pir Netanel: We all have 'ups and downs' in our lives that are within the range of our general level of maturity. For some, even a serious depression might not change the behaviors that characterize one's maturity.

What would actually make us lose a *maqam?* I don't know; but I imagine it might involve relieving ourselves of the tensions caused by the competing drives of our animal and divine natures in a critical moment of decision. Our humanity is held in that tension. If we escape the tension in a critical moment—perhaps abandoning fidelity in a moment of animal desire, or yielding to unjust cruelty in a moment of anger, or abandoning an important relationship or responsibility out of fear—inasmuch as these actions demonstrate some immaturity, lack of endurance or fear, we might lose a *maqam.*

Every one of us has a 'voice' that tells us whether we have crossed that line or not, and we *'know it'* whether we acknowledge it or not.

If we ever get into the place of believing that the level of maturity or knowledge we have achieved is fixed and absolute, it is a psychological set-up, a guarantee for dropping a level. Thus, the *maqam* is relative. We cannot see it as fixed without destabilizing it. We cannot see ourselves as being complete or 'enlightened' without losing that 'enlightenment.'[16]

Question: We have been discussing the relationship between Sufism and Judaism and their different paths; is one path more important than the other?

Pir Netanel: It is not the paths that matter. The prophet Hosea (14:9) says, *Yesharim darkey Ha-Shem, ve-tzaddikim yeyleku bam, reshayim yikashlu bam,* "Straight-forward are the ways of God; the righteous walk in them, the wicked stumble in them."

You see, there is not just *one* way, not just *one* path; but "ways." There is more than one way to get to God. There are many religions, many spiritual traditions, and many lineages within those traditions. "The righteous walk in them, the wicked stumble in them."

This suggests that the "ways of God," the critical or effective means of getting to God, do not necessarily deliver us to God by themselves. They don't make us "righteous" either; for it says, "the righteous *walk* in them, and the wicked *stumble.*"

Neither are the righteous those who never fall; for we are also told in Proverbs (24:16), "seven times will the righteous fall and rise again." The righteous are not perfect; it is just that they *"rise again."* According to a Hasidic teaching of Rabbi Shneur Zalman of Liadi, based on this verse, "The *tzaddik* is one who walks."[17] That is to say, the righteous person goes up and down, rising and falling, as we do when we walk. To walk is to go up and down (between heaven and earth), rising and falling.

So, again, the righteous are not those who never fall.

What then are the "wicked," according to this teaching? The wicked are those who make of "the ways of God" a stumbling block, owing to their wickedness; or we might say, because they are stuck or fixed in a particular mindset.

You see, the one who walks is righteous because they continue on, moving forward, always walking the path. They fall, but they get up again and walk.

The wicked are stopped, stuck, and fixed in their views. Maybe they believe that they have 'the answer,' 'the truth,' 'enlightenment!' Or maybe they believe that they cannot fall! Or maybe they believe that, having fallen, there is no getting up. But this is itself 'stumbling' on the path, the very thing that keeps one from reaching the goal.

So while the path itself may lead to the goal, it must be 'walked.'[18]

Appendix A

"Seclusion" from the *Kifayat al-Abidin* of Rabbi Avraham Maimuni ha-Nagid *

Seclusion *(khalwah)* is among the most distinguished of the elevated paths to God. It is the way of the friends of God *(awliya)*, and through it, the prophets *(anbiya)* achieved union *(wusul)* with God.[1] However, before we go any further, we must first distinguish between external seclusion *(khalwah zahirah)* and internal seclusion *(khalwah batinah)*.

Internal Seclusion

The sole purpose of *external* seclusion is the attainment of *internal* seclusion, which is the final rung on the ladder to God, and itself constitutes union with God. Internal seclusion refers to the complete sincerity of heart for which David prayed, saying, "God, create in me a pure heart, and renew my spirit *(ru'aḥ)* within me" (Ps. 51:12), and as Assaf attained, saying, "My body and my heart are emptied; God is the rock of my heart and my eternal portion." (73:26) Thus, we empty the heart and the mind of everything except God, allowing them to fill with God's exalted divinity.[2]

We accomplish this through a partial withdrawal of our senses, the detachment of our impulses from worldly things,

* A translation by the author, ca. 2017, for the Wisdom of the Prophets: Sufism and Judaism event.

reorienting them instead toward God alone, filling the mind with God, and using the imagination to support its observation of God's majestic existence in such things as the awesomeness of the sea, encompassing an abundance of life, and the magnificent movement of the heavens and the stars of the sphere![3]

Now, with regard to the clearing of the heart and mind of everything other than God, Assaf has said, "My body and my heart are emptied"; and with regard to withdrawing the impulses from everything other than God, he has said, "Whom have I in heaven but you? And beside you, I desire nothing upon the earth" (Ps. 73:25); and with regard to directing all our impulses to God alone, Yesha'ayahu has said, "To your name *(shem)* and your remembrance *(zekher)* is the desire of my soul. My soul *(nefesh)* desires you in the night, and my breath *(ru'aḥ)* seeks you in earnest." (Isa. 26:8-9) Furthermore, David has said, "My soul thirsts for you; my body yearns for you," (Ps. 63:2) and he later adds, "My soul *clings* to you." (63:9)

With regard to the quieting of the senses, it is written, "I have made a covenant with my eyes"[4] (Job 31:1) and the righteous "shut their eyes to evil." (Isa. 33:15) As David says, "Turn my eyes away from seeing what is false." (Ps. 119:37) And concerning the need to restrain the senses and desires for the sake of keeping the mind on God, Elisha said to [his disciple] Gehazi, "If you meet anyone, do not greet them; and if anyone greets you, do not respond." (2 Kings 4:29) *Understand this well.*

Moreover, the prophets and their disciples also used musical instruments and melodies to achieve internal seclusion, to awaken their desire for God, and to purify their interior from everything other than God.[5] Similarly, it is said of the Temple service—may it soon be restored—"David and his captains designated the sons of Assaf, Heyman, and Yedutun, who prophesied with harps, lyres, and cymbals for service." (1 Chron. 25:1)

Appendix B

Simple Intructions for *Khalwah Batinah*

1. Carry out the proper ablutions, washing the hands and feet, before beginning.
2. Sit down and whisper: "Create in me a pure heart, God, and renew my spirit within me."
3. Close your eyes and find a quiet, natural breathing rhythm, allowing yourself to attune to its peaceful movements.
4. Take a moment and allow your heart to imagine God's majestic existence in such things as the awesomeness of the sea, the magnificent vault of the heavens, or some other inspiring vista in nature.
5. Then, in the darkness of your senses, silently introduce one of the divine names into your heart on the in-breath. Do not attempt to 'hold' the divine name.
6. When you become aware of other thoughts, feelings or sensations entering your consciousness, do not entertain them in any way.
7. Simply return your attention to the divine name, taking hold of it as a refuge from these other thoughts, feelings, or sensations.
8. At the end of your period of seclusion, whisper: "My body and my heart are emptied; God is the rock of my heart and my eternal portion."
9. Remain in silence for a few moments before rising from your meditation.

Notes

Chapter 1: The Holy Name of God

1. Heard from my teacher, Rabbi Zalman Schachter-Shalomi, *z"l*, who first read it in Eliyahu de Vidas' *Reshit Ḥokhmah*, but who sometimes cited the book *Osseh Feleh* ('Working Wonders') compiled by Ezra Yaffe and Yitzchok Bikel.

2. Heard from Samuel Avital of the distinguished Abitbol family. His grandfather was Eliyahu Abitbol, a respected merchant and kabbalist.

3. Gershom Scholem. "Shabbetai Zevi." *Encyclopedia Judaica* (Vol. 14). Jerusalem: Keter Publishing House, 1972: 1231-38.

4. Gershom Scholem. "Doenmeh." *Encyclopedia Judaica* (Vol. 6). Jerusalem: Keter Publishing House, 1972: 148-50.

5. Saiyid Athar Abbas Rizvi. *A History of Sufism in India: Volume I: Early Sufism and its History in India to A.D. 1600*. New Delhi: Munshiram Manoharlal Publishers, 2012: 318-19.

6. Saiyid Athar Abbas Rizvi. *A History of Sufism in India: Volume II: From Sixteenth Century to Modern Century*. New Delhi: Munshiram Manoharlal Publishers, 1992: 475-79.

7. See Diana Lobel. *A Sufi-Jewish Dialogue: Philosophy and Mysticism in Baḥya ibn Paqūda's Duties of the Heart.* Philadelphia, PA: University of Pennsylvania Press, 2007: 196-201 for a clarification of specific influences and originality in Baḥya.

8. For an example, see Menahem Mansoor. *Book of Direction to the Duties of the Heart.* London: Routledge and Kegan Paul, 1973: 277.

9. "The farthest limit (achieved by) human reason through the principles of the Illumination of His sublimity is bewilderment. The ultimate end of the journey of the wayfarers and disciples in their search for proximity to His awesome beauty is astonishment. Abandoning hope in the principle of (striving for) the knowledge of Him is the denial of His attributes while the claim to a perfect knowledge of Him is the imagining of a similitude and a likening. The portion for all the eyes that would gaze upon the beauty of His

essence is bedazzlement, and the fruit of the contemplation of the wonders of His creation to all intellects is necessary knowledge." Abu Hamed Muḥammad al-Ghazzali. *On Knowing Yourself* (Great Books of the Islamic World). Kazi Publishing, Inc. Kindle Edition.

10. Lobel, *A Sufi-Jewish Dialogue,* 11.

11. Night vigils were also known in Judaism.

12. See Bachya ibn Pakuda. *Duties of the Heart.* Tr. Yaakov Feldman. Northvale, NJ: Jason Aronson, 1996: 453-54.

13. Ibn Pakuda, *Duties of the Heart,* 454.

14. Adapted from ibid., 463.

15. Ibid., 454.

16. Ibid.

17. Ibid.

18. See Y. Tzvi Langermann. "From Private Devotion to Communal Prayer: New Light on Abraham Maimonides' Synagogue Reforms." *Ginzei Qedem* 1 (2005): 35-41.

19. Langermann, "From Private Devotion to Communal Prayer," 39-41.

20. S. D. Goitein. *Jews and Arabs: Their Contacts Through the Ages.* New York, NY: Schocken Books, 1955: 6, 10, 127-38.

21. Lobel, *A Sufi-Jewish Dialogue,* xiii. Nevertheless, Baḥya is not named among Maimonides' sources. See Shlomo Pines' introduction to Maimonides' sources in Moses Maimonides. *The Guide to the Perplexed.* Tr. Shlomo Pines. Chicago, IL: The University of Chicago Press, 1963.

22. 'Obadyāh b. Abraham b. Moses Maimonides. *The Treatise of the Pool: Al-Maqāla al-Ḥawḍiyya.* Tr. Paul Fenton. London, UK: The Octagon Press, 1981: 3. See Abraham S. Halkin. "Ibn 'Aknin's Commentary to the Song of Songs." *Alexander Marx Jubilee Volume.* New York: Jewish Theological Seminary, 1950: 389-424.

23. See the letter of Yosef translated in Abraham Joshua Heschel. *Maimonides: A Biography.* Tr. Joachim Neugroschel. New York, NY: Farrar, Straus, Giroux, 1982: 190-91. Heschel mistakenly conflates Ceuta with Ibn 'Aqnin here (a common mistake until relatively recently).

24. Paul B. Fenton. "Abraham Maimonides (1187-1237): Founding a Mystical Dynasty." *Jewish Mystical Leaders and Leadership in the 13th Century*. Ed. Moshe Idel and Mortimer Ostow. Northvale, NJ: Jason Aronson Inc., 1998: 128.

25. Fenton, "Abraham Maimonides," 138.

26. Maimonides, *The Guide to the Perplexed,* 620, or *Guide* III: 51.

27. See the Dedication to ibid., 3-4, where Maimonides discusses why he has written the book, it being in response to the needs of his student Yosef, who rebelled against the systematic approach after two years, yearning to get right to the subject of his greatest concern. Also see Herbert A. Davidson. *Moses Maimonides: The Man and His Works.* Oxford, UK: Oxford University Press, 2005: 330-332 on this, and Julius Guttman. *Philosophies of Judaism: A History of Jewish Philosophy from Biblical Times to Franz Rosenzweig*. Tr. David W. Silverman. New York, NY: Schocken Books, 1973: 215-218 on Yosef's work prior to meeting Maimonides.

28. 'Pious ones,' the parallel term in Judaism to 'Sufi.'

29. See Elisha R. Russ-Fishbane. *Between Politics and Piety: Abraham Maimonides and His Times.* Dissertation, Harvard University, 2009: 270 note 39. In the Bodleian manuscript, it only says, *sāḥibī,* 'my companion.'

30. See Russ-Fishbane, *Between Politics and Piety*, 270, where he discusses whether Avraham he-Ḥasid was a colleague or spiritual mentor or the previous leader of the pietists.

31. Ibid., 157 note 27.

32. Fenton, "Abraham Maimonides," 130.

33. Russ-Fishbane, *Between Politics and Piety,* 102 note 13.

34. Fenton, "Abraham Maimonides," 131, 153.

35. Maimonides, *The Treatise of the Pool,* 13, 59 note 53.

36. Ibid., 13, 59 note 54. Russ-Fishbane, *Between Politics and Piety,* 280.

37. Maimonides, *The Treatise of the Pool,* 13, 59 and note 55.

38. Ibid., 13, 59 note 56.

39. Ibid., 13, 59 note 57.

40. Ibid., 13, 59 note 58.

41. Ibid., 13-14, 59-60 notes 59-61.

42. Ibid., 15-16, 60-61 notes 62-71.

43. Ibid., 16-17, 61 note 72.

44. Ibid., 17, 61 notes 73-74. Paul Fenton. "Some Judeo-Arabic Fragments by Rabbi Abraham He-Ḥasīd, the Jewish Sufi." *Journal of Semitic Studies* XXVI/1 (Spring 1981): 53-54.

45. Samuel Rosenblatt (ed./tr.). *The High Ways to Perfection of Abraham Maimonides: Volume II.* Baltimore, MD: The Johns Hopkins Press, 1938: 320 (321), 422 (423). (The page number in parentheses refers to facing English translation of the Judeo-Arabic text.)

46. Rosenblatt, *The High Ways to Perfection II,* 322 (323), 422 (423), 266 (267), 320 (321).

47. H. Graetz. *History of the Jews: Vol. 3.* Philadelphia, PA: Jewish Publication Society of America, 1967: 495.

48. Fenton, "Abraham Maimonides," 153-54. S. D. Goitein. "A Treatise in Defense of the Pietists by Abraham Maimonides." *The Journal of Jewish Studies.* Vol. 16 (1966): 105.

49. Heard from his wife, Eve Ilsen, who was present on this occasion.

Chapter 2: Seeking Internal Seclusion

1. For overviews of his life and work, see Paul Fenton, "Abraham Maimonides (1187-1237): Founding a Mystical Dynasty," *Jewish Mystical Leaders and Leadership in the Thirteenth Century*: 127-54; and S. D. Goitein, "Abraham Maimonides and His Pietist Circle," *Jewish Medieval and Renaissance Studies.* Ed. Alexander Altmann. Cambridge, MA: Harvard University Press, 1967: 145-64.

2. Samuel Rosenblatt (ed./tr.). *The High Ways to Perfection of Abraham Maimonides: Volume II.* Baltimore, MD: The Johns Hopkins Press, 1938: 320 (321), 422 (423). (The page number in parentheses refers to facing English translation of the Judeo-Arabic text.)

3. A few of these Judeo-Arabic scholars include Samuel Rosenblatt, S. D. Goitein, Georges Vajda, Paul Fenton, and Elisha Russ-Fishbane. The spiritual seekers are often Jews inspired to find an authoritative medieval precursor for their own interest in Sufism, and for respectful dialogue between religious traditions.

4. In his wonderful introduction to 'Obadyah Maimonides' *The Treatise of the Pool: Al-Maqala al-Hawdiyya,* Paul Fenton gives an overview of 'Sufi-Hasidic' practices, but says, "It is most surprising that no description is found in the texts at our disposal of a Jewish ceremony comparable to the most characteristic of Sufi devotions, the *dhikr.*" However, in 2004, my teacher Rabbi Zalman Schachter-Shalomi gave me a recording of an informal talk by Paul Fenton from 1998 on *The Meditative Method of Dhikr: A Jewish-Sufi Mystical Practice.* In this talk, he mentions the lack of direct evidence of *zikr* in Judaism, and says, "This was lacking until, in my own research, I came across a certain number of documents that Jews too pronounce the name of God during *dhikr,* and this was only quite natural." I am unaware of what these documents might be, and I apologize if I have overlooked a later article or paper treating this subject. Fenton's excellent talk discusses parallel words and concepts and pursues Jewish *zikr* mostly by way of Rabbi Avraham Abulafia's teachings.

5. Moses Maimonides. *The Guide to the Perplexed.* Tr. Shlomo Pines. Chicago, IL: The University of Chicago Press, 1963: 620, or *Guide* III: 51. Paul Fenton. "Some Judeo-Arabic Fragments by Rabbi Abraham He-Ḥasīd, the Jewish Sufi." *Journal of Semitic Studies* XXVI/1 (Spring 1981): 53-54.

6. Regarding a *zikr* ceremony conducted by Jews, Paul Fenton writes, "One can only assume that such a ceremony would have met with severe disapproval from more conservative circles in view of its strictly Islamic character." 'Obadyāh b. Abraham b. Moses Maimonides. *The Treatise of the Pool: Al-Maqāla al-Ḥawḍiyya.* Tr. Paul Fenton. London, UK: The Octagon Press, 1981: 17. How much more so then if it was performed in Arabic?

7. Conversation with Zalman Schachter-Shalomi after he had received and read a copy of the first edition of Gregory Blann's *Garden of Mystic Love.* He passed the book on to me with a photocopy of a page with *ain keloheynu* on it.

8. Aryeh Kaplan. *Meditation and the Bible.* York Beach, ME: Samuel Weiser, 1978: 5-9. Though Kaplan mentions the possible importance of Sufism to the passage, he does not consider it in the light of the most significant Sufi practices, i.e., *dhikr* and *fikr.*

9. 'Twilight language' refers to coded phrasing and word use that allows an author to transmit and conceal at the same time. Thus,

it requires one of two keys to unlock it: 'pointing-out instructions' from another initiate, or a prior acquaintance with the practice or a similar one. The term is used most often in discussions of Hindu and Buddhist tantric texts.

10. See Rosenblatt, *The High Ways to Perfection II,* 382 (383).

11. See Elisha R. Russ-Fishbane. *Between Politics and Piety: Abraham Maimonides and His Times*. Dissertation, Harvard University, 2009: 145, see note 189.

12. Fenton, "Abraham Maimonides," 132-34, 139. S. D. Goitein. "A Treatise in Defense of the Pietists by Abraham Maimonides." *The Journal of Jewish Studies.* Vol. 16 (1966): 108.

13. Fenton, "Abraham Maimonides," 139.

14. Ibid.,147-48, where he examines the use of the word *bid'ah* by S. D. Goitein and G. Cohen in this situation.

15. Goitein, "A Treatise in Defense of the Pietists," 108. Fenton, "Abraham Maimonides," 140.

16. As translated in Fenton, "Abraham Maimonides," 148.

17. Rosenblatt, *The High Ways to Perfection II,* 266 (267), 320 (321), 322 (323), 422 (423).

18. Such as *Mishnah, Tamid* 6:1,2.

19. My own rendering of the Judeo-Arabic text in Rosenblatt, *The High Ways to Perfection II,* 382.

20. The Arabic word *wusul* can also mean 'arrive,' 'reach,' 'join,' or 'commune' as in a sharing with God.

21. My own rendering of the Judeo-Arabic text in Rosenblatt, *The High Ways to Perfection II,* 382, 384.

22. This is similar to what the Sufi apologist, Abu Ḥamid al-Ghazzali says in his *Ihyā' 'Ulūm al-Dīn* (II:6)—"internal seclusion is the emptying of the heart and thought of all else except Allah." Maimonides, *The Treatise of the Pool,* 60 note 70.

23. The verse continues, "not to gaze on a maiden." Thus, we may infer that the instruction relates to refraining from following after the senses and one's desire-based impulses.

24. Fragment of the *Kifāyat* (Book II, Part II). See Avraham ben HaRambam. *The Guide to Serving God.* Tr. Yaakov Wincelberg. New

York, NY: Feldheim Publishers, 2008: 547. Sitting in meditation is also mentioned in Maimonides, *The Treatise of the Pool*, 104, "Know my son, that if thou desirest to achieve the state of solitude *(ḥalwa)* (126) and a worldly affair crosseth thy mind whilst thou art *seated* in contemplation, I urge thee to expel and banish it from thine abode and bar the door in its face; 'above all that thou guardest, keep thy heart'. (Pr. IV:23)

25. See Maimonides, *The Treatise of the Pool*, 104.

26. They may also have had a more conventional practice of vocal *zikr (zikr jahri);* but it does not seem to be suggested here.

27. We find there a 'spaciousness' around the divine name, a sacred vacuum left by it, without that positive content of the name absorbing or filling it. It is difficult to say there is a state that is no-thought, because mostly we replace the many with one; but here we do not even hold the one. Here there is 'presence' without a clear or defined content or object.

28. I freely admit that I was for many years a student of Father Thomas Keating, the founder of the Centering Prayer movement, which may have influenced my interpretation.

29. Russ-Fishbane, *Between Politics and Piety*, 295.

30. *Maqāla al-Ḥawdiyya*, 19b. See Maimonides, *The Treatise of the Pool*, 102.

31. Ibid., 8b. See Maimonides, *The Treatise of the Pool*, 84.

32. Russ-Fishbane, *Between Politics and Piety*, 294-95.

33. Quoted in Rosenblatt, *The High Ways to Perfection II*, 383, and HaRambam, *The Guide to Serving God*, 491.

34. The custom of facing Jerusalem is based on the verse, "they pray to you in the direction of the city which you have chosen and the house which I have built to your name." (2 Chr. 6:34)

35. Fragment of the *Kifāyat* (Book II, Part II). See HaRambam, *The Guide to Serving God*, 547.

36. This verse is also quoted in the *Kifāyat* (Bk IV, Pt II), 30a, in support of leaders kneeling during the *Amidah.* See Rosenblatt, *The High Ways to Perfection II*, 75, and HaRambam, *The Guide to Serving God*, 173.

37. Based upon the posture recommended in Javad Nurbakhsh. *In the Paradise of the Sufis.* New York, NY: Khaniqahi-Nimatullahi

Publications, 1979: 79, which seemed appropriate.

38. See Rosenblatt, *The High Ways to Perfection II,* 385, and HaRambam, *The Guide to Serving God,* 493.

39. See ibid., 385, and HaRambam. *The Guide to Serving God,* 493.

40. See ibid., 385, and HaRambam. *The Guide to Serving God,* 491.

41. See ibid., 385, and HaRambam. *The Guide to Serving God,* 493.

42. *Maqāla,* 20b (also 11b &13a). See Maimonides, *The Treatise of the Pool,* 104 (also 89 & 92).

43. Ibid., 20b. See Maimonides, *The Treatise of the Pool,* 104.

44. See Rosenblatt, *The High Ways to Perfection II,* 385, and HaRambam, *The Guide to Serving God,* 493.

45. See ibid., 383, 385, nd HaRambam, *The Guide to Serving God,* 491.

Chapter 3: A Hidden Dialogue

1. Ya'akov Yosef of Polonoyye. *Toldot Ya'akov Yosef.* Ed. Varsovie. 1881: Parshat Bo, Fol. 51b and 52d.

2. The same point is made in Diana Lobel. *A Sufi-Jewish Dialogue: Philosophy and Mysticism in Baḥya ibn Paqūda's Duties of the Heart.* Philadelphia, PA: University of Pennsylvania Press, 2007: ix.

3. See al-Hujwiri. *Revelation of the Mystery (Kashf al-Mahjub).* Tr. Reynold A. Nicholson. Accord, NY: Pir Press, 1999: 200.

4. Nathan of Nemirov. *Rabbi Nachman's Wisdom: Shevachay HaRan & Sichos HaRan.* Ed. Zvi Aryeh Rosenfeld. Tr. Aryeh Kaplan. Brooklyn, NY, 1973: 113..

5. This is in accord with his grandson, Rebbe Naḥman of Bratzlav's own assessment, when he says, "You must learn this lesson from my grandfather. A confusing thought may enter your mind, but if you stand firm, G-d will send you another thought to encourage you." Nathan of Nemirov. *Rabbi Nachman's Wisdom: Shevachay HaRan & Sichos HaRan.* Ed. Zvi Aryeh Rosenfeld. Tr. Aryeh Kaplan. Brooklyn, NY, 1973: 114.

6. Nosson of Nemirov, *Shivhhei ha-RaN,*., 2:17. See Nathan of Nemirov,

Rabbi Nachman's Wisdom, 56-57. Reb Nosson goes on to speculate that some thought the Rebbe had suggested that this was the Evil One incarnate, but he is not sure of this and does not commit to this interpretation. This passage is laregely reproduced from Zalman Schachter-Shalomi and Netanel Miles-Yépez. *A Hidden Light: Stories and Teachings of Early Ḥ̣aBaD and Bratzlav Hasidism.* Santa Fe, NM: Gaon Books, 2011: 266-68.

7. Here I am reproducing much of what I wrote in Schachter-Shalomi, *A Hidden Light*, 265-66. The professor was Zvi Mark, the author of *Mysticism and Madness: The Religious Thought of Rabbi Nachman of Bratslav.*

8. For the Simḥah Bunem version, see Martin Buber. *Tales of the Hasidim: The Later Masters.* Tr. Olga Marx. New York, NY: Schocken Books, 1948: 245-46, and the brief version of Rebbe Naḥman, Nachman of Breslov. *Rabbi Nachman's Stories (Sippurey Ma'asioth).* Tr. Aryeh Kaplan. Monsey, NY: Breslov Research Institute, 1983: 478.

9. Heinrich Zimmer. *Myths and Symbols in Indian Art and Civilization.* Ed. Joseph Campbell. New York, NY: Pantheon Books, 1946: 219-21.

10. Joseph Campbell, ed.. *The Portable Arabian Nights.* New York, NY: Viking Press, 1952: 321

11. Jorge Luis Borges. *Collected Fictions.* Andrew Hurley. New York, NY: Viking, 1998: 56-57.

12. See Massud Farzan. *The Tale of the Reed Pipe: Teachings of the Sufis.* New York, NY: E.P. Dutton, 1974: 70-71.

13. Schachter-Shalomi, *A Hidden Light*, 318.

14. See Idries Shah. *Tales of the Dervishes: Teaching-Stories of the Sufi Masters Over the Past Thousand Years.* London, UK: Jonathan Cape, 1967: 21-22, and Farzan, *The Tale of the Reed Pipe*, 92-93.

15. Shah, *Tales of the Dervishes*, 22.

16. See Nachman of Breslov, *Rabbi Nachman's Stories*, 481.

17. Heard from my teacher, Zalman Schachter-Shalomi, *z"l*, on numerous occasions.

18. See Martin Buber. *The Origin and Meaning of Hasidism.* Tr. Maurice Friedman. New York, NY: Horizon Press, 1960: 221-22, and Martin Buber. *Tales of the Hasidim: The Early Masters.* Tr. Olga Marx. New York, NY: Schocken Books, 1947: 199-200.

19. Buber, *The Origin and Meaning of Hasidism*, 222-23.

20. See ibid., 222.

21. Ibid., 222-23.

22. Alter of Teplik, *Meshivat Nefesh*, Pt. II *(Likkutey Halakhot)* 69. See Nachman of Breslov. *Restore My Soul*. Tr. Avraham Greenbaum. Monsey, NY: Breslov Research Institute, 1980: 85-86.

23. Lobel, *A Sufi-Jewish Dialogue*, 11.

24. My own rendering of the teaching. See Abu Ḥamed Muhammad al-Ghazzali. *On Knowing Yourself* (Great Books of the Islamic World). Kazi Publishing, Inc.. Kindle Edition.

25. See Martin Buber. *Hasidism and Modern Man*. Ed. & Tr. Maurice Friedman. New York, NY: Horizon Books, 1958: 182.

26. Ca. 2009 interview with Rabbi Marc Soloway for the documentary *A Fire in the Forest: The Life and Legacy of the Ba'al Shem Tov.* Directed by Chuck Davis and Netanel Miles-Yépez. Boulder, CO: Throughline Productions & Albion-Andalus Productions, 2012.

27. See Zalman Schachter-Shalomi and Netanel Miles-Yépez. *A Heart Afire: Stories and Teachings of the Early Hasidic Masters.* Philadelphia, PA: Jewish Publication Society, 2009: 142-43.

28. I entered Reb Zalman's office one day and he handed me a print-out with a very rough translation of this passage and a couple notes suggesting a connection to the "Toward the One." I still have the print-out and reconstructed the passage from Reb Zalman's rough translation. I believe it is translated from Yitzhak Rafael. *Sefer ha-Ḥasidut*. Tel Aviv, Israel: Avraham Zioni, 1972: 199. Another passage he translated from Zvi Hirsh of Nadverna related to the Sufi notion of *'ishq*, "A magnet works because of love, and does not have to give any other reasons for attracting a *ḥeshek;* this is a love that has no reasons."

29. Muzaffer Ozak. *Blessed Vigin Mary: Hazreti Maryam*. Wesport, CT: Pir Press, 1991: ix, based on the Qur'an 2:285 and 4:150-51.

30. Alter of Teplik, *Hishtap'khut ha-Nefesh,* 4 *(Likkutei MaHaRaN Tinyana* 96). See Nachman of Breslov. *Outpouring of the Soul: Rabbi Nachman's Path in Meditation*. Tr. Aryeh Kaplan. Breslov Research Institute, 1980: 24.

31. Translated from Reb Elazar Bein's notes in Zalman M. Schachter-Shalomi. *Gate to the Heart: A Manual of Contemplative Jewish Practice*. Ed.

Netanel Miles-Yépez and Robert Micha'el Esformes. Boulder, CO: Albion-Andalus Books, 2013: 17.

Chapter 4: Reb Zalman's Journey "Toward the One"

1. Schachter-Shalomi, Zalman, with Edward Hoffman. *My Life in Jewish Renewal: A Memoir.* Boulder, Colorado: Rowman & Littlefield Publishers, 2012: 25-34, 43-48, 53-56.

2. Ibid., 87-92.

3. See Zalman M. Schachter-Shalomi and Netanel Miles-Yépez. "Deep Encounter, Part 5 of 12. Islam." March 3rd, 2002. (Recording: JRRZ0001S0101N008). Zalman M. Schachter-Shalomi Collection of the University of Colorado at Boulder Archives. Reb Zalman may have made the acquaintance of various Perennialist Sufis by this point, having heard Seyyed Hossein Nasr (b.1933) speak, and having been introduced to Jewish *zikr* by Leo Schaya (1916-1985), though the dates of these meetings are uncertain.

4. Schachter-Shalomi, "Deep Encounter, Part 5 of 12. Islam."

5. Ibid.

6. At that time, the two organizations springing from Murshid S.A.M. and Pir Vilayat were closely associated, and it was not uncommon for Pir Moineddin to advise others to first seek initiation with his elder, Pir Vilayat.

7. See Schachter-Shalomi, "Deep Encounter, Part 5 of 12. Islam."

8. Taken from the published article, Zalman Schachter-Shalomi and Netanel Miles-Yépez. "Translating the Invocation of the Toward the One into the Hebrew of the Jewish Tradition." *Seven Pillars House of Wisdom.* June 10, 2009. (http://www.sevenpillarshouse.org) This article was published as if written by Reb Zalman and myself, but was originally written by me. It is here restored to the original version.

For Reb Zalman, the "Toward the One" was somewhat like the Aramaic *L'Shem Yiḥud* of the Jewish mystical tradition, which said before carrying out various commandments: *L'Shem yiḥud kudshah b'rikh Hu u'Shekhintey b'deḥilu u'reḥimu l'yaḥed shem Y"H b'V"H b'yiḥudah*

shelim b'shem kol Yisra'el. 'I do this for the sake of the conscious-uniting of the transcendent holy one with the manifest Presence, *Yod Heh* with *Vav Heh*, thus giving pleasure to the act of creation.'

9. The former translations he personally had printed in small red stapled booklets entitled "Baul Songs from India" which he gave to those he thought might benefit from them. Though I never saw a translation of the *Dhammapada,* he is described as translating it into a notebook in Rodger Kamenetz. *The Jew in the Lotus: A Poet's Rediscovery of Jewish Identity in Buddhist India*. New York, NY: HarperSanFrancisco, 1994: 18, "My first sight of Zalman Schachter had been in the JFK airport. Sitting on the floor, legs stretched out, he was scribbling in pencil on a small notebook. In preparation for the trip, Marc Lieberman had sent each of us *The Dhammapada,* a collection of classic Buddhist psalms. Reb Zalman was already at work translating them into Hebrew."

10. Arthur Green, with Ebn Leader, Ariel Evan Mayse, and Or N. Rose. *Speaking Torah: Spiritual Teachings from Around the Maggid's Table: Volume 1: Genesis, Exodus, Leviticus*. Woodstock, VT: Jewish Lights Publishing, 2013: xv.

11. My teacher, Rabbi Zalman Schachter-Shalomi, *z"l,* told me this explicitly, ca. 2009.

12. The Hebrew *takhlit,* 'ultimate purpose,' does not feel right in this context, according to Reb Zalman.

13. The Hebrew word, *emet,* is actually comprised of three letters—*aleph-mem-tav*—the beginning, middle and last letters of the Hebrew alphabet. In Jewish mysticism, this seeming coincidence is understood to suggest that *emet*, 'truth,' is the beginning, middle, and end, the all and everything. It is this notion that seemed to parallel 'love' in the Sufi tradition as a kind of ground concept, underlying all things.

14. There is no true parallel for 'harmony' in Hebrew. Reb Zalman said that he could have used *aḥdut,* 'oneness,' but felt that it was a very modern word.

15. This has the sense of 'Who form—thickening into shape—the master.'

Chapter 5: Hyphenating Sufism and Judaism

1. Founded in 1974 by the Tibetan Buddhist master, Chögyam Trungpa Rinpoche (1939-1987), the Naropa Intstitute, officially became Naropa University in the year 2000.

2. The truth was that I had no intention of leaving Boulder, as I had come there to meet him; but he knew nothing of this at the time.

3. This would become the book, *Wrapped in a Holy Flame: Teachings and Tales of the Hasidic Masters,* published in 2003.

4. Quoted from the notes I took on that occasion.

5. I believe I also met Murshida Devi Tide that fall at a Sufi gathering in Boulder. She was the Secretary General of the Sufi Order under Pir Vilayat in his last years.

6. Since this was written, the Inayati Order has changed its organizational name to the Inayatiyya.

7. The Sufi Order. *The Leader's Manual: Volume One: Leadership in the Sufi Order* and *Volume Two: Spiritual Practices Taught by the Sufi Order.* Revised 1990. Thomas A. O'Kane. *Making Your Ideal a Reality: A Study of the Counseling Approach Developed by Pir Vilayat Khan*. Master's Thesis, Goddard College, October 12, 1980, and Thomas Atum O'Kane. *Transpersonal Dimensions of Transformation: A Study of the Contributions Drawn from the Sufi Order Teachings and Training to the Emerging Field of Transpersonal Psychology*. Union Graduate Institute, November 9, 1987.

8. I learned the form of the Chishti-Inayati *zikr* from Murshid Atum O'Kane, and refined my understanding of it reading the oral teachings of Pir Vilayat Inayat-Khan, particularly as given in a wonderful little booklet the Sufi Order offered to new initiates in those years.

9. Puran Bair. *Living from the Heart: Heart Rhythm Meditation for Energy, Clarity, Peace, Joy, and Inner Power*. New York, NY: Three Rivers Press, 1998: 15.

10. I first met Imam Feisal Abdul-Rauf at "The Way of Contemplation & Meditation" seminar we put on in Aspen, Colorado, August 23-25th, 2002, and Shaykh Kabir Helminski at "The Way of the Mystic" seminar we put on with Naropa University in Boulder, Colorado, November 8-10th, 2002.

11. This was the Sufi Order Publications edition, ca. 1979, which he

gifted to me after my ordination.

12. The Sufi Publishing Company edition from 1974, which later came to me.

13. I do not know from whom he learned this practice, though I would suspect Pir Moineddin Jablonski.

14. Reb Zalman was not perfectly clear about which he had written on the *tallit*, '*kodesh*' or '*koheyn*.' He may have had his reasons for the differences, perhaps wanting to stress 'holiness' over a functional identity as 'priest.'

15. On his next visit to Boulder, Murshid Atum signed the ordination document.

16. In 2002, this meant a CD-ROM with most of the initiatic writings of Hazrat Inayat Khan, as well as those of Murshid Samuel Lewis. This was the beginning of my real study of Hazrat Inayat Khan's work, and my introduction to the teachings of the Ruhaniat. Though I would later meet Pir Shabda Kahn on his various visits to Boulder, I would not begin to form a real relationship with him until 2016.

17. Pamela Hakima Mumby was the Sufi Order representative for the Denver Metro Area in those years. We were on good terms and met fairly often over the next few years.

18. As noted in the previous chapter, Reb Zalman had requested that his friend, Pir Moineddin Jablonski of the Ruhaniat Order, confirm his initiation in 1975. On March 12th, 2017, I requested that Pir Shabda Kahn and Murshid Wali Ali Meyer both initiate me into the Sufi Ruhaniat Order to strengthen my own relationship to them, and in recognition of Reb Zalman's earlier connection the Sufi Ruhaniat Order. This was performed at the grave of Murshida Rabia Martin in Colma, California, after we co-led a pilgrimage there.

19. Pir Vilayat Inayat-Khan would pass a few months later on June 17th, 2004.

20. It was a weekend called "Sufism and Jewish Renewal," October 26-27th, 2002, at the Spice of Life facility in Boulder, Colorado. I believe Llewellyn Vaughn-Lee was only there for one session.

21. I have made minor edits to this passage from Reb Zalman's letter for consistency with the text.

22. This is a reference to the "Jewish renewal" movement, of which he was considered the founder.

Chapter 6: The S'firot in Sufi Zikr

1. Reb Zalman had originally (probably unintentionally) transposed *Ya Raḥim* and *Ya Raḥmin*, giving *Ya Raḥim* for compassion and *Ya Raḥman* for mercy. I have rearranged them here, as the correspondence of meaning is what he intended.

2. This description of the practice was preserved in a journal of teachings and practices I kept in those years. Later, Reb Zalman and I discerned a set of Hebrew *waza'if* to go with the *s'firot* and the days of the week.

3. Aryeh Kaplan, ed. and tr.. *Sefer Yetzirah: The Book of Creation*. York Beach, ME. Samuel Weiser, Inc., 1993: 38.

4. See Zalman Schachter-Shalomi and Netanel Miles-Yépez. *A Hidden Light: Stories and Teachings of Early HaBaD and Bratzlav Ḥasidism.* Santa Fe, NM: Gaon Books, 2011: 18-19.

5. See Moses Maimonides. *The Guide to the Perplexed.* Tr. Shlomo Pines. Chicago, IL: The University of Chicago Press, 1963: 7; Moses Maimonides. *The Guide for the Perplexed.* Tr. M. Friedlander. New York, NY: Dover Publications, 1956: 3; or *Guide,* Introduction Pt. I.

6. Schachter-Shalomi, *A Hidden Light,* 192.

7. As noted by her during my talk, "The Merging of Two Oceans: Sufism and Hasidism II," on April 29th, 2017, at Wisdom of the Prophets: Sufism & Judaism.

8. This is my own distillation and understanding of numerous descriptions of the *s'firot*. See Aryeh Kaplan. *Innerspace: Introduction to Kabbalah, Meditation and Prophecy*. Ed. Abraham Sutton. Jerusalem, Israel: Moznaim Publishing Corporation, 1991: 37-48.

9. Wali Ali Meyer, Bilal Hyde, Faisal Muqaddam, and Shabda Kahn. *Physicians of the Heart: A Sufi View of the Ninety-Nine Names of Allah.* San Francisco, CA: Sufi Ruhaniat International, 2011: 38.

10. Kaplan, *Innerspace,* 62.

11. Meyer, *Physicians of the Heart,* 158.

12. Ibid., 38-39.

13. *Yā Manṣūr! Amit,* meaning, 'O victorious! Bring death.'

14. Meyer, *Physicians of the Heart,* 269-70.

15. Ibid., 54.

16. Ibid., 56.

17. Ibid., 39.

18. *Raḥim* and *Raḥman* are adjusted here as well, but without the s'firotic associations.

19. Occasionally, Reb Zalman also put Ruth in *malkhut,* according to my friend and fellow student of Reb Zalman, Rabbi Ruth Kagan, because she is the "mother of royalty," and because she is also the progenitor of King David. Esther could also be placed here. Reb Ruth notes that Reb Zalman wanted Rebecca and Sarah to be connected to their husbands across the structure, because the right hand always moves with left leg, and the left hand with the right leg. Our friend, Rabbi Tirzah Firestone puts Esther in *netzaḥ.* Correspondence with Ruth Gan Kagan and Tirzah Firestone, May 5-8th, 2021.

Chapter 7: One God, Many Worlds

1. A favorite story of Ḥabad-Lubavitcher Ḥasidim that I first heard from my teacher, Rabbi Zalman Schachter-Shalomi, *z"l.* A written account of the same incident is found in the diaries of the sixth Lubavitcher Rebbe.

2. "Our sages revealed from Scripture that there are universes beyond number. This means that each of them is an infinity in itself. The finite is not boundless, and thus may be counted. But since as we have it from Scripture that they cannot be counted, those universes are known to be boundless and infinite." Yosef Yitzhak Schneersohn, tr. Zalman Schachter-Shalomi, "A Letter on the Four Worlds."

3. In an annotation to his translation of the sixth Lubavitcher Rebbe's "A Letter on The Four Worlds," Reb Zalman writes: "The Hebrew word for 'world' or 'universe' is *ōlām.* Ḥasidism teaches us that *ōlām* and *he-elem,* meaning 'obscuring' or 'hiding,' are related. Each universe, having its own dimensions, thus hides that which transcends it."

4. In his "Letter on the Four Worlds," the sixth Lubavitcher Rebbe writes, "And now it will make sense when we call the highest of the four worlds, *atzilut*, a 'world.' By this we mean that it is limited within its own confines; because what we mean by 'world,' is that no matter how vast (or even infinite) the universe is, it is confined and bound to itself." Thus, it is not about its 'boundaries,' but it's essence.

5. Robert Frager. *Heart, Self, and Soul: The Sufi Psychology of Growth, Balance, and Harmony*. Wheaton, IL: Quest Books, 1999: x-xi.

6. Most Sufi texts place *haqiqah* before *ma'rifah*, but this is really about how these are being taught. Reb Zalman preferred this schema ending with *haqiqah*, where one's individual ego is wholly obscured by the Truth. Other Sufis emphasize *Ma'rifah* or gnosis as the result of having tasted the Truth. See Gregory Blann. *The Garden of Mystic Love: Volume I: The Origin and Formation of the Great Sufi Orders.* Boulder, CO: Albion-Andalus Books, 2014: 232-33. In Hasan Lufti Shushud, *Masters of Wisdom in Central Asia: Teachings from the Sufi Path of Liberation*, Rochester, VT: Inner Traditions, 2014: 173, *Ma'rifah* is presented as the unitive experience, and *Haqiqah* as Reality.

7. In as much as Kabbalah was absorbed into Ḥasidism, especially as taught by Rabbi Dov Baer, the Maggid of Mezritch, and his disciple, Rabbi Shneur Zalman of Liadi, founder of the Ḥabad lineage.

8. As *Assiyah* is derived from the root, *Ayin-Shin-Heh*, meaning, 'to make.'

9. In *Adornment of Hearts* Westport, CT: Pir Press, 1991, 49, Shaykh Muzaffer Ozak speaks of "The Visible World, the World of Gross Body." But the sixth Lubavitcher Rebbe writes in his "Letter on the Four Worlds," "Thus, we can also see that the lowest of all worlds, the world of *Assiyah*, which is also a spiritual one, and which contains no physical matter, deserves the same term, 'world.'"

10. Zalman M. Schachter-Shalomi. *Gate to the Heart: A Manual of Contemplative Jewish Practice.* Boulder, CO: Albion-Andalus Books, 2013: 14. Also Zalman M. Schachter-Shalomi. "Kabbalah and Transpersonal Psychiatry." *Textbook of Transpersonal Psychiatry and Psychology.* New York, NY: Basic Books, 1996: 123.

11. Aryeh Kaplan. *Innerspace: Introduction to Kabbalah, Meditation and Prophecy.* Jerusalem: Moznaim, 1991: 27.

12. Scott Kugle, ed. *Sufi Meditation and Contemplation: Timeless Wisdom*

from Mughal India. New Lebanon, NY: Suluk Press, 2012: 137.

13. Saiyid Athar Abbas Rizvi. *A History of Sufism in India: Volume I: Early Sufism and its History in India to AD 1600.* New Delhi: Munshiram Manoharlal Publishers, 1997: 369.

14. Vilayat Inayat Khan. *Awakening Through the Planes: The Developmental Stages.* Seattle, WA: Sufi Order International, 1998: 6, 7, 8. In Zia Inayat-Khan, ed., *Caravan of Souls: An Introduction to the Sufi Path of Hazrat Inayat Khan,* New Lebanon, NY: Suluk Press, 2013: 124, Hazrat Inayat Khan says: "This is the consciousness dependent on our senses. Whatever we see by means of the eye, or hear by means of the ear, whatever we smell and taste, all these experiences, which we gain by the help of the material body, prove to us that this is a particular plane of consciousness, or a particular kind of experience of consciousness."

15. Ozak, *Adornment of Hearts,* 49: "The World of Ideas, the World of Angels of Subtle Body."

16. Schachter-Shalomi, *Gate to the Heart,* 14.

17. Kugle, *Sufi Meditation and Contemplation,* 139.

18. "The Compass of Truth" in Kugle, *Sufi Meditation and Contemplation,* 138.

19. Adin Steinsaltz. *The Thirteen Petalled Rose: A Discourse on the Essence of Jewish Existence and Belief.* New York: Basic Books, 1980: 8.

20. Inayat Khan, *Awakening Through the Planes,* 41.

21. Ozak, *Adornment of Hearts,* 49.

22. Schachter-Shalomi, *Gate to the Heart,* 14.

23. Steinsaltz, *The Thirteen Petalled Rose,* 17.

24. "The Compass of Truth" in Kugle, *Sufi Meditation and Contemplation,* 154.

25. Ibid.

26. The notion that the effect can occur before the cause, or that the future can effect the present or past.

27. Inayat Khan, *Awakening Through the Planes,* 49.

28. This interpretation is based on the notion that *atzilut* is derived from the root, *etzel,* meaning, 'nearness.'

29. Schachter-Shalomi, *Gate to the Heart,* 14.

30. Steinsaltz, *The Thirteen Petalled Rose,* 22.

31. Ozak, *Adornment of Hearts,* 49, "The World of Dominion comes after the World of Divinity."

32. Inayat Khan, *Awakening Through the Planes,* 61.

33. Vilayat Inayat Khan. *That Which Transpires Behind That Which Appears: The Experience of Sufism.* New Lebanon, NY: Omega, 1994: 83.

34. Schachter-Shalomi, *Gate to the Heart,* 14.

35. When we say *"nafs"* here, we are using the word differently than when we talk about *nafs* as ego.

36. Schachter-Shalomi, *Gate to the Heart,* 9.

37. Ibid. Also discussed in Hazrat Inayat Khan's *Gathas* (Part IV: Pasi Anfas, "The Power of Breath.")

38. Steinsaltz, *The Thirteen Petalled Rose,* 8-9.

39. A phrase and concept introduced in his book, *Understanding Media: The Extensions of Man.* New York: Signet Books, 1964.

40. Steinsaltz, *The Thirteen Petalled Rose,* 11-12, 16-17.

41. See Zalman Schachter-Shalomi and Netanel Miles-Yépez. *A Heart Afire: Stories and Teachings of the Early Hasidic Masters.* Philadelphia, PA: Jewish Publication Society, 2009: 58-59, where Reb Zalman and I discuss the Ba'al Shem Tov's report on a spiritual ascent to the Lower *Gan Eden,* where he met with both the "souls of the deceased and the living." In his "Letter on the Four Worlds," the sixth Lubavitcher Rebbe also writes, "All that we know about the Celestial Academy, in which the enlightened souls advance in learned fellowship, the order of progression and indoctrination of the newly arrived souls (those who have recently passed on), the abodes of the *tzaddikim* who preside over their followers and direct them to higher attainment, the proclamation, "Make way!" for those great souls who are about to pass over, the order in which the souls of the *tzaddikim* are made welcome *[. . .]* to *Gan Eden,* the conscious ascents of the souls of Rabbi Yitzhak Luria and the Ba'al Shem Tov *[. . .]* The whole host of things experienced and seen there, show that these worlds are somehow like this one, the lowest of them, the material world."

42. The notion of the Heavenly Court is based on Daniel 4:17: "This sentence is decreed by the Watchers, the verdict commanded by the Holy Ones." The Heavenly Court is often identified with the Counsel

of Souls *(nefashot shel tzaddakim,* lit. 'souls of the righteous') with whom God consulted before creation. The Counsel of Souls is generally thought to be comprised of the souls of the righteous who have ascended to heaven. See Howard Schwartz. *Tree of Souls: The Mythology of Judaism.* New York: Oxford UP, 2004: 160-62, 193-94, 208-09.

43. Likewise, the connections between persons in the world of action and souls in the world of knowing are suggested in various places. The Maggid of Mezritch suggests that when one studies the work of an author, whether living or dead, a kind of link is established between the two souls. Schachter-Shalomi, *A Heart Afire,* 211.

In the Kabbalah of the holy Ari, Rabbi Yitzhak Luria, the idea of *ibbur,* 'pregnancy,' "points to the sharing of a body by different souls that share same soul root," and how a soul above may infuse a person below with a particular inspiration. Zvi Ish-Shalom. *Radical Death: The Paradoxical Unity of Body, Soul and the Cosmos in Lurianic Kabbalah.* Dissertation: Brandeis University, 2013: 55.

In a similar vein, Hazrat Inayat Khan teaches: "If in the plane of the *jinn* a sympathetic link is established between two souls, it continues to exist. In this way it is natural for the spirit of Shakespeare to continue to inspire the Shakespeare personality on earth." Inayat Khan. *The Sufi Message of Hazrat Inayat Khan: Volume IV* ("The Mind-World") Surrey, England: Servire Publishing Company, 1978: 273.

44. See Zalman Schachter-Shalomi and Netanel Miles-Yépez. *A Hidden Light: Stories and Teachings of Early HaBaD and Bratzlav Hasidism.* Santa Fe, NM: Gaon Books, 2011: 72, 255-59, where I give a more detailed articulation of this idea and related concepts, and a similar presentation by Reb Zalman and I in *A Heart Afire,* 58-59.

45. Schachter-Shalomi, *A Heart Afire,* 297.

Chapter 8: Between the Animal and Divine Souls

1. By calling the work *Sefer Shel Beynonim,* Reb Shneur Zalman was sending a clear message to his Ḥasidim—he had written a book for them, and not for the perfectly righteous *tzaddikim.* As he says on the title page of the work, "For it is very near to you; it is in your mouth and in your heart to do it." That is to say, you are not so far from the

holy level of the *beynoni;* and it is within you to achieve.

2. Shneur Zalman of Liadi. *Tanya. "Sefer Shel Beynonim,"* Chapter 1.

3. Shneur Zalman of Liadi, *"Sefer Shel Beynonim,"* Ch. 1.

4. Ibid., Ch. 12.

5. Heard from my teacher, Rabbi Zalman Schachter-Shalomi, *z"l.* See Yosef Yitzchak Schneersohn. *Likkutei Dibburim: Volume 1.* Tr. Uri Kaploun. Kehot Publication Society, Brooklyn, NY: 1987: 61-62; also unnamed in Yosef Yitzchak Schneersohn. *Likkutei Dibburim: Volume 5.* Tr. Uri Kaploun. Kehot Publication Society, Brooklyn, NY: 2000: 148-49.

6. Heard from my teacher, Rabbi Zalman Schachter-Shalomi, *z"l.*

7. Shneur Zalman of Liadi, *"Sefer Shel Beynonim,"* Ch. 14.

8. Ibid., Ch. 12.

9. Heard from my teacher, Rabbi Zalman Schachter-Shalomi, *z"l.*

10. Charles Dickens. *Martin Chuzzelwit.* London: Chapman & Hall, 1844.

11. Yosef Wineberg. *Lessons in Tanya: Volume I.* Ed. Uri Kaploun. Trs. Levy Wineberg and Sholom B. Wineberg. Brooklyn, NY: Kehot Publication Society, 1982. 171. Also Adin Steinsaltz. *The Long Shorter Way: Discourses on Chasidic Thought.* Tr. Yehuda Hanegbi. Northvale, NJ: Jason Aronson, 1988: 85, and Adin Steinsaltz. *Opening the Tanya: Discovering the Moral and Mystical Teachings of a Classic Work of Kabbalah.* Ed. Meir Hanegbi. Tr. Yaacov Tauber. San Francisco, CA: Jossey-Bass, 2003: 288.

12. Shneur Zalman of Liadi, *"Sefer Shel Beynonim,"* Ch. 12.

13. Zalman Schachter-Shalomi and Netanel Miles-Yépez. *A Hidden Light: Stories and Teachings of Early HaBaD and Bratzlav Hasidism.* Santa Fe, NM: Gaon Books, 2011: 62-63.

Chapter 9: Threads of Connection

1. An experimental "Christmas *seder*" he led with a Christian minister.

2. This was a response to material and comments by Pir Zia Inayat-Khan on April 28th, 2017, in his session on "Exodus" during Wisdom

of the Prophets: Sufism and Judaism at the Abode of the Message in New Lebanon, New York. See Zia Inayat-Khan. *Mingled Waters: Sufism and the Mystical Unity of Religions.* New Lebanon, NY: Saluk Press, 2017: 138.

3. This was a response to material and comments by Pir Zia Inayat-Khan on April 28th, 2017, in his session on "Exodus" during Wisdom of the Prophets: Sufism and Judaism at the Abode of the Message in New Lebanon, New York. See Zia Inayat-Khan. *Mingled Waters: Sufism and the Mystical Unity of Religions.* New Lebanon, NY: Saluk Press, 2017: 140.

4. This was a response to material and comments by Pir Zia Inayat-Khan on April 28th, 2017, in his session on "Exodus" during Wisdom of the Prophets: Sufism and Judaism at the Abode of the Message in New Lebanon, New York.

5. This was a response to material and comments by Pir Zia Inayat-Khan on April 28th, 2017, in his session on "Exodus" during Wisdom of the Prophets: Sufism and Judaism at the Abode of the Message in New Lebanon, New York. A description of *ḥeshbon ha-nefesh* can be found in Zalman M. Schachter-Shalomi. *Gate to the Heart: A Manual of Contemplative Jewish Practice.* Eds. Netanel Miles-Yépez and Robert Micha'el Esformes. Boulder, CO: Albion-Andalus Books, 2013: 81-83.

6. This was a response to comments by Pir Zia Inayat-Khan on April 28th, 2017, in Rabbi Tirzah Firestone's session on "The Path of the Tzaddik: The All and the Nothing" during Wisdom of the Prophets: Sufism and Judaism at the Abode of the Message in New Lebanon, New York.

7. This was a response to material and comments by Pir Zia Inayat-Khan on April 29th, 2017, in his session on "A David Psalm" during Wisdom of the Prophets: Sufism and Judaism at the Abode of the Message in New Lebanon, New York. See Zia Inayat-Khan. *Mingled Waters: Sufism and the Mystical Unity of Religions.* New Lebanon, NY: Saluk Press, 2017: 148-49.

8. This was a response to material and comments by Pir Zia Inayat-Khan on April 29th, 2017, in his session on "A David Psalm" during

Wisdom of the Prophets: Sufism and Judaism at the Abode of the Message in New Lebanon, New York.

9. An anecdote in the Hasidic oral tradition heard from my teacher, Rabbi Zalman Schachter-Shalomi, *z"l*.

10. This was a response to material and comments by Pir Zia Inayat-Khan on April 30th, 2017, in his session on "Job" during Wisdom of the Prophets: Sufism and Judaism at the Abode of the Message in New Lebanon, New York. See Zia Inayat-Khan. *Mingled Waters: Sufism and the Mystical Unity of Religions.* New Lebanon, NY: Saluk Press, 2017: 161-62.

11. This was a response to an audience question on April 30th, 2017, in Pir Zia Inayat-Khan's session on "Job" during Wisdom of the Prophets: Sufism and Judaism at the Abode of the Message in New Lebanon, New York.

12. This was a response to an audience question on October 18th, 2016, from a talk at the Abode of the Message in New Lebanon, New York, called "Between the Animal and Divine Souls."

13. This was a response to an audience question on October 18th, 2016, from a talk at the Abode of the Message in New Lebanon, New York, called "Between the Animal and Divine Souls."

14. Zalman Schachter-Shalomi. *Sh'ma': A Concise Weekday Siddur for Praying in English.* Boulder, CO: Albion-Andalus Books, 2010: 29.

15. This was a response to a question from Peter Schein on October 18th, 2016, from a talk at the Abode of the Message in New Lebanon, New York, called "Between the Animal and Divine Souls."

16. This was a response to a question from Mikhail Horowitz on October 18th, 2016, from a talk at the Abode of the Message in New Lebanon, New York, called "Between the Animal and Divine Souls."

17. Heard from my teacher, Rabbi Zalman Schachter-Shalomi, *z"l*.

18. This was actually a sermon delivered by the author in a Universal Worship service on April 30th, 2017, during the Wisdom of the Prophets: Sufism and Judaism event at the Abode of the Message in New Lebanon, New York.

Apprendix A: "Seclusion"

1. See Moshe ben Maimun, *Mishneh Torah, Sefer ha-Madda–Yesodey ha-Torah* 7:4.

2. See *Mishneh Torah, Sefer ha-Madda–T'shuvah* 10:3; *Yesodey ha-Torah* 7:1.

3. In the Ptolemaic understanding of cosmology, the earth was seen as the center of the universe, and thus surrounded by a series of spheres which held the other celestial bodies, such as the stars.

4. The verse continues, "not to gaze on a maiden." Thus, it is about not following after the senses and one's lustful impulses.

5. See *Mishneh Torah, Sefer ha-Madda–Yesodey ha-Torah* 7:4; Hayyim ben Yosef Vital, *Sha'arey Kedushah* 4:2.

Glossary

Ādām Kadmōn – Heb., 'primordial human.' The 'blueprint' of creation.

'Aḥad, wāḥid, wa-samad – Ara., 'one, unique, and sufficient.'

ahavāh – Heb., 'love.'

aḥdut – Heb., 'oneness.'

ahl al-kitāb – Ara., 'people of the book.'

ahl aṣ-ṣuffah – 'people of the bench.' The companions of the Prophet Muḥammad who sat outside the *masjid* in Medina.

ain – Heb., 'there is not,' 'nothing.'

ain kadōneynū – Heb., 'nothing like our lord.'

ain kelōheynū – Heb., 'nothing like our God.'

ain sōf – Heb., 'infinite nothing,' 'without limits.' God.

al-'ālamūn – Ara., 'the world.'

'ālam (pl. *'ālamīn)* – Ara., 'world.'

'ālam al-jabarūt – Ara., 'world of power.' The world of knowledge in Sufism.

'ālam al-lāhūt – Ara., 'world of divinity.' The world of being in Sufism.

'ālam-i lazim – Ara., 'causal world.'

'ālam al-malakūt – Ara., 'world of angels.' The world of feeling in Sufism.

'ālam al-mithāl – Ara., 'world of the imagination.'

'ālam an-nāsūt – Ara., 'world of humanity.' The world of action in Sufism.

Al-ḥamdu lillāh – Ara., 'praise God.'

Allāh – Ara., 'God.'

Allāhu 'Akbar – Ara., 'God is greater.'

Amidah – Heb., 'standing.'

An al-Haqq! – Ara., 'I am the Truth!'

Anbiyā (sing. *nabī*) – Ara., 'prophets.'

ānī – Heb., 'I.'

anūsīm – Heb., 'forced.' A term for forced converts.

āpīkoros – Heb. (derived from Gr.), 'abandoned.' A heretic; one who has abandoned their faith.

'arba'īn – Ara., 'forty.' A forty-day Sufi retreat.

'ārōn kōdesh – Heb., 'holy ark.' The structure in which the Torah scroll is kept in the synagogue.

'arwāḥ – Ara., 'spirits.' The world of the spirits in Sufism.

'asmā' al-ḥusnā – Ara., 'beautiful names.' The ninety-nine names of God found in the Qur'ān.

asmā o sifat – Per.,/Ara., 'names and attributes.'

'attār – Ara., 'fragrance.'

ayīn – Heb., 'nothingness.' A way of describing God in Kabbalah.

bāb al-mahabba – Ara., 'gate of love'.

bāb al-tawḥīd – 'Ara., gate of unity'.

bākī – Heb., 'expert.'

baqā' – Ara., 'subsistence.' Returning from *fanā'* ('annihilation'), retaining the experience of the divine.

bar mītzvāh – Heb., 'son of the commandment.' A ceremony marking a son's coming into adult responsibility.

bawabat (sing. *bāb)* – Ara., 'gates.'

bay'ah – Ara., 'agreement,' 'covenant,' or 'deal.' Sufi initiation; also called, 'taking hand.'

beyt mīdrash – Heb., 'house of study.'

beynonī (pl. *beynonīm)* – Heb., 'in-Betweener,' 'average.'

bhakti yōga – San., 'discipline of devotion.'

bid'ah – Ara., 'innovation.' Heresy.

bidar – Ara., waking consciousness.

bīmāh – Heb. (derived from Ara.), 'dais,' 'platform.'

bīnāh – Heb., 'understanding.' One of the ten *s'fīrōt* or divine qualities in Kabbalah.

Bismillāh ar-Raḥmān ar-Raḥīm – Ara., 'In the name of the most compassionate, the most merciful.'

bittūl hā-yesh – Heb. 'nullification of existence.' In Hasidism, making the ego transparent to God.

cherāg – Per., 'candle' or 'light.' (See *chirāgh).*

chirāgh (f. *chirāghah)* – Per., 'candle' or 'light.' A religious functionary of Universal Worship in most Inayati lineages, and a broader vocational role in the Inayati-Maimuni lineage.

dā'at – Heb., 'knowledge.' Gnosis, esoteric, interior, or experiential knowledge. One of the ten *s'fīrōt* or divine qualities in Kabbalah.

dargāh – Per., 'burial shrine.' The burial place of a Sufi master; often a place of pilgrimage.

darvīsh (pl. *darāvīsh)* – Per., 'one who stands on the threshold.' A beggar. In the Sufi context, a beggar of God, or a mature Sufi. Also, dervish.

dāvvenen – Yid. (derived from Lat.), 'praying with feeling' or deep investment.

dayyān (pl. *dayyānīm)* – Heb., 'judge.' A judge in religious matters.

dīn – Heb., 'judgment.'

dishdāshah – Ara., a ankle-length garment with long sleeves.

dönmeh – Heb., 'apostates.' The followers of Shabbetai Zvi after his apostasy.

d'veykūt – Heb., 'cleaving,' 'clinging,' to God.

eḥād hā-manuy – Heb., the number one.

eḥād v'ain sheyni – Heb., 'one for whom there is no other.'

Eḥād, yaḥid, u'meyuḥad – Heb., 'One uniquely simple unity.'

emet – Heb., 'truth.' The concept of truth in Hebrew.

eretz Yisrā'ēl – Heb., 'land of Israel.'

etz ḥayyīm – Heb., 'tree of life.' In Kabbalah, a structure of dynamic relationships between ten divine qualities.

fanā' – Ara., 'annihilation.' Annihilation or obscuration of the self. Better understood as making the self transparent to God.

gemāra – Aram., 'completion.' Rabbinic commentary on the *Mishnah.*

gevūrāh – Heb., 'strength'. One of the ten *s'fīrōt* or divine qualities in Kabbalah.

ghazal – Ara., 'love poem'.

ghayb – Ara., 'unseen.'

g'mīllūt ḥassādim – Heb., 'deeds of loving-kindness'.

gūf – Heb., 'body,' 'flesh.'

ḤaBaD – Heb., an acrostic for *ḥokhmāh, bīnāh, dā'at,* 'wisdom,' 'understanding,' 'knowledge.'

ḥadīth (pl., *aḥādīth)* – Ara., 'report' or 'tradition.' A report of words or deeds of the prophet Muhammad in the Islamic tradition.

ḥaddrāl-ilāhiyya – Ara., 'divine presence.'

hāhūt – Ara., 'is-ness,' 'he-ness.' One of the 'upper' worlds of Sufism.

ḥāl (pl., *aḥwal)* – Ara., 'state.' A technical term in Sufism for temporary emotional states or states of consciousness.

halākhāh – 'Heb., way to walk.' Jewish law.

ḥalāl – Ara., 'permissible.' Things that are permissible in Islam, especially with regard to dietary laws.

haqīqah – Ara., 'truth,' 'reality.'

ḥāsīd (pl. *ḥāsīdīm)* – Heb., 'pious.'

ḥāsīdut – Heb., 'piety.' Hasidism.

ḥāyyāh – Heb., 'living essence.' The soul of being in Kabbalah.

ḥesed – Heb., 'loving-kindness.' One of the ten *s'fīrōt* or divine qualities in Kabbalah.

ḥeshbōn ha-nefesh – Heb., 'soul accounting.' A Hasidic contemplative practice for reviewing one's actions.

ḥikmat al-zawqiyya – Ara., 'tasted wisdom.' Sufism.

hitbōdedūt – Heb., 'self-isolation.' A prayer practice of freely expressing your intimate thoughts to God.

hōd – Heb., 'glory.' One of the ten *s'fīrōt* or divine qualities in Kabbalah.

ḥokhmāh – Heb., 'wisdom.' One of the ten *s'fīrōt* or divine qualities in Kabbalah. (See *ko'aḥ māh.)*

ibbur, Heb., 'pregnancy.'

'i'jāz – Ara., 'inimitability.'

ijāzah – Ara., 'authorization.'

iltazām ta'at Allāh – Ara., 'obedience to God.'

ikhlās al-'amal – Ara., 'sincerity in intention.'

'ilm – Ara., 'knowledge.'

ishrāqī – Ara., 'illuminationist.'

i'tibar – Ara., creation.

izn (idhn) – Ara., 'permission.' The soul of being in Sufism.

jasad – Ara., 'flesh.'

jihād – Ara., 'struggle.'

jihād al-'akbar – Ara., 'greater struggle.'

jihād al-asghar – Ara., 'lesser struggle.'

jinn (sing. *jini)* – 'concealed ones.' Spirit beings made of 'smokeless fire,' sharing many of the characteristics of human beings, but existing on another plane of reality.

jñāna yōga – San., 'discipline of knowledge.'

kabbālāh – 'receiving,' 'tradition.' The mystical tradition of Judaism.

Kālāh sh'eyri ū'l'vāvi; tzūr-l'vāvi v'ḥel'ki Elōhim l'ōlām. – Heb., "My body and my heart are emptied; God is the rock of my heart and my eternal portion." (Ps. 73:26)

karma yōga – San., 'discipline of action.'

kavānāh – Heb., 'intentionality.'

keter – Heb., 'crown'. One of the ten *s'fīrōt* or divine qualities in Kabbalah.

kindelākh – Yid., 'children.'

khalīfa (pl. *khulafā')* – Ara., 'deputy' or 'steward.' A successor and representative of a Sufi *shaykh* or *murshid.*

khalīl Allāh – Ara., 'friend of God.'

khalwah – Ara., 'seclusion' or 'isolation.' Sufi retreat.

khalwah bātinah – Ara., 'internal seclusion.'

khalwah zāhirah – Ara., 'external seclusion.'

khilāfat-nāma – Ara., 'letter of succession.' Document signifying succession as a Sufi master.

khwāb – Ara., 'dreaming.'

k'līppāh (pl. *k'līppōt)* – Heb., 'shell,' 'husk.'

ko'aḥ māh – Heb., 'power of what-ness!' (See *ḥokhmāh.)*

kōdesh l'Eyl Eliyōn – Heb., 'holy to God, Most High'.

kōheyn l'Eyl Eliyōn – Heb., 'priest to God, Most High.'

Lā – Ara., 'no.'

Lā 'ilāha 'illā llāh hū – Ara., 'There is no God; nevertheless, God is.' The basic creedal statement of Islam, and the phrase most often used in Sufi *zikr.*

lāqab – Ara., 'nickname.'

latīf – Ara., 'subtle.'

Lev tāhōr b'rā-li Elōhīm, v'rū'aḥ nākhōn ḥaddeysh b'kirbi. – Heb., "God, create in me a pure heart, and renew my spirit within me." (Ps. 51:12)

ma'asīōt (sing. *ma'aseh*) – Heb., deeds,' 'stories.' Hasidic stories.

mahabba – 'love.' Love in general, or love of God.

maḥshāvōt zārōt – Heb., 'strange thoughts.' Distracting thoughts.

majlis (pl. *majālis*)– Ara., 'private salon,' 'sitting room,' or 'council.'

majzūb (majdhūb) – Ara., 'intoxicated.' A Sufi who is as if intoxicated.

mālā – San., 'garland.' A string of 108 beads used by Hindu and Buddhist practitioners while repeating mantras.

malāk – Ara., 'messenger,' 'angel.'

malākh – Heb., 'messenger,' 'angel.'

malkhūt – Heb., 'kingdom', 'sovereignty.' One of the ten *s'fīrōt* or divine qualities in Kabbalah.

maqām (pl. *maqāmāt)* – Ara., 'place' or 'station.' A level of sustained integration achieved by a Sufi, and sometimes marked by a specific role or responsibility in the Sufi community.

maqbara (pl. *maqābir)* – Ara., 'mausoleum.'

ma'rifah – Ara., 'gnosis' or 'experiential knowledge.'

māshpīyya (pl. *māshpī'im)* – a mentor instructing him in basic *ḥasidut* in his stead.

matteh – Heb., 'staff.'

mawlā – Ara., 'master.'

mekubāl – Heb., 'receiver.' A kabbalist.

mentch – Yid., 'human.' A person of exceptional character.

meshālīm (sing. *māshāl)* – Heb., 'parables.'

meshreb – 'distinctive character.'

mikveh – Heb., 'gathering of water.' Ritual bath.

mītzvōt (sing. *mītzvāh)* – Heb., 'commandments.'

M'lō khōl hā-āretz k'vōdō. – 'The whole Earth is filled with God's Glory' (Isa. 6:3).

muḥāsaba – Ara., 'accounting,' 'reckoning.' A contemplative practice of self-examination in Sufism.

mujāhadat an-nafs – Ara., 'greater struggle is with the self .'

mulk – Ara., created world .

mu'minun – Ara., 'believers.' Monotheists, or believers in one God.

murīd (f. *murīda,* pl., *murīdun*) – Ara., 'seeker.' An initiate in a Sufi lineage.

murshid (f. *murshida*) – Ara., 'guide.' The leader of a Sufi community. Parallel to *shaykh,* and sometimes *pir.*

mūssar – Heb., 'discipline.' Jewish ethics and ethical literature.

mustagādd – Ara., new religious practice.

nafs – Ara., 'ego, 'self,' 'soul,' or 'essence.'

nagīd – Heb., 'prince,' 'ruler.' A title given to the head of all Egyptian Jewry in the time of Rabbi Avraham Maimuni.

nafas – Ara., 'breath,' 'wind,' 'spirit.' The soul of feeling in Sufism.

nefesh – Heb., 'soul.' Animating soul.

nefesh hā-behāmīt – Heb., 'animal soul' or nature.

nefesh ha-elōhīt – Heb., 'divine soul' or nature.

nefesh hā-sikhlīt – 'Heb., rational soul' or nature.

neshāmāh – Heb., 'breath,' 'soul.'

netzāḥ – Heb., 'victory.' One of the ten *s'fīrōt* or divine qualities in Kabbalah.

nītzōtzōt (sing. *nītzōtz)* – Heb., 'sparks' of holiness.

ōlām – Heb., 'world,' 'eternity.'

ōlām ha-assīyāh – Heb., 'world of making.' The world of action in Kabbalah.

ōlām ha-atzīlūt – Heb., 'world of nearness.' The world of action

in Kabbalah.

'ōlām hā-bā – Heb., 'world-to-come.' The afterlife in Judaism.

ōlām ha-b'rīyāh – Heb., 'world of creation.' The world of action in Kabbalah.

ōlām ha-yetzīrāh – Heb., 'world of formation.' The world of feeling in Kabbalah.

ōlāmōt (sing. *ōlām)* – Heb., 'worlds.' The four worlds of Kabbalah.

orvīn – Heb., 'ravens.'

pindar – Ara., world-as-believed.

pir – Per., 'elder.' The leader of a Sufi community, parallel to *shaykh* and murshid. In Inayati Sufism the head of an Inayati lineage (formal title, *pir-o-murshid)*.

piyyūtīm (sing. *piyyūt)* – Heb., 'poems.' Hebrew and Aramaic liturgical poems.

pogrōm – Rus., 'to destroy.' A violent attack against Jews aimed at their destruction or expulsion.

qiyām al-layl – Ara., 'stand at night.' A practice of the prophet Muhammad, meaning to rise during the night for prayer.

qiyām was-siyām – Ara., 'rising and fasting.' A Sufi practice of rising to fast through the night.

qurb – Ara., 'proximity.'

raḥma – Ara., 'womb,' 'mercy.'

rāja yōga – San., 'royal discipline.'

rāshā (pl. *reshayim)* – Heb., 'wicked.'

rāshā gamur – Heb., 'completely wicked person.'

rāshā sh'eino gamur – Heb., 'conditionally wicked person.'

rāshā v'ra lo – Heb., 'wicked person for whom it is bad.'

rāshā v'tov lo – Heb., wicked person for whom it is good.'

rayyis al-yaḥūd – Heb., leader of Egyptian Jewry. A title given to the head of all Egyptian Jewry in the time of Rabbi Avraham Maimuni.

rebbe (pl. *rebbe'im)* – Yid., 'master.' A Hasidic master. The equivalent of a Sufi *shaykh.*

rehal – Ara., a folding x-shaped bookstand used for the recitation from scripture.

Ribbōnō shel Ōlām – Heb., 'master of the world' or 'universe.' An expression used in Judaism for God.

rōsh he-ḥasīdīm – Heb., 'head of the Ḥasidim.'

rū'aḥ – Heb., 'wind,' 'spirit.' The soul of feeling in Kabbalah.

rūḥ – Ara., 'spirit.'

rūḥu ḥaiwāni – (Ara., 'animal soul.' The soul associated with the animal realm in Sufism.

rūḥu insāni – (Ara., 'human soul.' The soul associated with the human realm in Sufism.

rūḥu sultāni – (Ara., 'divine soul.' The soul associated with the realm of divinity in Sufism.

sābā – Heb., 'grandfather.'

sabr – Ara., 'patience.' One of the divine qualities according to Islam.

sāḥibunā fī derekh ha-Shem – Heb., our companion on the path of God.

sajjāda – Ara., 'prostration carpet.'

salāh – Ara., 'Islamic prayer.'

samā – Ara., 'hearing.' Practice of courting ecstasy with music and dance and the recitation of love poetry.

samādhi – San., 'one-pointed.' Meditative absorption.

seder – Heb., 'order,' 'arrangement.' The Passover meal and ritual.

s'fīrōt (sing. *s'fīrāh)* – Heb., divine attributes. The ten divine qualities of the *etz ḥayyīm* ('tree of life').

Shabbāt – Heb., 'to rest.' Sabbath.

shahādat – Ara., visible world .

shajara sharīf – Ara., 'noble tree.' The graphic depiction of a Sufi *silsila.*

shamāsh – Heb., 'attendant.' Synagogue attendant.

sharī'ah – Ara., "well-trodden path.' The religious law of Islam.

shaykh (f. *shaykha,* pl. *shuyūkh)* – Ara., 'elder.' The leader of a Sufi community, parallel to *pir* and *murshid.*

shem – Heb., 'name.'

shīur – Ara., 'lesson.' A Hasidic study session, usually learning from a text.

Sh'mā – Heb., 'hear,' 'listen.' The primary creedal statement of Judaism.

shukr – Ara., 'gratitude.' One of the divine qualities according to Islam.

silsila – Ara., 'chain.' The line of succession or the chain of transmission of a lineage.

sōd – Heb., 'secret.'

sūq – Ara., an open market.

takhlit – Heb., 'ultimate purpose.'

tallīt – Heb., prayer shawl.'

Tanya – Heb., 'It is taught.' The chief work of Rabbi Shneur Zalman of Liadi.

tarīqah (pl., *turuq)* – Ara., 'path' or 'order.' The Sufi path, or a particular Sufi lineage.

tawadu – Ara., humility before God.

tawakkul – Ara., 'trust' or 'reliance.' Trust in or reliance on God.

tawba – Ara., 'turning' or 'turning back.' Turning back to God, repentance, or conversion in Islam.

tawḥīd – Ara., 'unity' of God.

tesbīḥ – Ara., 'tool of glorification' or 'glorifier.' A string of ninety-nine beads used to keep count during *zikr.*

tif'eret – Heb., 'beauty.' One of the ten *s'fīrōt* or divine qualities

in Kabbalah.

tōkaḥah – Heb., 'reproof.'

t'shūvāh – Heb., 'repentance.'

tzāddīk (pl. *tzaddīkīm)* – Heb., 'righteous person.' A saint, spiritual master, or especially righteous person in Judaism.

tzāddīk gamur – Heb., 'completely righteous person.'

tzāddīk sh'eino gamur – Heb., 'conditionally righteous person.'

tzāddīk v'ra lo – Heb., 'righteous person for whom it is bad.'

tzāddīk v'tov lo – Heb., 'righteous person for whom it is good.'

tzimtzūm – Heb., 'contraction'. The Withdrawal or hiding of the divine light.

waḥdat al-wujūd – Ara., 'unity of all being' or 'existence.' The radical teaching of non-duality in Sufism. In Inayati Sufism, expressed by the phrase, 'the message.'

walī – Ara., 'friend,' 'guardian.'

wazīfa (pl. *wazā'if)* – Ara., mantra, sacred word or formula.

wusūl – Ara., 'approach,' 'union.'

wusūl nabawī – Ara., 'prophetic union.'

Yā Jamīl – Ara., 'o beautiful one.' One of the ninety-nine names of God.

Yā Khalīl – Ara., 'o friend.' One of the ninety-nine names of God.

Yā Mālik – Ara., 'o sovereign.' One of the ninety-nine names of God.

Yā Manṣūr – Ara., 'o victorious one.' One of the ninety-nine names of God.

Yā Manṣūr! Amit! – Ara., 'o victorious! Bring death!'

Yā Qahhār – Ara., 'prevailing.' One of the ninety-nine names of God.

Yā Raḥīm – Ara., 'o merciful one.' One of the ninety-nine names of God.

Yā Raḥmān – Ara., 'o compassionate one.' One of the ninety-nine names of God.

Yā Wadūd – Ara., 'o lover.' One of the ninety-nine names of God.

yeḥīdāh – Heb., 'only one.' The highest level of soul in Kabbalah, indistinguishable from God.

yesh mi'ain – Heb., 'existence from nothing.'

Yeshārīm darkey Hā-Shem, ve-tzadikkīm yeylekū bām, reshayim yikāshlū bām. – Heb., 'Straight-forward are the ways of God; the righteous walk in them, the wicked stumble in them.' (Hos. 14:9)

yesōd – Heb., 'foundation.' One of the ten *s'fīrōt* or divine qualities in Kabbalah.

zekher – Heb., 'remembrance.'

zikr (dhikr) – Ara., 'remembrance.' The practice of remembering God through repetition of a divine name or sacred formula.

zikr khafī – Ara., 'hidden' or 'silent remembrance.'

zuhd – Ara., 'asceticism,' 'detachment.'

Index

Abbaye (ca. 280-340), 150-51, 159

Abhai Chand (17th-century), 12

Abode of the Message, ix-xi, 3, 27, 49, 73, 87, 109, 149, 173, 212-13

Abraham (Avraham, Abrahamic), 28, 32, 54, 69, 92, 98, 122

Abdul Rauf, Feisal, 95, 203

Ādām Kadmōn, 137, 215

ahavāh, 83. 215

Ahron of Karlin (1736-1772), 63

ain kelōheynū, 28, 195, 215

ain sōf, 166-67, 215

'ālam al-jabarūt, 135-36, 139, 215

'ālam al-lāhūt, 132, 136-38, 139, 215

'ālam al-malakūt, 133-34, 139, 215

'ālam al-mithāl, 134, 215

'ālam an-nāsūt, 131-33, 139, 215

Alchemist, The, 55, 59

Al-Hallāj, Mansūr (ca. 858-922), 64, 138,

Al-Hidāyah ilā-Farā'id al-Qulūb (see *Duties of the Heart)*, 13-16, 17, 49-50, 66

Allāhu 'Akbar, 109, 110, 119, 122, 216

Al-Makki, Abu Talib (d. 996), 14

Almohad Caliphate, 10, 18

Al-Moumani, Sidi Hasan, of Balata, 23, 78, 92

Al-Muḥasibi, Abu 'Abdallah Harith (781-857), 14
Al-Sulamī, Muḥammad ibn al-Husayn (d. 1021), 64
Ali-Shah, Sayyid Sabir (d. 1818), 61-62
An al-Haqq, 138, 216
angels, 121-22, 140-41, 143, 150, 152, 156-58, 221
animal nature (see *nefesh hā-behāmīt),* 149-69, 182-86, 222
annihilation, 176, 216, 218
Answer to Job, 181
anūsīm, 10-11, 216
Arabian Nights (see *Kitāb Alf Laylah wa-Laylah),* 59, 199
Aristotelianism, 17
'asmā al-husnā (see ninety-nine 'beautiful names' of God), 109-10, 118-22, 216
Assaf (Asaph), 33, 34, 35, 187-88
Averroes (Abu al-Walid Muḥammad ibn Rushd, 1126-1198), 18
Avraham Abulafia, 195
Avraham he-Ḥasid (d. ca.1223), 19, 21, 193
Avraham of Kalisk (1741-1810), 50
Ayyubid government, 31
Ba'al Shem Tov (Yisra'el ben Eliezer, 1698-1760), 14, 49, 50, 51, 66, 67, 158, 169, 175, 176, 209
Badi ad-Din (see Shah Madar, b. 1315), 12
Baḥya ibn Paquda (11th-century C.E.), 13-17, 21, 49-50, 54, 65, 66, 191, 192, 198
Bair, Puran Khan, 78, 89, 94-95, 99
baqā', 176, 216
Bastian, Edward, 95
Baul singers, 79, 202
bay'ah (see initiation), 91-93, 216
Bektāshī, 78

beynonī, 149-69, 210-11, 217
beyt mīdrash, 80, 216
bid'ah, 31, 196, 217
bīnāh, 114-15, 117, 166, 217, 218
bittūl hā-yesh, 34, 176, 217
Borges, Jorge Luis, 59
breath, 35, 37-38, 41, 42, 43, 134, 140, 188, 189, 209, 222
Buber, Martin (1878-1965), 59, 63, 64, 65
Buddhism, 87
Cairo Genizah, 23
Centering Prayer, 38, 197
cherag (chirāgh), 78, 93-98, 217
Chishtī, x, 12, 61, 9, 92, 105, 203
Christianity, 10, 13, 32, 53, 54, 75, 95, 211
Coelho, Paulo, 55, 59
Contemplation, 13, 14, 15, 29, 30, 37, 43, 74, 98, 135, 166, 192, 197, 219, 222
Cordoba House, 95
dā'at, 112-13, 114-15, 117, 166, 217, 218
Dalālat al-Ḥā'irīn (see *Guide to the Perplexed),* 14, 18, 113, 192
Dārā Shikūh (1615-1659), ix, 13, 134, 136
dargāh, 12, 217
Darth Vader (see Anikin Skywalker), 162
David, King, 33, 34, 35, 36, 40, 41, 42, 123, 153, 177, 187, 188, 206, 212,
Dhammapada, 80, 202
Dhū'n-nūn al-Misrī (d. ca. 862), 15
Dickens, Charles, 161-62
divine nature (see *nefesh ha-elōhīt),* 149-69, 182-86
Dönmeh, 11, 217

Duties of the Heart (see *Al-Hidāyah ilā-Farā'id al-Qulūb*), 13-16, 17, 49-50, 66
ecstasy, 38, 167
Einstein, Albert,
Elijah (prophet),
Elisha (prophet),
emet,
'eshq,
etz ḥayyīm (see tree of life),
fanā',
Fenton, Paul,
Firestone, Tirzah,
Galante, Moshe, of S'fat (d. 1608),
Galante, Moshe, of Damascus (d. 1806),
Game Theory,
Gehazi,
Gershon of Kittov (1701-1761),
gevūrāh,
ghazal,
Ghazzālī, Abū Ḥāmid (ca.1058-1111),
God-ideal,
God's will,
God's wish,
Golden Age,
Goitein, S. D.,
Graetz, Heinrich,
"Ground Zero Mosque",
Guide to the Perplexed (see *Dalālat al-Ḥā'irīn),* 14, 18, 113, 192
Guide to the Servants of God (see Kifāyat al-'Ābidīn), 19, 22, 23, 27, 29, 31, 36, 40, 41, 187-88

Ḥabad Hasidism, 74, 111, 149-69, 206, 207, 218
Ḥabad-Lubavitch, 74, 114, 127, 128, 206, 207, 209
Ḥabad-Niezhin, 74
Haggai, 84
hāhūt, 137, 218
ḥāl, 167-68, 218
Halvetī-Jerrāhī Order, ix, 69, 78, 92
Hanan'el ben Shmuel, 19
Ḥanina ben Dosa, 3
haqīqah, 130-31, 207, 218
ḥāyyāh, 137, 139, 143, 219
Helminski, Camille, xi, 95
Helminski, Kabir, xi, 95, 203
heresy, 217
ḥesed, 109, 115-17, 118, 119, 122-23
ḥeshbōn ha-nefesh, 175-76, 212, 219
Hinduism, 12, 95, 196, 221
hitbōdedūt, 69, 219
hōd, 110, 117-18, 120-21, 219
ḥokhmāh, 113-15, 117, 166, 218, 219, 220
Holy Dervish, 3-10, 23
Hosea, 185
Ḥōvōt ha-Levāvōt (see *Duties of the Heart)*, 13-16, 17, 49-50, 66
Ibn 'Arabī, Muḥyīddīn (1165-1240), 12, 132, 174, 175
'i'jāz, 80, 84, 219
ijāzah, 95, 98, 105, 219
Ināyatī, 87, 88, 90, 91, 95, 99, 100, 101, 103, 104, 105, 109, 122, 127, 203, 217, 223

Inayat-Khan, Vilayat (1916-2004), ix, 76-78, 88, 89, 90, 92, 93, 94, 98, 100, 101, 102, 103, 131, 132, 133, 134, 136, 137, 201, 203, 204, 208

Inayat-Khan, Zia, ix, x-xi, 78, 90, 100-03, 211, 212, 213

Inayati-Maimuni Order, 27, 87-105, 217

Inayati Order (see Sufi Order), ix, 78, 90, 94, 99, 100, 101, 109, 203, 204

initiation (see *bay'ah),* 30, 76, 77, 78, 88, 90, 91-93, 95, 99, 101, 109, 201, 204, 216

Isaiah (Yesha'ayahu), 13, 35, 37, 41, 50, 188

ishrāqī, 12, 219

Islam, 10-12, 13-16, 22, 53, 55, 76, 89, 110, 131, 195, 201, 218, 220, 224, 225

izn, 139, 143-44

Jablonski, Moineddin (1942-2001), 75, 76, 78, 91, 201, 204

Jahān, Shāh (1592-1666), 13

jihād, 50, 65, 219

Job (Ayyūb), 35, 41, 178-82, 188, 213

John of the Cross (Juan de la Cruz, 1542-1591), 13, 177

Judeo-Arabic, 14, 18, 33, 49, 194, 196

Junayd of Baghdad (835-910), 15

Jung, Carl Gustav (1875-1961), 181

Kahn, Shabda, xi, 78, 99, 122, 204

Kahn, Solomon, 122

kavānāh, 50, 153, 220

Kekulé, August, 144

keter, 112-13, 220

khalīfa, 97-99, 220

khalīl Allāh, 92, 220, 226

khalwah, 21, 27, 29, 30, 33, 37, 39-45, 187-88, 189, 220

khalwah bātinah, 21, 27, 30, 33-45, 187-89, 220

khalwah zāhirah, 33, 187, 220

Khan, Inayat (1882-1927), 67, 68, 73, 75, 79, 82, 84, 88, 92, 95, 100, 132, 175, 184, 204, 208, 210

Khan, Mirza, 78

khilāfat-nāma, 101, 103, 220

Khizr, 61

Kifāyat al-'Ābidīn (see *Guide to the Servants of God),* 19, 22, 23, 27, 29, 31, 36, 40, 41, 187-88

Kimiya-yi Sa'ādat, 66

Kitāb Alf Laylah wa-Laylah (see *Arabian Nights),* 59

Lama Foundation, 27

Lewis, Samuel (Sufi Ahmed Murad) (1896-1971), 27, 75, 97, 204

Likkūtey Halākhōt, 65

Luria, Yitzhak (1534-1572), 175, 209, 210

Luzzatto, Moshe Ḥayyim (1707-1747), 83

mahabba, 15, 216, 221

Maimonides (see Moshe ben Maimun, 1138-1204), 17, 21, 101, 102, 113, 192

Maimuni, Avraham ben Moshe (1186-1237), 16-23, 27-45, 54, 102, 187-89

Maimuni, Ovadyah ben Avraham (1228-1265), 37, 39, 42, 43, 101, 102

Majma al-Bahrain, ix, x

Malachi, 84

Malkhi-tzedek (Melchizedek), 98

malkhūt, 110, 118, 121, 206, 221

Maqāla al-Ḥawdiyya, 37, 39, 42

maqām, 22, 167-68, 184-85, 221

Maqbara Hut, 27, 29, 221

ma'rifah, 130-31, 207, 221

Mark, Zvi, 199

Martin, Rabia, 204
Martin Chuzzlewit, 161-62
meditation, 27-45, 89, 91, 94-95, 96, 140, 145, 187-89, 197, 224
Melami, 78
Menaḥem Mendel of Vitebsk (ca. 1730-1788), 50
Mesnavī, 64
message, the, 84
Messiah, 11
Meyer, Wali Ali, xi, 78, 204
Moshe ben Maimun (see Maimonides 1138-1204), 17, 21, 101, 102, 113, 192
Muḥammad, Prophet (ca. 570-632), 14, 15, 49-50, 215, 218, 223
muḥāsaba, 175, 176
Mu'īn ad-Dīn Hasan Chishtī, Gharīb Nawāz (1141-1236), 12
Mullā Ṣadrā (ca. 1571-ca.1641), 12
mūssar, 14, 22, 222
My Love Stands Behind a Wall, 177
Myths and Symbols in Indian Art and Civilization, 59
nafas, 139, 140-41
nafs, 50, 139-40, 209, 222
nagīd, 19, 20, 27, 32, 187, 222
Naḥman of Bratzlav (1772-1810), 52-59, 60, 62, 69, 198
Naḥman of Horodenka (1680-ca.1766), 50-52
Naropa University (Institute), xii, 87, 88, 89, 93, 203
Nash, John, 144
Nasr, Seyyed Hossein (b.1933), 201
nefesh, 35, 37, 42, 132, 139-40, 154, 155, 157, 160, 161, 175, 188, 212, 219, 222
nefesh hā-behāmīt (see animal nature), 149-69, 182-86, 222
nefesh ha-elōhīt (see divine nature), 149-69, 182-86, 222

nefesh hā-sikhlīt (see rational nature), 149-69, 182-86, 222
Neo-Platonism, 17
neshāmāh, 135, 139, 142-43, 222
netzāḥ, 109, 117, 118, 120, 206, 222
ninety-nine 'beautiful names' of God (see *'asmā al-husnā)*, 109-10, 118-22, 216
non-dualism, 82, 226
Nosson of Nemirov (1780-1844), 65-66, 199
O'Kane, Thomas Atum, xi, 78, 89, 90-91, 92, 93, 94, 98, 99, 102, 203, 204
ōlām, 127-45, 206, 222, 223
ōlām ha-assīyāh, 131-33, 139, 207, 222
ōlām ha-atzīlūt, 136-38, 139, 207, 208, 222
ōlām ha-b'rīyāh, 135-36, 139, 223
ōlām ha-yetzīrāh, 133-35, 139, 223
Ozak, Muzaffer (1916-1985), 78, 92, 207
Physicicans of the Heart, 118
Pinḥas of Koretz (1726-1791), 67-68
Polen, Nehemia, 67
Potter, Harry, 162
Pran Nath, Pandit, 77
prostration, 6-7, 15, 16, 20, 21, 31-32, 224
Psalms *(Zabur)*, 6, 12, 16, 34, 177-78, 202
Qadirī-Rufai, 23, 78, 92
qiyām al-layl (qiyām was-siyām), 15, 21, 223
Qur'an, 10, 80, 88, 118, 178, 200
Qushayrī, Abū'l-Qāsim (986-ca.1072), 15, 18, 22
Rabbah bar Naḥmani (ca. 270-330), 150, 151, 152, 158
rāshā, 149-169, 182-86, 223
rāshā gamur, 153, 158, 162, 163, 223

rāshā sh'eino gamur, 153, 158, 160, 163, 223
rāshā v'ra lo, 151, 163, 223
rāshā v'tov lo, 151, 163, 223
rational nature (see *nefesh hā-sikhlīt)*, 149-69, 182-86
rayyis al-yaḥūd, 18, 19, 223
Riddle, Tom (see Voldemort), 162
rū'aḥ, 33, 35, 37, 38, 42, 82, 83, 84, 134, 139, 140-41, 187, 188, 224
rūḥ, 139, 142-43, 182-83, 224
Ruhaniat Order, 91, 99, 100, 122, 204
rūḥu ḥaiwāni, 182-83
rūḥu insāni, 182-83
rūḥu sultāni, 182-83
Rūmī, Jalāl ad-Dīn (1207-1273), 64, 142, 173
Sabbatean Judaism, 11, 65
sabr, 181, 224
Sarmad (ca. 1590-1661), 12-13
Schachter-Shalomi, Zalman (Sulayman) (1924-2014), ix, xi, 8, 23, 27, 28, 63, 67-69, 73-84, 87-105, 109, 110, 111, 118-23, 127-45, 160, 173, 175, 179-80, 182, 184, 191, 194, 195, 199, 200, 201, 202, 204, 205, 206, 207, 209, 211, 213
Schaya, Leo (1916-1985), 201
Schneersohn, Yosef Yitzhak (1880-1950), 74, 127, 206, 211
Sefārdī, 11, 82
Sēfer Shel Beynonim, 149-50, 210
Sēfer Yetzīrāh, 112
Semnani, Ashraf Jahangir (1285-1386), 12
seven wisdoms, 3, 4
s'fīrōt, 91, 98, 109-23, 166, 205, 206, 217, 218, 219, 220, 221, 222, 224, 225, 227
Shabbetai Zvi (1626-1676), 11, 217

Shah Madar (see Badi ad-Din, b. 1315), 12, 13
Shah, Idries (1924-1996), 61, 75
Shapira, Kalonymous Kalmish, of Piasetzno (1889-1943), 69-70
sharīʿah, 130-31, 225
Sh'mā, 8, 166, 184, 225
Shneur Zalman of Liadi (1745-1812), 149-69, 182-86, 207, 210, 225
Shneuri, Dov Baer, of Lubavitch (1773-1827), 114
shukr, 181, 225
Simḥah Bunem of P'shyskha (ca.1765-1827), 55, 59, 199
Skywalker, Anakin (see Darth Vader), 162
Skywalker, Luke, 162
Solomon (Sh'lomoh), King, 40
Song of Songs (Shīr hā-Shirīm), 17, 21, 176-77, 192
Spiritual Paths Foundation, 95
Sufi Choir, 75, 76
Sufi Order (see Inayati Order), ix, 78, 90, 94, 99, 100, 101, 109, 203, 204
Suhrawardī, Yahya (1154-1191), 12
takhlit, 202
tallīt, 98, 204, 225
Tanya, 149-69, 225
Toward the One, 67-68, 73-84, 92, 200, 201
Tapley, Mark, 161-62
tarīqah, 78, 101, 103, 105, 130-31, 225
tawba, 15, 225
tawḥīd, 15, 216
Temple, the, 36, 40, 188
Teresa of Ávila (1515-1582), 13
tesbīḥ, 91, 93, 225

thought experiments *(Gedankenexperiment),* 114-15
Thurman, Howard (1899-1981, 75
Tibetan Buddhism, 87, 203
tif'eret, 109, 116-17, 119, 225
tōkaḥah, 16, 226
Toldōt Ya'akov Yosef, 49
Trungpa, Chögyam, 87, 203
t'shūvāh, 5, 6, 20, 169, 226
twilight language, 29, 195-96
tzāddīk, 3, 5, 59, 68, 149-69, 182-86, 209, 210, 212, 226
tzāddīk gamur, 153, 154, 158, 162
tzāddīk sh'eino gamur, 153, 154, 158, 162
tzāddīk v'ra lo, 151
tzāddīk v'tov lo, 151
tzimtzūm, 89, 132, 226
unity of all being (see *waḥdat al-wujūd*), 12, 84, 226
Vaishnava sannyasins, 91
Vaughn-Lee, Llewellyn, 204
Vedanta, ix, 130
Voldemort (see Riddle, Tom), 162
waḥdat al-wujūd (see unity of all being), 12, 84, 226
wazīfa, 76, 90. 91, 226
wusūl, 21, 30, 33, 44, 187, 196, 226
Ya'akov Yosef of Polonoyye (d.1782), 49
yeḥīdāh, 137, 227
Yehudah ibn Tibbon (1120-ca. 1190), 14
yesh mi'ain, 176
Yeshārīm darkey Hā-Shem, 185-86, 227
yesōd, 110, 117, 118, 121, 123, 227
Yoga, 130, 140, 217, 220, 223

Yom Kippur, 23
Yosef, brother of Avraham he-Ḥasid, 19
Yosef ben Yehudah of Ceuta (ca.1160-1226), 18, 192, 193
Yosef ibn 'Aqnin (ca.1150-ca.1220), 17, 192
Zachariah, 84
Ze'ev Wolf, 53
zekher, 35, 37, 38, 42, 188, 227
Zen, 63
zikr, 15, 18, 21, 23, 27-45, 69, 70, 76, 78, 91, 92, 93, 96, 97, 100, 109-23, 140, 195, 197, 201, 203, 220, 225, 227
zikr jahrī, 197
zikr khafī, 38, 227
Zimmer, Heinrich, 59
Zvi Hirsh of Nadverna (d. 1802), 68, 200

Pir Netanel (Mu'in ad-Din) Miles-Yépez is the current head of the Inayati-Maimuni Order of Sufism.

An artist, writer, philosopher, and scholar of comparative religion, Pir Netanel first studied History of Religions at Michigan State University and then Contemplative Religion at the Naropa Institute before pursuing traditional studies and training in both Sufism and Hasidism with his *pir* and *rebbe*, Zalman Schachter-Shalomi, the famous pioneer in interfaith dialogue and comparative mysticism.

Pir Netanel is the author of *In the Teahouse of Experience: Nine Talks on the Path of Sufism* (2020), the translator of *My Love Stands Behind a Wall: A Translation of the Song of Songs and Other Poems* (2015), co-author of two critically acclaimed commentaries on Hasidic spirituality, *A Heart Afire: Stories and Teachings of the Early Hasidic Masters* (2009) and *A Hidden Light: Stories and Teachings of Early HaBaD and Bratzlav Hasidism* (2011), and the editor of various works on Sufism and InterSpirituality.

Currently, Pir Netanel lives in Boulder, Colorado, where he is a professor in the Department of Religious Studies at Naropa University, and from which he leads the Inayati-Maimuni Order.

www.ingramcontent.com/pod-product-compliance
Lightning Source LLC
Chambersburg PA
CBHW021440070526
44577CB00002B/232
* 9 7 8 1 9 5 3 2 2 0 1 0 3 *